HISTORY

OF

THE EXPEDITION

UNDER THE COMMAND OF

CAPTAINS LEWIS
AND CLARK

TO

THE SOURCES OF THE MISSOURI, ACROSS THE ROCKY
MOUNTAINS, DOWN THE COLUMBIA RIVER
TO THE PACIFIC IN 1804–6

*A REPRINT OF THE EDITION OF 1814 TO
WHICH ALL THE MEMBERS OF THE
EXPEDITION CONTRIBUTED*

WITH MAPS

IN THREE VOLUMES

VOL. II.

NEW AMSTERDAM BOOK COMPANY
PUBLISHERS: NEW YORK, 1902

Contents.

VOL. II.

CHAPTER XIII.

CHAPTER XIV.

CONTENTS.

CONTENTS.

CHAPTER XVI.

CHAPTER XVII.

CONTENTS.

CHAPTER XVIII.

CHAPTER XIX.

CONTENTS.

CHAPTER XX.

CHAPTER XXI.

CONTENTS.

CONTENTS.

CHAPTER XXIV.

LEWIS AND CLARK'S EXPEDITION UP THE MISSOURI.

CHAPTER XIII.

The name of the Missouri changed, as the river now divides itself into three forks, one of which is called after Jefferson, the other Madison, and the other after Gallatin—Their general character—The party ascend the Jefferson branch—Description of the river Philosophy which enters into the Jefferson—Captain Lewis and a small party go in advance in search of the Shoshonees—Description of the country, &c. bordering on the river—Captain Lewis still preceding the main party in quest of the Shoshonees—A singular accident which prevented captain Clark from following captain Lewis's advice, and ascending the middle fork of the river—Description of Philanthropy river, another stream running into the Jefferson—Captain Lewis and a small party having been unsuccessful in their first attempt, set off a second time in quest of the Shoshonees.

Sunday, July 28.—Captain Clark continued very unwell during the night, but was somewhat relieved this morning. On examining the two streams it became difficult to decide which was the larger or the real Missouri; they are each ninety yards wide and so perfectly similar in character and appearance that they seem to have been formed in the same mould. We were therefore induced to discontinue the name of Missouri, and gave to the southwest branch the name of Jefferson in honour of the president of the United States, and the projector of the enterprise: and called the middle branch Madison, after James Madison secretary of state. These two, as well as Gallatin river, run with great velocity and throw

11

out large bodies of water. Gallatin river is however the most rapid of the three, and though not quite as deep, yet navigable for a considerable distance. Madison river though much less rapid than the Gallatin, is somewhat more rapid than the Jefferson; the beds of all of them are formed of smooth pebble and gravel, and the waters are perfectly transparent. The timber in the neighbourhood would be sufficient for the ordinary uses of an establishment, which, however, it would be advisable to build of brick, as the earth appears calculated for that purpose, and along the shores are some bars of fine pure sand. The greater part of the men, having yesterday put their deer skins in water, were this day engaged in dressing them, for the purpose of making clothing. The weather was very warm, the thermometer in the afternoon was at 90° above 0, and the mosquitoes more than usually inconvenient: we were, however, relieved from them by a high wind from the southwest, which came on at four o'clock, bringing a storm of thunder and lightning, attended by refreshing showers, which continued till after dark. In the evening the hunters returned with eight deer and two elk; and the party who had been sent up the Gallatin, reported that after passing the point, where it escaped from captain Lewis's view yesterday, it turned more towards the east, as far as they could discern the opening of the mountains, formed by the valley which bordered it. The low grounds were still wide but not so extensive as near its mouth, and though the stream is rapid and much divided by islands, it is still sufficiently deep for navigation with canoes. The low grounds, although not more than eight or nine feet above the water, seem never to be overflowed, except a part on the

12

west side of the middle fork, which is stony and seems occasionally inundated, are furnished with great quantities of small fruit, such as currants and gooseberries: among the last of which is a black species, which we observe not only in the meadows but along the mountain rivulets. From the same root rise a number of stems to the height of five or six feet, some of them particularly branched and all reclining. The berry is attached by a long peduncle to the stem, from which they hang of a smooth ovate form, as large as the common garden gooseberry, and as black as jet, though the pulp is of a bright crimson colour. It is extremely acid: the form of the leaf resembles that of the common gooseberry, though larger. The stem is covered with very sharp thorns or briars: the grass too is very luxuriant and would yield fine hay in parcels of several acres. The sand-rushes will grow in many places as high as a man's breast, and as thick as stalks of wheat; it would supply the best food during the winter to cattle of any trading or military post.

Sacajawea, our Indian woman, informs us that we are encamped on the precise spot where her countrymen, the Snake Indians, had their huts five years ago, when the Minnetarees of Knife river first came in sight of them, and from which they hastily retreated three miles up the Jefferson, and concealed themselves in the woods. The Minnetarees, however, pursued and attacked them, killed four men, as many women, and a number of boys; and made prisoners of four other boys, and all the females, of whom Sacajawea was one: she does not, however, show any distress at these recollections, nor any joy at the prospect of being restored to her country; for she seems to possess the folly or the philosophy of not suffering her feelings to extend beyond the anxiety of having plenty to eat and a few trinkets to wear.

Monday 29.—This morning the hunters brought in some fat deer of the long-tailed red kind, which are quite as large as those of the United States, and are, indeed, the only kind we have found at this place: there are numbers of the sandhill cranes feeding in the meadows; we caught a young one of the same colour as the red deer, which, though it had nearly attained its full growth could not fly; it is very fierce and strikes a severe blow with its beak. The kingfisher has become quite common on this side of the falls: but we have seen none of the summer duck since leaving that place. The mallard duck, which we saw for the first time on the 20th instant, with their young, are now abundant, though they do not breed on the Missouri, below the mountains. The small birds already described are also abundant in the plains; here too, are great quantities of grasshoppers or crickets; and among other animals, a large ant with a reddish brown body and legs, and a black head and abdomen, who build little cones of gravel, ten or twelve inches high, without a mixture of sticks, and but little earth. In the river we see a great abundance of fish, but we cannot tempt them to bite by any thing on our hooks. The whole party have been engaged in dressing skins, and making them into moccasins and leggings. Captain Clark's fever has almost left him, but he still remains very languid and has a general soreness in his limbs. The latitude of our camp, as the mean of two observations of the meridian altitude of the sun's lower limb with octant by back observation, is N. 45° 24′ 8″ 5.

Tuesday 30.—Captain Clark was this morning much restored; and, therefore, having made all

14

the observations necessary to fix the longitude, we reloaded our canoes, and began to ascend Jefferson river. The river now becomes very crooked, and forms bends on each side; the current too is rapid, and cut into a great number of channels, and sometimes shoals, the beds of which consist of coarse gravel. The islands are unusually numerous: on the right are high plains occasionally forming cliffs of rocks and hills; while the left was an extensive low ground and prairie intersected by a number of bayous or channels falling into the river. Captain Lewis, who had walked through it with Chaboneau, his wife, and two invalids, joined us at dinner, a few miles above our camp. Here the Indian woman said was the place where she had been made prisoner. The men being too few to contend with the Minnetarees, mounted their horses, and fled as soon as the attack began. The women and children dispersed, and Sacajawea as she was crossing at a shoal place, was overtaken in the middle of the river by her pursuers. As we proceeded, the low grounds were covered with cottonwood and a thick underbrush, and on both sides of the river, except where the high hills prevented it, the ground was divided by bayous, which are dammed up by the beaver, which are very numerous here. We made twelve and a quarter miles, and encamped on the north side. Captain Lewis proceeded after dinner, through an extensive low ground of timber and meadow land intermixed; but the bayous were so obstructed by beaver dams, that in order to avoid them he directed his course towards the high plain on the right. This he gained with some difficulty, after wading up to his waist through the mud and water of a number of beaver dams. When he desired to rejoin the canoes he found the underbrush so thick, and the river so crooked, that this, joined to the difficulty of passing the beaver dams, induced him to go on and endeavour to intercept the river at some point where it might be more collected into one channel and approach nearer to the high plain. He arrived at the bank about sunset, having gone only six miles in a direct course from the canoes: but he saw no traces of the men, nor did he receive any answer to his shouts nor the firing of his gun. It was now nearly dark; a duck lighted near him and he shot it. He then went on the head of a small island where he found some driftwood, which enabled him to cook his duck for supper, and he laid down to sleep on some willow brush. The night was cool, but the driftwood gave him a good fire, and he suffered no inconvenience except from the mosquitoes.

Wednesday 31.—The next morning he waited till after seven o'clock, when he became uneasy lest we should have gone beyond his camp last evening and determined to follow us. Just as he had set out with this intention, he saw one of the party in advance of the canoes; although our camp was only two miles below him, in a straight line, we could not reach him sooner, in consequence of the rapidity of the water and the circuitous course of the river. We halted for breakfast, after which captain Lewis continued his route. At the distance of one mile from our encampment we passed the principal entrance of a stream on the left, which rises in the snowy mountains to the southwest, between Jefferson and Madison rivers, and discharges itself by seven mouths, five below, and one three miles above this, which is the largest, and about thirty yards wide: we called it Philosophy river. The water of it is abundant and perfectly clear, and the bed like that of the Jefferson consists of pebble and gravel. There is some timber in the bottoms of the river, and vast numbers of otter and beaver, which build on its smaller mouths and the bayous of its neighbourhood. The Jefferson continues as yesterday, shoaly and rapid, but as the islands though numerous are small, it is however more collected into one current than it was below, and is from ninety to one hundred and twenty yards in width. The low ground has a fertile soil of rich black loam, and contains a considerable quantity of timber, with the bullrush and cattail flag very abundant in the moist parts, while the drier situations are covered with fine grass, tansy, thistles, onions, and flax. The uplands are barren, and without timber: the soil is a light yellow clay intermixed with small smooth pebble and gravel, and the only produce is the prickly-pear, the sedge, and the bearded grass, which is as dry and inflammable as tinder. As we proceeded the low grounds became narrower, and the timber more scarce, till at the distance of ten miles the high hills approach and overhang the river on both sides, forming cliffs of a hard black granite, like almost all those below the limestone cliffs at the three forks of the Missouri: they continue so for a mile and three quarters, where we came to a point of rock on the right side, at which place the hills again retire, and the valley widens to the distance of a mile and a half. Within the next five miles we passed four islands, and reached the foot of a mountain in a bend of the river to the left: from this place we went a mile and a quarter to the entrance of a small run discharging itself on the left, and encamped on an island just above it, after making seventeen and three quarter miles.

We observe some pine on the hills on both sides of our encampment, which are very lofty. The only game which we have seen are one bighorn, a few antelopes, deer, and one brown bear, which escaped from our pursuit. Nothing was, however, killed to-day, nor have we had any fresh meat except one beaver for the last two days, so that we are now reduced to an unusual situation, for we have hitherto always had a great abundance of flesh.

Thursday, August 1.—We left our encampment early, and at the distance of a mile, reached a point of rocks on the left side, where the river passes through perpendicular cliffs. Two and three quarter miles further we halted for breakfast under a cedar tree in a bend to the right: here as had been previously arranged, captain Lewis left us, with sergeant Gass, Chaboneau, and Drewyer, intending to go on in advance in search of the Shoshonees. He began his route along the north side of the river over a high range of mountains, as captain Clark who ascended them on the 26th had observed from them a large valley spreading to the north of west, and concluded that on leaving the mountain the river took that direction; but when he reached that valley, captain Lewis found it to be the passage of a large creek falling just above the mountain into the Jefferson, which bears to the southwest. On discovering his error, he bent his course towards that river, which he reached about two in the afternoon, very much exhausted with heat and thirst. The mountains were very bare of timber, and the route lay along the steep and narrow hollows of the mountain, exposed to the mid-day sun, without air, or shade, or water. Just as he arrived there a flock of elk passed, and they killed

18

two of them, on which they made their dinner, and left the rest on the shore for the party in the canoes. After dinner they resumed their march, and encamped on the north side of the river, after making seventeen miles; in crossing the mountains captain Lewis saw a flock of the black or dark brown pheasant, of which he killed one. This bird is one third larger than the common pheasant of the Atlantic States; its form is much the same. The male has not however the tufts of long black feathers on the sides of the neck so conspicuous in the Atlantic pheasant, and both sexes are booted nearly to the toes. The colour is a uniform dark brown with a small mixture of yellow or yellowish brown specks on some of the feathers, particularly those of the tail, though the extremities of these are perfectly black for about an inch. The eye is nearly black, and the iris has a small dash of yellowish brown; the feathers of the tail are somewhat longer than those of our pheasant, but the same in number, eighteen, and nearly equal in size, except that those of the middle are somewhat the longest; their flesh is white and agreeably flavoured.

He also saw among the scattered pine near the top of the mountain, a blue bird about the size of a robin, but in action and form something like a jay; it is constantly in motion, hopping from spray to spray, and its note which is loud and frequent, is, as far as letters can represent it, char ah! char ah! char ah!

After breakfast we proceeded on: at the distance of two and a quarter miles the river enters a high mountain, which forms rugged cliffs of nearly perpendicular rocks. These are of a black granite at the lower part, and the upper consists of a light coloured freestone; they continue from the point of rocks close to the river for nine miles, which we passed before breakfast, during which the current is very strong. At nine and a quarter miles we passed an island, and a rapid with a fall of six feet, and reached the entrance of a large creek on the left side. In passing this place the towline of one of the canoes broke just at the shoot of the rapids, swung on the rocks and had nearly upset. To the creek as well as the rapid we gave the name of Frazier, after Rober Frazier one of the party: here the country opens into a beautiful valley from six to eight miles in width: the river then becomes crooked and crowded with islands; its low grounds wide and fertile, but though covered with fine grass from nine inches to two feet high; possesses but a small proportion of timber, and that consists almost entirely of a few narrow-leafed cottonwood distributed along the verge of the river. The soil of the plain is tolerably fertile, and consists of a black or dark yellow loam. It gradually ascends on each side to the bases of two ranges of high mountains which lie parallel to the river; the tops of them are yet in part covered with snow, and while in the valley we are nearly suffocated with heat during the day, and at night the air is so cold that two blankets are not more than sufficient covering. In passing through the hills we observed some large cedar trees, and some juniper also. From Frazier's creek we went three and three quarter miles, and encamped on the left side, having come thirteen miles. Directly opposite our camp is a large creek which we call Field's creek, from Reuben Fields, one of our men. Soon after we halted two of the hunters went out and returned with five deer, which, with one bighorn, we killed in coming through the mountain on which we dined;

and the elk left by captain Lewis. We were again well supplied with fresh meat. In the course of the day we saw a brown bear but were not able to shoot him.

Friday, August 2.—Captain Lewis, who slept in the valley a few miles above us, resumed his journey early, and after making five miles and finding that the river still bore to the south, determined to cross it in hopes of shortening the route: for the first time therefore he waded across it, although there are probably many places above the falls where it might be attempted with equal safety. The river was about ninety yards wide, the current rapid, and about waist deep: the bottom formed of smooth pebble with a small mixture of coarse gravel. He then continued along the left bank of the river till sunset and encamped, after travelling twenty-four miles. He met no fresh tracks of Indians. Throughout the valley are scattered the bones and excrement of the buffalo of an old date, but there seems no hope of meeting the animals themselves in the mountains: he saw an abundance of deer and antelope, and many tracks of elk and bear. Having killed two deer they feasted sumptuously, with a dessert of currants of different colours; two species of red, others yellow, deep purple, and black: to these were added black gooseberries and deep purple serviceberries, somewhat larger than ours, from which it differs also in colour, size, and the superior excellence of its flavour. In the low grounds of the river were many beaver-dams formed of willow brush, mud, and gravel, so closely interwoven that they resist the water perfectly: some of them were five feet high and overflowed several acres of land.

In the meantime we proceeded on slowly, the

current being so strong as to require the utmost
exertions of the men to make any advance even
with the aid of the cord and pole, the wind being
from the northwest. The river is full of large and
small islands, and the plain cut by great numbers
of bayous or channels, in which are multitudes of
beaver. In the course of the day we passed some
villages of barking squirrels: we saw several rattlesnakes in the plain; young ducks, both of the
duckon-mallard and red-headed fishing duck species; some geese; also the black woodpecker, and
a large herd of elk. The channel, current, banks,
and general appearance of the river, are like that
of yesterday. At fourteen and three quarter miles
we reached a rapid creek or bayou about thirty
yards wide, to which we gave the name of Birth
creek. After making seventeen miles we halted in
a smooth plain in a bend towards the left.

Saturday, 3.—Captain Lewis continued his
course along the river through the valley, which
continued much as it was yesterday, except that
it now widens to nearly twelve miles: the plains
too are more broken and have some scattered pine
near the mountains, where they rise higher than
hitherto. In the level parts of the plains and the
river bottoms there is no timber except small
cottonwood near the margin, and an undergrowth of narrow-leafed willow, small honeysuckle, rosebushes, currants, serviceberry, and
gooseberry, and a little of a small species of birch;
it is a finely indented oval of a small size and a
deep green colour; the stem is simple, ascending
and branching, and seldom rises higher than ten
or twelve feet. The mountains continue high on
each side of the valley, but their only covering is
a small species of pitch-pine with a short leaf,
growing on the lower and middle regions, while

22

for some distance below the snowy tops there is neither timber nor herbage of any kind. About eleven o'clock Drewyer killed a doe on which they breakfasted, and after resting two hours continued till night, when they reached the river near a low ground more extensive than usual. From the appearance of the timber captain Lewis supposed that the river forked above him, and therefore encamped with an intention of examining it more particularly in the morning. He had now made twenty-three miles, the latter part of which were for eight miles through a high plain covered with prickly pears and bearded grass, which rendered the walking very inconvenient: but even this was better than the river bottoms we crossed in the evening, which, though apparently level, were formed into deep holes as if they had been rooted up by hogs, and the holes were so covered with thick grass that they were in danger of falling at every step. Some parts of these low grounds, however, contain turf or peat of an excellent quality for many feet deep apparently, as well as the mineral salts which we have already mentioned on the Missouri. They saw many deer, antelopes, ducks, geese, some beaver, and great traces of their work, and the small birds and curlews as usual. The only fish which they observed in this part of the river is the trout and a species of white fish with a remarkably long small mouth, which one of our men recognize as the fish called in the eastern states the bottlenose.

On setting out with the canoes we found the river as usual much crowded with islands, the current more rapid as well as shallower, so that in many places they were obliged to man the canoes double, and drag them over the stone and gravel of the channel. Soon after we set off captain Clark who was walking on shore observed a fresh track which he knew to be that of an Indian from the large toes being turned inwards, and on following it found that it led to the point of a hill from which our camp of last night could be seen. This circumstance strengthened the belief that some Indian had strayed thither, and had run off alarmed at the sight of us. At two and a quarter miles, is a small creek in a bend towards the right, which runs down from the mountains at a little distance; we called it Panther creek from an animal of that kind killed by Reuben Fields at its mouth. It is precisely the same animal common to the western parts of the United States, and measured seven and a half feet from the nose to the extremity of the tail. Six and three quarter miles beyond this stream is another on the left formed by the drains which convey the melted snows from a mountain near it, under which the river passes, leaving the low grounds on the right side, and making several bends in its course. On this stream are many large beaver dams. One mile above it is a small run on the left, and after leaving which begins a very bad rapid, where the bed of the river is formed of solid rock: this we passed in the course of a mile, and encamped on the lower point of an island. Our journey had been only thirteen miles, but the badness of the river made it very laborious, as the men were compelled to be in the water during the greater part of the day. We saw only deer, antelopes, and the common birds of the country.

Saturday 4.—This morning captain Lewis proceeded early, and after going southeast by east for four miles reached a bold running creek, twelve yards wide, with clear cold water, furnished apparently by four drains from the snowy mountains on the left: after passing this creek he changed his direction to southeast, and leaving the valley in which he had travelled for the last two days, entered another which bore east. At the distance of three miles on this course he passed a handsome little river, about thirty yards wide, which winds through the valley: the current is not rapid nor the water very clear, but it affords a considerable quantity of water, and appears as if it might be navigable for some miles. The banks are low, and the bed formed of stone and gravel. He now changed his route to southwest, and passing a high plain which separates the valleys, returned to the more southern or that which he had left: in passing this he found a river about forty-five yards wide, the water of which has a whitish blue tinge, with a gentle current, and a gravelly bottom. This he waded and found it waist deep. He then continued down it, till at the distance of three quarters of a mile he saw the entrance of the small river he had just passed; as he went on two miles lower down, he found the mouth of the creek he had seen in the morning. Proceeding further on three miles, he arrived at the junction of this river, with another which rises from the southwest, runs through the south valley about twelve miles before it forms its junction, where it is fifty yards wide: we now found that our camp of last night was about a mile and a half above the entrance of this large river, on the right side. This is a bold, rapid, clear stream, but its bed is so much obstructed by gravelly bars, and subdivided by islands, that the navigation must be very insecure, if not impracticable. The other or middle stream, has about two-thirds its quantity of water, and is more gentle, and may be safely navigated. As far as it could be observed, its course was about south-west, but the opening of the valley induced him to believe that farther above it turned more towards the west. Its water is more turbid and warmer than that of the other branch, whence it may be presumed to have its sources at a greater distance in the mountains, and to pass through a more open country. Under this impression he left a note recommending to captain Clark the middle fork, and then continued his course along the right side of the other, or more rapid branch. After travelling twenty-three miles he arrived near a place where the river leaves the valley and enters the mountains. Here he encamped for the night. The country he passed is like that of the rest of this valley, though there is more timber in this part on the rapid fork than there has been on the river in the same extent since we entered it; for on some parts of the valley the Indians seem to have destroyed a great proportion of the little timber there was, by setting fire to the bottoms. He saw some antelopes, deer, cranes, geese and ducks of the two species common to this country, though the summer duck has ceased to appear, nor does it seem to be an inhabitant of this part of the river.

We proceeded soon after sunrise: the first five miles we passed four bends on the left, and several bayous on both sides. At eight o'clock we stopped to breakfast, and found the note captain Lewis had written on the 2d instant. During the next four miles, we passed three small bends of the river to the right, two small islands, and two bayous on the same side. Here we reached a bluff on the left; our next course was six miles to our encampment. In this course we met six circular bends on the right, and several small bayous, and

halted for the night in a low ground of cottonwood on the right. Our days journey, though
only fifteen miles in length, was very fatiguing.
The river is still rapid and the water though clear
is very much obstructed by shoals or ripples at
every two or three hundred yards: at all these
places we are obliged to drag the canoes over the
stones as there is not a sufficient depth of water
to float them, and in the other parts the currents
obliges us to have recourse to the cord. But as
the brushwood on the banks will not permit us to
walk on shore, we are under the necessity of
wading through the river as we drag the boats.
This soon makes our feet tender, and sometimes
occasions severe falls over the slippery stones; and
the men by being constantly wet are becoming
more feeble. In the course of the day the hunters
killed two deer, some geese and ducks, and the
party saw antelopes, cranes, beaver and otter.

Monday 5.—This morning Chaboneau com-
plained of being unable to march far to-day, and
captain Lewis therefore ordered him and sergeant
Gass to pass the rapid river and proceed through
the level low ground, to a point of high timber on
the middle fork, seven miles distant, and wait his
return. He then went along the north side of the
rapid river about four miles, where he waded it,
and found it so rapid and shallow that it would
be impossible to navigate it. He continued along
the left side for a mile and a half, when the mountains came close on the river, and rise to a considerable height with a partial covering of snow.
From this place the course of the river was to the
east of north. After ascending with some difficulty a high point of the mountain, he had a
pleasing view of the valley he had passed, and
which continued for about twenty miles further

on each side of the middle fork, which then seemed
to enter the mountains, and was lost to the view.
In that direction, however, the hills which terminate the valley are much lower than those along
either of the other forks, particularly the rapid
one, where they continue rising in ranges above
each other as far as the eye could reach. The
general course too of the middle fork, as well as
that of the gap which it forms on entering the
mountains, is considerably to the south of west;
circumstances which gave a decided preference to
this branch as our future route. Captain Lewis
now descended the mountain, and crossed over to
the middle fork, about five miles distant, and
found it still perfectly navigable. There is a very
large and plain Indian road leading up it, but it
has at present no tracks, except those of horses
which seem to have used it last spring. The river
here made a great bend to the southeast, and he
therefore directed his course, as well as he could,
to the spot where he had directed Chaboneau and
Gass to repair, and struck the river about three
miles above their camp. It was now dark, and
he, therefore, was obliged to make his way
through the thick brush of the pulpy-leafed thorn
and the prickly pear, for two hours before he
reached their camp. Here he was fortunate
enough to find the remains of some meat, which
was his only food during the march of twenty-five
miles to-day. He had seen no game of any sort
except a few antelopes who were very shy. The
soil of the plains is a meagre clay, of a light yellow colour, intermixed with a large proportion of
gravel, and producing nothing but twisted or
bearded grass, sedge and prickly pears. The
drier parts of the low grounds are also more indifferent in point of soil than those further down

28

the river, and although they have but little grass, are covered with southern wood, pulpy-leafed thorn, and prickly pears, while the moist parts are fertile, and supplied with fine grass and sand-rushes.

We passed within the first four and a quarter miles three small islands, and the same number of bad rapids. At the distance of three quarters of a mile is another rapid of difficult passage: three miles and three quarters beyond this are the forks of the river, in reaching which we had two islands and several bayous on different sides to pass. Here we had come nine miles and a quarter. The river was straighter and more rapid than yesterday, the labour of the navigation proportionally increased, and we therefore proceeded very slowly, as the feet of several of the men were swollen, and all were languid with fatigue. We arrived at the forks about four o'clock, but unluckily captain Lewis's note had been left on a green pole which the beaver had cut down and carried off with the note, an accident which deprived us of all information as to the character of the two branches of the river. Observing therefore that the northwest fork was most in our direction, and contained as much water as the other, we ascended it; we found it extremely rapid, and its waters were scattered in such a manner, that for a quarter of a mile we were forced to cut a passage through the willowbrush that leaned over the little channels and united at the top. After going up it for a mile we encamped on an island which had been overflowed, and was still so wet that we were compelled to make beds of brush to keep ourselves out of the mud. Our provision consisted of two deer which had been killed in the morning.

Tuesday 6.—We proceeded up the northwest

fork, which we found still very rapid, and divided
by several islands, while the plains near it were
intersected by bayous. After passing with much
difficulty over stones and rapids, we reached a
bluff on the right, at the distance of nine miles,
our general course south 30° west, and halted for
breakfast. Here we were joined by Drewyer, who
informed us of the state of the two rivers and of
captain Lewis's note, and we immediately began
to descend the river in order to take the other
branch. On going down one of the canoes upset,
and two others filled with water, by which all the
baggage was wet, and several articles irrevocably
lost. As one of them swung round in a rapid
current, Whitehouse was thrown out of her, and
whilst down the canoe passed over him, and had
the water been two inches shallower would have
crushed him to pieces; but he escaped with a
severe bruise of his leg. In order to repair these
misfortunes we hastened to the forks, where we
were joined by captain Lewis, and then passed
over to the left side opposite to the entrance of
the rapid fork, and encamped on a large gravelly
bar, near which there was plenty of wood. Here
we opened and exposed to dry all the articles
which had suffered from the water; none of them
were completely spoiled except a small keg of
powder; the rest of the powder, which was distributed in the different canoes was quite safe,
although it had been under the water upwards of
an hour. The air is indeed so pure and dry that
any wood-work immediately shrinks, unless it is
kept filled with water; but we had placed our
powder in small canisters of lead, each containing
powder enough for the canister when melted into
bullets, and secured with cork and wax, which
answered our purpose perfectly.

Captain Lewis had risen very early, and having nothing to eat, sent out Drewyer to the woodland on the left in search of a deer, and directed sergeant Gass to keep along the middle branch to meet us if we were ascending it. He then set off with Chaboneau towards the forks, but five miles above them, hearing us on the left, struck the river as we were descending, and came on board at the forks.

In the evening we killed three deer and four elk, which furnished us once more with a plentiful supply of meat. Shannon, the same man who was lost before for fifteen days, was sent out this morning to hunt, up the northwest fork; when we decided on returning, Drewyer was directed to go in quest of him, but he returned with information that he had gone several miles up the river without being able to find Shannon. We now had the trumpet sounded, and fired several guns, but he did not return, and we fear he is again lost.

Wednesday 7.—We remained here this morning for the purpose of making some celestial observations, and also in order to refresh the men, and complete the drying of the baggage. We obtained a meridian altitude which gave the latitude of our camp as north 45° 2′ 43″ 8. We were now completely satisfied that the middle branch was the most navigable, and the true continuation of the Jefferson. The northwest fork seems to be the drain of the melting snows of the mountains, its course cannot be so long as the other branch, and although it contains now as great a quantity of water, yet the water has obviously overflowed the old bed, and spread into channels which leave the low grounds covered with young grass, resembling that of the adjoining lands, which are not inundated; whence we readily infer that the

31

supply is more precarious than that of the other branch, the waters of which though more gentle are more constant. This northwest fork we called Wisdom river.

As soon as the baggage was dried, it was reloaded on board the boats, but we now found it so much diminished, that we would be able to proceed with one canoe less. We therefore hauled up the superfluous one into a thicket of brush where we secured her against being swept away by the high tide. At one o'clock all set out, except captain Lewis who remained till the evening in order to complete the observation of equal altitudes: we passed several bends of the river both to the right and left, as well as a number of bayous on both sides, and made seven miles by water, though the distance by land is only three. We then encamped on a creek which rises in a high mountain to the northeast, and after passing through an open plain for several miles, discharges itself on the left, where it is a bold running stream twelve yards wide. We called it Turf creek, from the number of bogs and the quantity of turf on its waters. In the course of the afternoon there fell a shower of rain attended with thunder and lightning, which lasted about forty minutes, and the weather remained so cloudy all night that we were unable to take any lunar observations. Uneasy about Shannon, we sent R. Fields in search of him this morning, but we have as yet no intelligence of either of them. Our only game to-day was one deer.

Thursday 8.—There was a heavy dew this morning. Having left one of the canoes, there are now more men to spare for the chase: and four were sent out at an early hour, after which we proceeded. We made five miles by water along two

islands and several bayous, but as the river formed
seven different bends towards the left, the distance
by land was only two miles south of our encampment. At the end of that course we reached the
upper principal entrance of a stream which we
called Philanthropy river. This river empties itself into the Jefferson on the southeast side, by
two channels a short distance from each other:
from its size and its southeastern course, we presume that it rises in the Rocky mountains near
the sources of the Madison. It is thirty yards
wide at its entrance, has a very gentle current,
and is navigable for some distance. One mile
above this river we passed an island, a second at
the distance of six miles further, during which the
river makes a considerable bend to the east.
Reuben Fields returned about noon with information that he had gone up Wisdom river till its
entrance into the mountains, but could find nothing of Shannon. We made seven miles beyond the
last island, and after passing some small bayous,
encamped under a few high trees on the left, at
the distance of fourteen miles above Philanthropy
river by water, though only six by land. The
river has in fact become so very crooked that
although by means of the pole which we now use
constantly we make a considerable distance, yet
being obliged to follow its windings, at the end of
the day, we find ourselves very little advanced on
our general course. It forms itself into small circular bends, which are so numerous that within
the last fourteen miles we passed thirty-five of
them, all inclining towards the right; it is however much more gentle and deep than below Wisdom river, and its general width is from thirty-five
to forty-five yards. The general appearance of the
surrounding country is that of a valley five or six

miles wide, enclosed between two high mountains. The bottom is rich, with some small timber on the islands and along the river, which consists rather of underbrush, and a few cottonwood, birch, and willow-trees. The high grounds have some scattered pine, which just relieve the general nakedness of the hills and the plain, where there is nothing except grass. Along the bottoms we saw to-day a considerable quantity of the buffalo clover, the sunflower, flax, green sward, thistle and several species of rye grass, some of which rise to the height of three or four feet. There is also a grass with a soft smooth leaf which rises about three feet high, and bears its seed very much like the timothy, but it does not grow luxuriantly nor would it apparently answer so well in our meadows as that plant. We preserved some of its seed, which are now ripe, in order to make the experiment. Our game consisted of deer and antelope, and we saw a number of geese and ducks just beginning to fly, and some cranes. Among the inferior animals we have an abundance of the large biting or hare fly, of which there are two species, one black, the other smaller and brown, except the head which is green. The green or blowing flies unite with them in swarms to attack us, and seem to have relieved the eye-gnats who have now disappeared. The mosquitoes too are in large quantities, but not so troublesome as they were below. Through the valley are scattered bogs, and some very good turf, the earth of which the mud is composed is of a white or bluish white colour, and seems to be argilaceous. On all the three rivers, but particularly on the Philanthropy, are immense quantities of beaver, otter and muskrat. At our camp there was an abundance of rosebushes and briars, but so little timber that we

were obliged to use willow brush for fuel. The
night was again cloudy which prevented the lunar
observations.

On our right is the point of a high plain, which
our Indian woman recognizes as the place called
the Beaver's-head from a supposed resemblance to
that object. This she says is not far from the
summer retreat of her countrymen, which is on a
river beyond the mountains, and running to the
west. She is therefore certain that we shall meet
them either on this river, or on that immediately
west of its source, which judging from its present
size, cannot be far distant. Persuaded of the
absolute necessity of procuring horses to cross
the mountains, it was determined that one of us
should proceed in the morning to the head of the
river, and penetrate the mountains till he found
the Shoshonees or some other nation who could
assist us in transporting our baggage, the greater
part of which we shall be compelled to leave without the aid of horses.

Friday 9.—The morning was fair and fine. We
set off early, and proceeded on very well, though
there were more rapids in the river than yesterday. At eight o'clock we halted for breakfast,
part of which consisted of two fine geese killed
before we stopped. Here we were joined by Shannon for whose safety we had been so uneasy. The
day on which he left us on his way up Wisdom
river, after hunting for some time and not seeing
the party arrive, he returned to the place where
he had left us. Not finding us there he supposed
we had passed him, and he therefore marched up
the river during all the next day, when he was
convinced that we had not gone on, as the river
was no longer navigable. He now followed the
course of the river down to the forks, and then

took the branch which we are pursuing. During the three days of his absence, he had been much wearied with his march, but had lived plentifully, and brought the skins of three deer. As far as he had ascended Wisdom river it kept its course obliquely down towards the Jefferson. Immediately after breakfast, captain Lewis took Drewyer, Shields and M'Neal, and slinging their knapsacks they set out with a resolution to meet some nation of Indians before they returned, however long they might be separated from the party. He directed his course across the low ground to the plain on the right, leaving the Beaver's-head about two miles to the left. After walking eight miles to the river, which they waded, they went on to a commanding point from which he saw the place at which it enters the mountain, but as the distance would not permit his reaching it this evening, he descended towards the river, and after travelling eight miles further, encamped for the evening some miles below the mountain. They passed before reaching their camp a handsome little stream formed by some large springs which rise in the wide bottom on the left side of the river. In their way they killed two antelopes, and took with them enough of the meat for their supper and breakfast the next morning.

In the meantime we proceeded, and in the course of eleven miles from our last encampment passed two small islands, sixteen short round bends in the river, and halted in a bend towards the right where we dined. The river increases in rapidity as we advance, and is so crooked that the eleven miles, which have cost us so much labour, only bring us four miles in a direct line. The weather became overcast towards evening, and we experienced a slight shower attended with thunder and lightning. The three hunters who were sent out killed only two antelopes; game of every kind being scarce.

Saturday, 10.—Captain Lewis continued his route at an early hour through the wide bottom along the left bank of the river. At about five miles he passed a large creek, and then fell into an Indian road leading towards the point where the river entered the mountain. This he followed till he reached a high perpendicular cliff of rocks where the river makes its passage through the hills, and which he called the Rattlesnake cliff, from the number of that animal which he saw there: here he kindled a fire and waited the return of Drewyer, who had been sent out on the way to kill a deer: he came back about noon with the skin of three deer and the flesh of one of the best of them. After a hasty dinner they returned to the Indian road which they had left for a short distance to see the cliff. It led them sometimes over the hills, sometimes in the narrow bottoms of the river, till at the distance of fifteen miles from the Rattlesnake cliffs they reached a handsome open and level valley, where the river divided into two nearly equal branches. The mountains over which they passed were not very high, but are rugged and continue close to the river side. The river, which before it enters the mountain was rapid, rocky, very crooked, much divided by islands, and shallow, now becomes more direct in its course as it is hemmed in by the hills, and has not so many bends nor islands, but becomes more rapid and rocky, and continues as shallow. On examining the two branches of the river it was evident that neither of them was navigable further. The road forked with the river; and captain Lewis therefore sent a man up each of them for a short distance, in order that by comparing their respective information he might be able to take that which seemed to have been most used this spring. From their account he resolved to choose that which led along the southwest branch of the river which was rather the smaller of the two: he accordingly wrote a note to captain Clark informing him of the route, and recommending his staying with the party at the forks till he should return: This he fixed on a dry willow pole at the forks of the river, and then proceeded up the southwest branch; but after going a mile and a half the road became scarcely distinguishable, and the tracks of the horses which he had followed along the Jefferson were no longer seen. Captain Lewis therefore returned to examine the other road himself, and found that the horses had in fact passed along the western or right fork which had the additional recommendation of being larger than the other.

This road he concluded to take, and therefore sent back Drewyer to the forks with a second letter to captain Clark apprising him of the change, and then proceeded on. The valley of the west fork through which he now passed, bears a little to the north of west, and is confined within the space of about a mile in width, by rough mountains and steep cliffs of rock. At the distance of four and a half miles it opens into a beautiful and extensive plain about ten miles long and five or six in width: this is surrounded on all sides by higher rolling or waving country, intersected by several little rivulets from the mountains, each bordered by its wide meadows. The whole prospect is bounded by these mountains, which nearly surround it, so as to form a beautiful cove about sixteen or eighteen miles in diameter. On entering this cove the river bends to the northwest, and bathes the foot of the hills to the right. At this place they halted for the night on the right side of the river, and having lighted a fire of dry willow brush, the only fuel which the country affords, supped on a deer. They had travelled to-day thirty miles by estimate: that is ten to the Rattle-snake cliff, fifteen to the forks of Jefferson river, and five to their encampment. In this cove some parts of the low grounds are tolerably fertile, but much the greater proportion is covered with prickly pear, sedge, twisted grass, the pulpy-leafed thorn, southern-wood, and wild sage, and like the uplands have a very inferior soil. These last have little more than the prickly pear and the twisted or bearded grass, nor are there in the whole cove more than three or four cottonwood trees, and those are small. At the apparent extremity of the bottom above, and about ten miles to the west-ward, are two perpendicular cliffs rising to a con-siderable height on each side of the river, and at this distance seem like a gate. In the meantime we proceeded at sunrise, and found the river not so rapid as yesterday, though more narrow and still very crooked, and so shallow that we were obliged to drag the canoes over many ripples in the course of the day. At six and a half miles we had passed eight bends on the north, and two small bayous on the left, and came to what the Indians call the Beaver's head, a steep rocky cliff about one hundred and fifty feet high, near the right side of the river. Opposite to this at three hundred yards from the water is a low cliff about fifty feet in height, which forms the extremity of a spur of the mountain about four miles distant on the left. At four o'clock we were overtaken by a heavy shower of rain, attended with thunder, lightning and hail. The party were defended from

39

the hail by covering themselves with willow bushes, but they got completely wet, and in this situation, as soon as the rain ceased, continued till we encamped. This we did at a low bluff on the left, after passing in the course of six and a half miles, four islands and eighteen bends on the right, and a low bluff and several bayous on the same side. We had now come thirteen miles, yet were only four on our route towards the mountains. The game seems to be declining, for our hunters procured only a single deer, though we found another for us that had been killed three days before by one of the hunters during an excursion, and left for us on the river.

CHAPTER XIV.

Captain Lewis proceeds before the main body in search of the Shoshonees—His ill success on the first interview—The party with captain Lewis at length discover the source of the Missouri—Captain Clark with the main body still employed in ascending the Missouri or Jefferson river—Captain Lewis's second interview with the Shoshonees attended with success—The interesting ceremonies of his first introduction to the natives, detailed at large—Their hospitality—Their mode of hunting the antelope—The difficulties encountered by captain Clark and the main body in ascending the river—The suspicions entertained of captain Lewis by the Shoshonees, and his mode of allaying them—The ravenous appetites of the savages illustrated by a singular adventure—The Indians still jealous, and the great pains taken by captain Lewis to preserve their confidence—Captain Clark arrives with the main body exhausted by the difficulties which they underwent.

Sunday, August 11.—Captain Lewis again proceeded on early, but had the mortification to find that the track which he followed yesterday soon disappeared. He determined therefore to go on to the narrow gate or pass of the river which he had seen from the camp, in hopes of being able to recover the Indian path. For this purpose he waded across the river, which was now about twelve yards wide, and barred in several places by the dams of the beaver, and then went straight forward to the pass, sending one man along the river to his left, and another on the right, with orders to search for the road, and if they found it to let him know by raising a hat on the muzzle of their guns. In this order they went along for about five miles, when captain Lewis perceived with the greatest delight a man on horseback at the distance of two miles coming down the plain

41

towards them. On examining him with the glass, captain Lewis saw that he was of a different nation from any Indians we had hitherto met: he was armed with a bow and a quiver of arrows; mounted on an elegant horse without a saddle, and a small string attached to the under jaw answered as a bridle. Convinced that he was a Shoshonee, and knowing how much of our success depended on the friendly offices of that nation, captain Lewis was full of anxiety to approach without alarming him, and endeavour to convince him that he was a white man. He therefore, proceeded on towards the Indian at his usual pace, when they were within a mile of each other the Indian suddenly stopped, captain Lewis immediately followed his example, took his blanket from his knapsack, and holding it with both hands at the two corners, threw it above his head and unfolded it as he brought it to the ground as if in the act of spreading it. This signal which originates in the practice of spreading a robe or a skin, as a seat for guests to whom they wish to show a distinguished kindness, is the universal sign of friendship among the Indians on the Missouri and the Rocky mountains. As usual, captain Lewis repeated this signal three times: still the Indian kept his position, and looked with an air of suspicion on Drewyer and Shields who were now advancing on each side. Captain Lewis was afraid to make any signal for them to halt, lest he should increase the suspicions of the Indian, who began to be uneasy, and they were too distant to hear his voice. He, therefore, took from his pack some beads, a looking-glass and a few trinkets, which he had brought for the purpose, and leaving his gun advanced unarmed towards the Indian. He remained in the same position till cap-

tain Lewis came within two hundred yards of
him, when he turned his horse, and began to move
off slowly; captain Lewis then called out to him,
in as loud a voice as he could, repeating the word,
tabba bone! which in the Shoshonee language
means white man; but looking over his shoulder
the Indian kept his eyes on Drewyer and Shields,
who were still advancing, without recollecting the
impropriety of doing so at such a moment, till
captain Lewis made a signal to them to halt:
this Drewyer obeyed, but Shields did not observe
it, and still went forward: seeing Drewyer halt
the Indian turned his horse about as if to wait for
captain Lewis who now reached within one hundred and fifty paces, repeating the word tabba
bone, and holding up the trinkets in his hand, at
the same time stripping up the sleeve of his shirt
to show the colour of his skin. The Indian suffered him to advance within one hundred paces,
then suddenly turned his horse, and giving him the
whip, leaped across the creek and disappeared in
an instant among the willow bushes: with him
vanished all the hopes which the sight of him had
inspired of a friendly introduction to his countrymen. Though sadly disappointed by the impru-
dence of his two men, captain Lewis determined
to make the incident of some use, and therefore
calling the men to him they all set off after the
track of the horse, which they hoped might lead
them to the camp of the Indian who had fled, or
if he had given the alarm to any small party,
their track might conduct them to the body of the
nation. They now fixed a small flag of the United
States on a pole, which was carried by one of the
men as a signal of their friendly intentions, should
the Indians observe them as they were advancing.
The route lay across an island formed by a nearly

equal division of the creek in the bottom: after reaching the open grounds on the right side of the creek, the track turned towards some high hills about three miles distant. Presuming that the Indian camp might be among these hills, and that by advancing hastily he might be seen and alarm them, captain Lewis sought an elevated situation near the creek, had a fire made of willow brush, and took breakfast. At the same time he prepared a small assortment of beads, trinkets, awls, some paint and a looking glass, and placed them on a pole near the fire, in order that if the Indians returned they might discover that the party were white men and friends. Whilst making these preparations a very heavy shower of rain and hail came on, and wet them to the skin: in about twenty minutes it was over, and captain Lewis then renewed his pursuit, but as the rain had made the grass which the horse had trodden down rise again, his track could with difficulty be distinguished. As they went along they passed several places where the Indians seemed to have been digging roots to-day, and saw the fresh track of eight or ten horses, but they had been wandering about in so confused a manner that he could not discern any particular path, and at last, after pursuing it about four miles along the valley to the left under the foot of the hills, he lost the track of the fugitive Indian. Near the head of the valley they had passed a large bog covered with moss and tall grass, among which were several springs of pure cold water: they now turned a little to the left along the foot of the high hills, and reached a small creek where they encamped for the night, having made about twenty miles, though not more than ten in a direct line from their camp of last evening.

The morning being rainy and wet we did not set out with the canoes till after an early breakfast. During the first three miles we passed three small islands, six bayous on different sides of the river, and the same number of bends towards the right. Here we reached the lower point of a large island which we called Three-thousand-mile island, on account of its being at that distance from the mouth of the Missouri. It is three miles and a half in length, and as we coasted along it we passed several small bends of the river towards the left, and two bayous on the same side. After leaving the upper point of Three-thousand-mile island, we followed the main channel on the left side, which led us by three small islands and several small bayous, and fifteen bends towards the right. Then at the distance of seven miles and a half we encamped on the upper end of a large island near the right. The river was shallow and rapid, so that we were obliged to be in the water during a great part of the day, dragging the canoes over the shoals and ripples. Its course too was so crooked, that notwithstanding we had made fourteen miles by water, we were only five miles from our encampment of last night. The country consists of a low ground on the river about five miles wide, and succeeded on both sides by plains of the same extent which reach to the base of the mountains. These low grounds are very much intersected by bayous, and in those on the left side is a large proportion of bog covered with tall grass, which would yield a fine turf. There are very few trees, and those small narrow-leafed cottonwood: the principal growth being the narrow-leafed willow, and currant bushes, among which were some bunches of privy near the river. We saw a number of geese, ducks, beaver, otter, deer and antelopes, of all which one beaver was killed with a pole from the boat, three otters with a tomahawk, and the hunters brought in three deer and an antelope.

Monday, 12.—This morning as soon as it was light captain Lewis sent Drewyer to reconnoitre if possible the route of the Indians: in about an hour and a half he returned, after following the tracks of the horse which we had lost yesterday to the mountains, where they ascended and were no longer visible. Captain Lewis now decided on making the circuit along the foot of the mountains which formed the cove, expecting by that means to find a road across them, and accordingly sent Drewyer on one side, and Shields on the other. In this way they crossed four small rivulets near each other, on which were some bowers or conical lodges of willow brush, which seemed to have been made recently. From the manner in which the ground in the neighbourhood was torn up the Indians appeared to have been gathering roots; but captain Lewis could not discover what particular plant they were searching for, nor could he find any fresh track, till at the distance of four miles from his camp he met a large plain Indian road which came into the cove from the northeast, and wound along the foot of the mountains to the southwest, approaching obliquely the main stream he had left yesterday. Down this road he now went towards the southwest: at the distance of five miles it crossed a large run or creek, which is a principal branch of the main stream into which it falls, just above the high cliffs or gates observed yesterday, and which they now saw below them: here they halted and breakfasted on the last of the deer, keeping a small piece of pork in reserve against accident:

they then continued through the low bottom
along the main stream near the foot of the mountains on their right. For the first five miles the
valley continues towards the southwest from two
to three miles in width; then the main stream,
which had received two small branches from the
left in the valley, turns abruptly to the west
through a narrow bottom between the mountains.
The road was still plain, and as it led them directly on towards the mountain the stream gradually became smaller, till after going two miles it
had so greatly diminished in width that one of the
men in a fit of enthusiasm, with one foot on each
side of the river, thanked God that he had lived
to bestride the Missouri. As they went along
their hopes of soon seeing the waters of the
Columbia arose almost to painful anxiety, when
after four miles from the last abrupt turn of the
river, they reached a small gap formed by the high
mountains which recede on each side, leaving
room for the Indian road. From the foot of one
of the lowest of these mountains, which rises with
a gentle ascent of about half a mile, issues the
remotest water of the Missouri. They had now
reached the hidden sources of that river, which
had never yet been seen by civilized man; and as
they quenched their thirst at the chaste and icy
fountain—as they sat down by the brink of that
little rivulet, which yielded its distant and modest
tribute to the parent ocean, they felt themselves
rewarded for all their labours and all their difficulties. They left reluctantly this interesting spot,
and pursuing the Indian road through the interval
of the hills, arrived at the top of a ridge, from
which they saw high mountains partially covered
with snow still to the west of them. The ridge on
which they stood formed the dividing line between
47

the waters of the Atlantic and Pacific oceans.
They followed a descent much steeper than that
on the eastern side, and at the distance of three
quarters of a mile reached a handsome bold creek
of cold clear water running to the westward.
They stopped to taste for the first time the waters
of the Columbia; and after a few minutes followed
the road across steep hills and low hollows, till
they reached a spring on the side of a mountain:
here they found a sufficient quantity of dry willow
brush for fuel, and therefore halted for the night;
and having killed nothing in the course of the day
supped on their last piece of pork, and trusted to
fortune for some other food to mix with a little
flour and parched meal, which was all that now
remained of their provisions. Before reaching the
fountain of the Missouri they saw several large
hawks nearly black, and some of the heath cocks:
these last have a long pointed tail, and are of a
uniform dark brown colour, much larger than the
common dunghill fowl, and similar in habits and
the mode of flying to the grouse or prairie hen.
Drewyer also wounded at the distance of one hundred and thirty yards an animal which we had
not yet seen, but which after falling recovered
itself and escaped. It seemed to be of the fox
kind, rather larger than the small wolf of the
plains, and with a skin in which black, reddish
brown, and yellow, were curiously intermixed.
On the creek of the Columbia they found a species
of currant which does not grow as high as that
of the Missouri, though it is more branching, and
its leaf, the under disk of which is covered with a
hairy pubescence, is twice as large. The fruit is of
the ordinary size and shape of the currant, and
supported in the usual manner, but is of a deep
purple colour, acid, and of a very inferior flavour.

We proceeded on in the boats, but as the river was very shallow and rapid, the navigation is extremely difficult, and the men who are almost constantly in the water are getting feeble and sore, and so much wore down by fatigue that they are very anxious to commence travelling by land. We went along the main channel which is on the right side, and after passing nine bends in that direction, three islands and a number of bayous, reached at the distance of five and a half miles the upper point of a large island. At noon there was a storm of thunder which continued about half an hour; after which we proceeded, but as it was necessary to drag the canoes over the shoals and rapids, made but little progress. On leaving the island we passed a number of short bends, several bayous, and one run of water on the right side, and having gone by four small and two large islands, encamped on a smooth plain to the left near a few cottonwood trees: our journey by water was just twelve miles, and four in a direct line. The hunters supplied us with three deer and a fawn.

Tuesday 13.—Very early in the morning captain Lewis resumed the Indian road, which led him in a western direction, through an open broken country; on the left was a deep valley at the foot of a high range of mountains running from southeast to northwest, with their sides better clad with timber than the hills to which we have been for some time accustomed, and their tops covered in part with snow. At five miles distance, after following the long descent of another valley, he reached a creek about ten yards wide, and on rising the hill beyond it had a view of a handsome little valley on the left, about a mile in width, through which they judged, from the appearance of the timber, that some stream of water most probably passed. On the creek they had just left were some bushes of the white maple, the sumach of the small species with the winged rib, and a species of honeysuckle, resembling in its general appearance and the shape of its leaf the small honeysuckle of the Missouri, except that it is rather larger, and bears a globular berry, about the size of a garden pea, of a white colour, and formed of a soft white mucilaginous substance, in which are several small brown seeds irregularly scattered without any cell, and enveloped in a smooth thin pellicle.

They proceeded along a waving plain parallel to this valley for about four miles, when they discovered two women, a man and some dogs on an eminence at the distance of a mile before them. The strangers first viewed them apparently with much attention for a few minutes, and then two of them sat down as if to await captain Lewis's arrival. He went on till he reached within about half a mile, then ordered his party to stop, put down his knapsack and rifle, and unfurling the flag advanced alone towards the Indians. The females soon retreated behind the hill, but the man remained till captain Lewis came within a hundred yards from him, when he too went off, though captain Lewis called out tabba bone! loud enough to be heard distinctly. He hastened to the top of the hill, but they had all disappeared. The dogs however were less shy, and came close to him; he therefore thought of tying a handkerchief with some beads round their necks, and then let them loose to convince the fugitives of his friendly disposition, but they would not suffer him to take hold of them, and soon left him. He now made a signal to the men, who joined him, and then all followed the track of the Indians, which led along a continuation of the same road they had been already travelling. It was dusty and seemed to have been much used lately both by foot passengers and horsemen. They had not gone along it more than a mile when on a sudden they saw three female Indians, from whom they had been concealed by the deep ravines which intersected the road, till they were now within thirty paces of each other; one of them a young woman immediately took to flight, the other two, an elderly woman and a little girl, seeing we were too near for them to escape, sat on the ground, and holding down their heads seemed as if reconciled to the death which they supposed awaited them. The same habit of holding down the head and inviting the enemy to strike, when all chance of escape is gone, is preserved in Egypt to this day. Captain Lewis instantly put down his rifle, and advancing towards them, took the woman by the hand, raised her up, and repeated the word tabba bone! at the same time stripping up his shirt sleeve to prove that he was a white man, for his hands and face had become by constant exposure quite as dark as their own. She appeared immediately relieved from her alarm, and Drewyer and Shields now coming up, captain Lewis gave them some beads, a few awls, pewter mirrors, and a little paint, and told Drewyer to request the woman to recall her companion who had escaped to some distance, and by alarming the Indians might cause them to attack him without any time for explanation. She did as she was desired, and the young woman returned almost out of breath: captain Lewis gave her an equal portion of trinkets, and painted the tawny cheeks of all three of them with vermillion, a ceremony

51

which among the Shoshonees is emblematic of peace. After they had become composed, he informed them by signs of his wish to go to their camp in order to see their chiefs and warriors; they readily obeyed, and conducted the party along the same road down the river. In this way they marched two miles, when they met a troop of nearly sixty warriors mounted on excellent horses riding at full speed towards them. As they advanced captain Lewis put down his gun, and went with the flag about fifty paces in advance. The chief who with two men were riding in front of the main body, spoke to the women, who now explained that the party was composed of white men, and showed exultingly the presents they had received. The three men immediately leaped from their horses, came up to captain Lewis and embraced him with great cordiality, putting their left arm over his right shoulder and clasping his back, applying at the same time their left cheek to his, and frequently vociferating ah hi e! ah hi e! "I am much pleased, I am much rejoiced." The whole body of warriors now came forward, and our men received the caresses, and no small share of the grease and paint of their new friends. After this fraternal embrace, of which the motive was much more agreeable than the manner, captain Lewis lighted a pipe and offered it to the Indians who had now seated themselves in a circle around the party. But before they would receive this mark of friendship they pulled off their moccasins, a custom as we afterwards learnt, which indicates the sacred sincerity of their professions when they smoke with a stranger, and which imprecates on themselves the misery of going barefoot forever if they are faithless to their words, a penalty by no means light to those who rove over the thorny

52

plains of their country. It is not unworthy to remark the analogy which some of the customs of
those wild children of the wilderness bear to those
recorded in holy writ. Moses is admonished to
pull off his shoes, for the place on which he stood
was holy ground. Why this was enjoined as an
act of peculiar reverence; whether it was from the
circumstance that in the arid region in which the
patriarch then resided, it was deemed a test of
the sincerity of devotion to walk upon the burning
sands barefooted, in some measure analogous to
the pains inflicted by the prickly pear, does not
appear. After smoking a few pipes, some trifling
presents were distributed amongst them, with
which they seemed very much pleased, particularly
with the blue beads and the vermillion. Captain
Lewis then informed the chief that the object of
his visit was friendly, and should be explained as
soon as he reached their camp; but that in the
meantime as the sun was oppressive, and no
water near, he wished to go there as soon as possible. They now put on their moccasins, and
their chief, whose name was Cameahwait, made a
short speech to the warriors. Captain Lewis
then gave him the flag, which he informed him
was among white men the emblem of peace, and
now that he had received it was to be in future
the bond of union between them. The chief then
moved on, our party followed him, and the rest of
the warriors in a squadron, brought up the rear.
After marching a mile they were halted by the
chief, who made a second harangue, on which six
or eight young men rode forward to their camp,
and no further regularity was observed in the
order of march. At the distance of four miles
from where they had first met, they reached the
Indian camp, which was in a handsome level

meadow on the bank of the river. Here they were introduced into an old leathern lodge which the young men who had been sent from the party had fitted up for their reception. After being seated on green boughs and antelope skins, one of the warriors pulled up the grass in the centre of the lodge so as to form a vacant circle of two feet diameter, in which he kindled a fire. The chief then produced his pipe and tobacco, the warriors all pulled off their moccasins, and our party was requested to take off their own. This being done, the chief lighted his pipe at the fire within the magic circle, and then retreating from it began a speech several minutes long, at the end of which he pointed the stem towards the four cardinal points of the heavens, beginning with the east and concluding with the north. After this ceremony he presented the stem in the same way to captain Lewis, who supposing it an invitation to smoke, put out his hand to receive the pipe, but the chief drew it back, and continued to repeat the same offer three times, after which he pointed the stem first to the heavens, then to the centre of the little circle, took three whiffs himself, and presented it again to captain Lewis. Finding that this last offer was in good earnest, he smoked a little, the pipe was then held to each of the white men, and after they had taken a few whiffs was given to the warriors. This pipe was made of a dense transparent green stone, very highly polished, about two and a half inches long, and of an oval figure, the bowl being in the same situation with the stem. A small piece of burnt clay is placed in the bottom of the bowl to separate the tobacco from the end of the stem, and is of an irregularly round figure, not fitting the tube perfectly close, in order that the smoke may pass with facility.

The tobacco is of the same kind with that used by the Minnetarees, Mandans and Ricaras of the Missouri. The Shoshonees do not cultivate this plant, but obtain it from the Rocky mountain Indians, and some of the bands of their own nation who live further south. The ceremony of smoking being concluded, captain Lewis explained to the chief the purposes of his visit, and as by this time all the women and children of the camp had gathered around the lodge to indulge in a view of the first white men they had ever seen, he distributed among them the remainder of the small articles he had brought with him. It was now late in the afternoon, and our party had tasted no food since the night before. On apprising the chief of this circumstance, he said that he had nothing but berries to eat, and presented some cakes made of serviceberry and chokecherries which had been dried in the sun. On these captain Lewis made a hearty meal, and then walked down towards the river: he found it a rapid clear stream forty yards wide and three feet deep; the banks were low and abrupt, like those of the upper part of the Missouri, and the bed formed of loose stones and gravel. Its course, as far as he could observe it, was a little to the north of west, and was bounded on each side by a range of high mountains, of which those on the east are the lowest and most distant from the river.

The chief informed him that this stream discharged itself at the distance of half a day's march, into another of twice its size, coming from the southwest; but added, on further inquiry, that there was scarcely more timber below the junction of those rivers than in this neighbourhood, and that the river was rocky, rapid, and so closely confined between high mountains, that it

55

was impossible to pass down it, either by land or water to the great lake, where as he had understood the white men lived. This information was far from being satisfactory; for there was no timber here that would answer the purpose of building canoes, indeed not more than just sufficient for fuel, and even that consisted of the narrow-leafed cottonwood, the red and the narrow-leafed willow, the chokecherry, serviceberry and a few currant bushes such as are common on the Missouri. The prospect of going on by land is more pleasant; for there are great numbers of horses feeding in every direction round the camp, which will enable us to transport our stores if necessary over the mountains. Captain Lewis returned from the river to his lodge, and on his way an Indian invited him into his bower and gave him a small morsel of boiled antelope and a piece of fresh salmon roasted. This was the first salmon he had seen, and perfectly satisfied him that he was now on the waters of the Pacific. On reaching this lodge, he resumed his conversation with the chief, after which he was entertained with a dance by the Indians. It now proved, as our party had feared, that the men whom they had first met this morning had returned to the camp and spread the alarm that their enemies, the Minnetarees of fort de Prairie, whom they call Pahkees, were advancing on them. The warriors instantly armed themselves and were coming down in expectation of an attack, when they were agreeably surprised by meeting our party. The greater part of them were armed with bows and arrows, and shields, but a few had small fusils, such as are furnished by the northwest company traders, and which they had obtained from the Indians on the Yellowstone, with whom they are now at peace.

They had reason to dread the approach of the Pahkees, who had attacked them in the course of this spring and totally defeated them. On this occasion twenty of their warriors were either killed or made prisoners, and they lost their whole camp except the leathern lodge which they had fitted up for us, and were now obliged to live in huts of a conical figure made with willow brush. The music and dancing, which was in no respect different from those of the Missouri Indians, continued nearly all night; but captain Lewis retired to rest about twelve o'clock, when the fatigues of the day enabled him to sleep though he was awaked several times by the yells of the dancers.

Whilst all these things were occurring to captain Lewis we were slowly and laboriously ascending the river. For the first two and a half miles we went along the island opposite to which we encamped last evening, and soon reached a second island behind which comes in a small creek on the left side of the river. It rises in the mountains to the east and forms a handsome valley for some miles from its mouth, where it is a bold running stream about seven yards wide: we called it M'Neal's creek, after Hugh M'Neal one of our party. Just above this stream and at the distance of four miles from our camp is a point of limestone rock on the right, about seventy feet high, forming a cliff over the river. From the top of it the Beaver's-head bore north 24° east twelve miles distant, the course of Wisdom river, that is the direction of its valley through the mountains is north 25° west, while the gap through which the Jefferson enters the mountains is ten miles above us on a course south 18° west. From this limestone rock we proceeded along several islands, on both sides, and after making twelve miles ar-

rived at a cliff of high rocks on the right, opposite
to which we encamped in a smooth level prairie,
near a few cottonwood trees; but were obliged to
use the dry willow brush for fuel. The river is
still very crooked, the bends short and abrupt,
and obstructed by so many shoals, over which the
canoes were to be dragged, that the men were in
the water three-fourths of the day. They saw
numbers of otter, some beaver, antelopes, ducks,
geese, and cranes, but they killed nothing except a
single deer. They, however, caught some very fine
trout, as they have done for several days past.
The weather had been cloudy and cool during the
forepart of the day, and at eight o'clock a shower
of rain fell.

Wednesday 14.—In order to give time for the
boats to reach the forks of Jefferson river, captain
Lewis determined to remain here and obtain all
the information he could collect with regard to
the country. Having nothing to eat but a little
flour and parched meal, with the berries of the
Indians, he sent out Drewyer and Shields, who
borrowed horses from the natives, to hunt for a
few hours. About the same time the young warriors set out for the same purpose. There are but
few elk or blacktailed deer in this neighbourhood, and as the common red-deer secrete themselves in the bushes when alarmed, they are soon
safe from the arrows, which are but feeble weapons against any animals which the huntsmen cannot previously run down with their horses. The
chief game of the Shoshonees, therefore, is the
antelope, which when pursued retreats to the open
plains, where the horses have full room for the
chase. But such is its extraordinary fleetness and
wind that a single horse has no possible chance of
outrunning it, or tiring it down; and the hunters

are therefore obliged to resort to stratagem. About twenty Indians, mounted on fine horses, and armed with bows and arrows, left the camp; in a short time they descried a herd of ten antelopes: they immediately separated into little squads of two or three, and formed a scattered circle round the herd for five or six miles, keeping at a wary distance, so as not to alarm them till they were perfectly enclosed, and usually selecting some commanding eminence as a stand. Having gained their positions, a small party rode towards the herd, and with wonderful dexterity the huntsman preserved his seat, and the horse his footing, as he ran at full speed over the hills, and down the steep ravines, and along the borders of the precipices. They were soon outstripped by the antelopes, which on gaining the other extremity of the circle were driven back and pursued by the fresh hunters. They turned and flew, rather than ran in another direction; but there too, they found new enemies. In this way they were alternately pursued backwards and forwards, till at length, notwithstanding the skill of the hunters, they all escaped, and the party after running for two hours returned without having caught any thing, and their horses foaming with sweat. This chase, the greater part of which was seen from the camp, formed a beautiful scene; but to the hunters is exceedingly laborious, and so unproductive, even when they are able to worry the animal down and shoot him, that forty or fifty hunters will sometimes be engaged for half a day without obtaining more than two or three antelopes. Soon after they returned, our two huntsmen came in with no better success. Captain Lewis therefore made a little paste with the flour, and the addition of some berries formed a very palatable repast. Having now secured the good will of Cameahwait, captain Lewis informed him of his wish that he would speak to the warriors and endeavour to engage them to accompany him to the forks of Jefferson river, where by this time another chief with a large party of white men were waiting his return: that it would be necessary to take about thirty horses to transport the merchandise; that they should be well rewarded for their trouble; and that when all the party should have reached the Shoshonee camp they would remain some time among them, and trade for horses, as well as concert plans for furnishing them in future with regular supplies of merchandise. He readily consented to do so, and after collecting the tribe together he made a long harangue, and in about an hour and a half returned, and told captain Lewis that they would be ready to accompany him in the morning.

As the early part of the day was cold, and the men stiff and sore from the fatigues of yesterday: we did not set out till seven o'clock. At the distance of a mile we passed a bold stream on the right, which comes from a snowy mountain to the north, and at its entrance is four yards wide, and three feet in depth: we called it Track creek: at six miles further we reached another stream which heads in some springs at the foot of the mountains on the left. After passing a number of bayous and small islands on each side, we encamped about half a mile by land below the Rattlesnake cliffs. The river was cold, shallow, and as it approached the mountains formed one continued rapid, over which we were obliged to drag the boats with great labour and difficulty. By using constant exertions we succeeded in making fourteen miles, but this distance did not carry us more than six and a half in a straight line: several of the men have received wounds and lamed themselves in hauling the boats over the stones. The hunters supplied them with five deer and an antelope.

Thursday 15.—Captain Lewis rose early, and having eaten nothing yesterday except his scanty meal of flour and berries felt the inconveniences of extreme hunger. On inquiry he found that his whole stock of provisions consisted of two pounds of flour. This he ordered to be divided into two equal parts, and one half of it boiled with the berries into a sort of pudding: and after presenting a large share to the chief, he and his three men breakfasted on the remainder. Cameahwait was delighted at this new dish: he took a little of the flour in his hand tasted and examined it very narrowly, asking if it was made of roots; captain Lewis explained the process of preparing it, and he said it was the best thing he had eaten for a long time.

This being finished, captain Lewis now endeavoured to hasten the departure of the Indians who still hesitated, and seemed reluctant to move, although the chief addressed them twice for the purpose of urging them: on inquiring the reason, Cameahwait told him that some foolish person had suggested that he was in league with their enemies the Pahkees, and had come only to draw them into ambuscade, but that he himself did not believe it: captain Lewis felt uneasy at this insinuation: he knew the suspicious temper of the Indians, accustomed from their infancy to regard every stranger as an enemy, and saw that if this suggestion were not instantly checked, it might hazard the total failure of the enterprise. Assuming therefore a serious air, he told the chief that he was sorry to find they placed so little confidence in him, but that he pardoned their suspicions because they were ignorant of the character of white men, among whom it was disgraceful to lie or entrap even an enemy by falsehood; that if they continued to think thus meanly of us they might be assured no white men would ever come to supply them with arms and merchandise; that there was at this moment a party of white men waiting to trade with them at the forks of the river; and that if the greater part of the tribe entertained any suspicion, he hoped there were still among them some who were men, who would go and see with their own eyes the truth of what he said, and who, even if there was any danger, were not afraid to die. To doubt the courage of an Indian is to touch the tenderest string of his mind, and the surest way to rouse him to any dangerous achievement. Cameahwait instantly replied, that he was not afraid to die, and mounting his horse, for the third time harangued the warriors: he told them that he was resolved to go if he went alone, or if he were sure of perishing; that he hoped there were among those who heard him some who were not afraid to die, and who would prove it by mounting their horses and following him. This harangue produced an effect on six or eight only of the warriors, who now joined their chief. With these captain Lewis smoked a pipe, and then fearful of some change in their capricious temper set out immediately. It was about twelve o'clock when his small party left the camp, attended by Cameahwait and the eight warriors: their departure seemed to spread a gloom over the village; those who would not venture to go were sullen and melancholy, and the women were crying and imploring the Great

Spirit to protect their warriors as if they were going to certain destruction: yet such is the wavering inconstancy of these savages, that captain Lewis's party had not gone far when they were joined by ten or twelve more warriors, and before reaching the creek which they had passed on the morning of the 13th, all the men of the nation and a number of women had overtaken them, and had changed from the surly ill temper in which they were two hours ago, to the greatest cheerfulness and gaiety. When they arrived at the spring on the side of the mountain where the party had encamped on the 12th, the chief insisted on halting to let the horses graze; to which captain Lewis assented and smoked with them. They are excessively fond of the pipe, in which however they are not able to indulge much as they do not cultivate tobacco themselves, and their rugged country affords them but few articles to exchange for it. Here they remained for about an hour, and on setting out, by engaging to pay four of the party, captain Lewis obtained permission for himself and each of his men to ride behind an Indian; but he soon found riding without stirrups more tiresome than walking, and therefore dismounted, making the Indian carry his pack. About sunset they reached the upper part of the level valley in the cove through which he had passed, and which they now called Shoshonee cove. The grass being burnt on the north side of the river they crossed over to the south, and encamped about four miles above the narrow pass between the hills noticed as they traversed the cove before. The river was here about six yards wide, and frequently dammed up by the beaver. Drewyer had been sent forward to hunt, but he returned in the evening unsuccessful, and their only supper therefore was the remaining pound of flour stirred in a little boiling water, and then divided between the four white men and two of the Indians.

In order not to exhaust the strength of the men, captain Clark did not leave his camp till after breakfast. Although he was scarcely half a mile below the Rattlesnake cliffs he was obliged to make a circuit of two miles by water before he reached them. The river now passed between low and rugged mountains and cliffs formed of a mixture of limestone and a hard black rock, with no covering except a few scattered pines. At the distance of four miles is a bold little stream which throws itself from the mountains down a steep precipice of rocks on the left. One mile further is a second point of rocks, and an island, about a mile beyond which is a creek on the right, ten yards wide and three feet three inches in depth, with a strong current: we called it Willard's creek after one of our men, Alexander Willard. Three miles beyond this creek, after passing a high cliff on the right opposite to a steep hill, we reached a small meadow on the left bank of the river. During its passage through these hills to Willard's creek the river had been less tortuous than usual, so that in the first six miles to Willard's creek we had advanced four miles on our route. We continued on for two miles, till we reached in the evening a small bottom covered with clover and a few cottonwood trees: here we passed the night near the remains of some old Indian lodges of brush. The river is as it has been for some days shallow and rapid; and our men, who are for hours together in the river, suffer not only from fatigue, but from the extreme coldness of the water, the temperature of which is as low as that of the freshest springs in our country. In walking along the side of the river, captain Clark was very near being bitten twice by rattlesnakes, and the Indian woman narrowly escaped the same misfortune. We caught a number of fine trout; but the only game procured to-day was a buck, which had a peculiarly bitter taste, proceeding probably from its favourite food, the willow.

Friday, 16.—As neither our party nor the Indians had any thing to eat, captain Lewis sent two of his hunters ahead this morning to procure some provision: at the same time he requested Cameahwait to prevent his young men from going out, lest by their noise they might alarm the game; but this measure immediately revived their suspicions: it now began to be believed that these men were sent forward in order to apprise the enemy of their coming, and as captain Lewis was fearful of exciting any further uneasiness, he made no objection on seeing a small party of Indians go on each side of the valley under pretence of hunting, but in reality to watch the movements of our two men: even this precaution however did not quiet the alarms of the Indians, a considerable part of whom returned home, leaving only twenty-eight men and three women. After the hunters had been gone about an hour, captain Lewis again mounted with one of the Indians behind him, and the whole party set out; but just as they passed through the narrows they saw one of the spies coming back at full speed across the plain: the chief stopped and seemed uneasy, the whole band were moved with fresh suspicions, and captain Lewis himself was much disconcerted, lest by some unfortunate accident some of their enemies might have perhaps straggled that way. The young Indian had scarcely breath to say a few words as he came up, when the whole troop dashed forward as fast as their horses could carry them; and captain Lewis astonished at this movement was borne along for nearly a mile before he learnt with great satisfaction that it was all caused by the spy's having come to announce that one of the white men had killed a deer. Relieved from his anxiety he now found the jolting very uncomfortable; for the Indian behind him being afraid of not getting his share of the feast had lashed the horse at every step since they set off; he therefore reined him in and ordered the Indian to stop beating him. The fellow had no idea of losing time in disputing the point, and jumping off the horse ran for a mile at full speed. Captain Lewis slackened his pace, and followed at a sufficient distance to observe them. When they reached the place where Drewyer had thrown out the intestines, they all dismounted in confusion and ran tumbling over each other like famished dogs: each tore away whatever part he could and instantly began to eat it; some had the liver, some the kidneys, in short no part on which we are accustomed to look with disgust escaped them: one of them who had seized about nine feet of the entrails was chewing at one end, while with his hand he was diligently clearing his way by discharging the contents at the other. It was indeed impossible to see these wretches ravenously feeding on the filth of animals, and the blood streaming from their mouths, without deploring how nearly the condition of savages approaches that of the brute creation: yet though suffering with hunger they did not attempt, as they might have done, to take by force the whole deer, but contented themselves with what had been thrown away by the hunter. Captain Lewis

now had the deer skinned, and after reserving a
quarter of it gave the rest of the animal to the
chief to be divided among the Indians, who immediately devoured nearly the whole of it without cooking. They now went forward towards
the creek where there was some brushwood to
make a fire, and found Drewyer who had killed a
second deer: the same struggle for the entrails was
renewed here, and on giving nearly the whole deer
to the Indians, they devoured it even to the soft
part of the hoofs. A fire being made captain
Lewis had his breakfast, during which Drewyer
brought in a third deer: this too, after reserving
one quarter, was given to the Indians, who now
seemed completely satisfied and in good humour.
At this place they remained about two hours to
let the horses graze, and then continued their
journey, and towards evening reached the lower
part of the cove, having on the way shot an antelope, the greater part of which was given to the
Indians. As they were now approaching the
place where they had been told by captain Lewis
they would see the white men, the chief insisted on
halting: they therefore all dismounted, and Cameahwait with great ceremony and as if for ornament, put tippets or skins round the necks of our
party, similar to those worn by themselves. As
this was obviously intended to disguise the white
men, captain Lewis in order to inspire them with
more confidence put his cocked hat and feather on
the head of the chief, and as his own over-shirt
was in the Indian form, and his skin browned by
the sun, he could not have been distinguished
from an Indian: the men followed his example,
and the change seemed to be very agreeable to the
Indians.

In order to guard however against any disap-

67

pointment captain Lewis again explained the possibility of our not having reached the forks in consequence of the difficulty of the navigation, so that if they should not find us at that spot they might be assured of our not being far below. They again all mounted their horses and rode on rapidly, making one of the Indians carry their flag, so that we might recognise them as they approached us; but to the mortification and disappointment of both parties on coming within two miles of the forks, no canoes were to be seen. Uneasy lest at this moment he should be abandoned, and all his hopes of obtaining aid from the Indians be destroyed, captain Lewis gave the chief his gun, telling him that if the enemies of his nation were in the bushes he might defend himself with it; that for his own part he was not afraid to die, and that the chief might shoot him as soon as they discovered themselves betrayed. The other three men at the same time gave their guns to the Indians, who now seemed more easy, but still wavered in their resolutions. As they went on towards the point, captain Lewis perceiving how critical his situation had become, resolved to attempt a stratagem which his present difficulty seemed completely to justify. Recollecting the notes he had left at the point for us, he sent Drewyer for them with an Indian who witnessed his taking them from the pole. When they were brought, captain Lewis told Cameahwait that on leaving his brother chief at the place where the river issues from the mountains, it was agreed that the boats should not be brought higher than the next forks we should meet; but that if the rapid water prevented the boats from coming on as fast as they expected, his brother chief was to send a note to the first forks above him to let

68

him know where the boats were; that this note had been left this morning at the forks, and mentioned that the canoes were just below the mountains, and coming slowly up in consequence of the current. Captain Lewis added, that he would stay at the forks for his brother chief, but would send a man down the river, and that if Cameah-wait doubted what he said, one of their young men would go with him whilst he and the other two remained at the forks. This story satisfied the chief and the greater part of the Indians, but a few did not conceal their suspicions, observing that we told different stories, and complaining that the chief exposed them to danger by a mistaken confidence. Captain Lewis now wrote by the light of some willow brush a note to captain Clark, which he gave to Drewyer, with an order to use all possible expedition in ascending the river, and engaged an Indian to accompany him by a promise of a knife and some beads. At bedtime the chief and five others slept round the fire of captain Lewis, and the rest hid themselves in different parts of the willow brush to avoid the enemy, who they feared would attack them in the night. Captain Lewis endeavoured to assume a cheerfulness he did not feel to prevent the despondency of the savages: after conversing gayly with them he retired to his mosquito bier, by the side of which the chief now placed himself: he lay down, yet slept but little, being in fact scarcely less uneasy than his Indian companions. He was apprehensive that finding the ascent of the river impracticable, captain Clark might have stopped below the Rattlesnake bluff, and the messenger would not meet him. The consequence of disappointing the Indians at this moment would most probably be, that they would retire and secrete themselves in the mountains, so as to prevent our having an opportunity of recovering their confidence: they would also spread a panic through all the neighbouring Indians, and cut us off from the supply of horses so useful and almost so essential to our success: he was at the same time consoled by remembering that his hopes of assistance rested on better foundations than their generosity—their avarice, and their curiosity. He had promised liberal exchanges for their horses; but what was still more seductive, he had told them that one of their countrywomen who had been taken with the Minnetarees accompanied the party below; and one of the men had spread the report of our having with us a man perfectly black, whose hair was short and curled. This last account had excited a great degree of curiosity, and they seemed more desirous of seeing this monster than of obtaining the most favourable barter for their horses.

In the meantime we had set out after breakfast, and although we proceeded with more ease than we did yesterday, the river was still so rapid and shallow as to oblige us to drag the large canoes during the greater part of the day. For the first seven miles the river formed a bend to the right so as to make our advance only three miles in a straight line; the stream is crooked, narrow, small, and shallow, with highlands occasionally on the banks, and strewed with islands, four of which are opposite to each other. Near this place we left the valley, to which we gave the name of Serviceberry valley, from the abundance of that fruit now ripe which is found in it. In the course of the four following miles we passed several more islands and bayous on each side of the river, and reached a high cliff on the right. Two and a half miles beyond this the cliffs approach on both sides and form a very considerable rapid near the entrance of a bold running stream on the left. The water was now excessively cold, and the rapids had been frequent and troublesome. On ascending an eminence captain Clark saw the forks of the river and sent the hunters up. They must have left it only a short time before captain Lewis's arrival, but fortunately had not seen the note which enabled him to induce the Indians to stay with him. From the top of this eminence he could discover only three trees through the whole country, nor was there along the sides of the cliffs they had passed in the course of the day, any timber except a few small pines: the low grounds were supplied with willow, currant bushes, and serviceberries. After advancing half a mile further we came to the lower point of an island near the middle of the river, and about the centre of the valley: here we halted for the night, only four miles by land, though ten by water, below the point where captain Lewis lay. Although we had made only fourteen miles, the labours of the men had fatigued and exhausted them very much: we therefore collected some small willow brush for a fire, and lay down to sleep.

CHAPTER XV.

Affecting interview between the wife of Chaboneau and the chief of the Shoshonees—Council held with that nation, and favourable result—The extreme navigable point of the Missouri mentioned—General character of the river and of the country through which it passes—Captain Clark in exploring the source of the Columbia falls in company with another party of Shoshonees—The geographical information acquired from one of that party—Their manner of catching fish—The party reach Lewis river—The difficulties which captain Clark had to encounter in his route—Friendship and hospitality of the Shoshonees—The party with captain Lewis employed in making saddles, and preparing for the journey.

Saturday, August 17.—Captain Lewis rose very early, and despatched Drewyer and the Indian down the river in quest of the boats. Shields was sent out at the same time to hunt, while M'Neal prepared a breakfast out of the remainder of the meat. Drewyer had been gone about two hours, and the Indians were all anxiously waiting for some news, when an Indian who had straggled a short distance down the river, returned with a report that he had seen the white men, who were only a short distance below, and were coming on. The Indians were all transported with joy, and the chief in the warmth of his satisfaction renewed his embrace to captain Lewis, who was quite as much delighted as the Indians themselves; the report proved most agreeably true. On setting out at seven o'clock, captain Clark with Chaboneau and his wife walked on shore, but they had not gone more than a mile before captain Clark saw Sacajawea, who was with her husband one hundred yards ahead, begin to dance and show

72

every mark of the most extravagant joy, turning round him and pointing to several Indians, whom he now saw advancing on horseback, sucking her fingers at the same time to indicate that they were of her native tribe. As they advanced captain Clark discovered among them Drewyer dressed like an Indian, from whom he learned the situation of the party. While the boats were performing the circuit, he went towards the forks with the Indians, who as they went along, sang aloud with the greatest appearance of delight. We soon drew near to the camp, and just as we approached it a woman made her way through the crowd towards Sacajawea, and recognising each other, they embraced with the most tender affection. The meeting of these two young women had in it something peculiarly touching, not only in the ardent manner in which their feelings were expressed, but from the real interest of their situation. They had been companions in childhood, in the war with the Minnetarees they had both been taken prisoners in the same battle, they had shared and softened the rigours of their captivity, till one of them had escaped from the Minnetarees, with scarce a hope of ever seeing her friend relieved from the hands of her enemies. While Sacajawea was renewing among the women the friendships of former days, captain Clark went on, and was received by captain Lewis and the chief, who after the first embraces and salutations were over, conducted him to a sort of circular tent or shade of willows. Here he was seated on a white robe; and the chief immediately tied in his hair six small shells resembling pearls, an ornament highly valued by these people, who procured them in the course of trade from the seacoast. The moccasins of the whole party were then taken off, and after much ceremony the smoking began. After this the conference was to be opened, and glad of an opportunity of being able to converse more intelligibly, Sacajawea was sent for; she came into the tent, sat down, and was beginning to interpret, when in the person of Cameahwait she recognised her brother: she instantly jumped up, and ran and embraced him, throwing over him her blanket and weeping profusely: the chief was himself moved, though not in the same degree. After some conversation between them she resumed her seat, and attempted to interpret for us, but her new situation seemed to overpower her, and she was frequently interrupted by her tears. After the council was finished, the unfortunate woman learnt that all her family were dead except two brothers, one of whom was absent, and a son of her eldest sister, a small boy, who was immediately adopted by her. The canoes arriving soon after, we formed a camp in a meadow on the left side, a little below the forks; took out our baggage, and by means of our sails and willow poles formed a canopy for our Indian visitors. About four o'clock the chiefs and warriors were collected, and after the customary ceremony of taking off the moccasins and smoking a pipe, we explained to them in a long harangue the purposes of our visit, making themselves one conspicuous object of the good wishes of our government, on whose strength as well as its friendly disposition we expatiated. We told them of their dependence on the will of our government for all future supplies of whatever was necessary either for their comfort or defence; that as we were sent to discover the best route by which merchandise could be conveyed to them, and no trade would be begun before our return, it was mutually advantageous that we

74

should proceed with as little delay as possible; that we were under the necessity of requesting them to furnish us with horses to transport our baggage across the mountains, and a guide to show us the route, but that they should be amply remunerated for their horses, as well as for every other service they should render us. In the meantime our first wish was, that they should immediately collect as many horses as were necessary to transport our baggage to their village, where, at our leisure we would trade with them for as many horses as they could spare.

The speech made a favourable impression: the chief in reply thanked us for our expressions of friendship towards himself and his nation, and declared their willingness to render us every service. He lamented that it would be so long before they should be supplied with firearms, but that till then they could subsist as they had heretofore done. He concluded by saying that there were not horses here sufficient to transport our goods, but that he would return to the village to-morrow, and bring all his own horses, and encourage his people to come over with theirs. The conference being ended to our satisfaction, we now enquired of Cameahwait what chiefs were among the party, and he pointed out two of them. We then distributed our presents: to Cameahwait we gave a medal of the small size, with the likeness of President Jefferson, and on the reverse a figure of hands clasped with a pipe and tomahawk: to this was added an uniform coat, a shirt, a pair of scarlet leggings, a carrot of tobacco, and some small articles. Each of the other chiefs received a small medal struck during the presidency of general Washington, a shirt, handkerchief, leggings, a knife, and some tobacco. Medals of the same sort were also presented to two young warriors, who though not chiefs were promising youths and very much respected in the tribe. These honorary gifts were followed by presents of paint, moccasins, awls, knives, beads and looking-glasses. We also gave them all a plentiful meal of Indian corn, of which the hull is taken off by being boiled in lye; and as this was the first they had ever tasted, they were very much pleased with it. They had indeed abundant sources of surprise in all they saw: the appearance of the men, their arms, their clothing, the canoes, the strange looks of the negro, and the sagacity of our dog, all in turn shared their admiration, which was raised to astonishment by a shot from the airgun: this operation was instantly considered as *a great medicine,* by which they as well as the other Indians mean something emanating directly from the Great Spirit, or produced by his invisible and incomprehensible agency. The disp ay of all these riches had been intermixed with inquiries into the geographical situation of their country; for we had learnt by experience, that to keep the savages in good temper their attention should not be wearied with too much business; but that the serious affairs should be enlivened by a mixture of what is new and entertaining. Our hunters brought in very seasonably four deer and an antelope, the last of which we gave to the Indians, who in a very short time devoured it. After the council was over, we consulted as to our future operations. The game does not promise to last here for a number of days, and this circumstance combined with many others to induce our going on as soon as possible. Our Indian information as to the state of the Columbia is of a very alarming kind, and our first object is of course to ascertain the practicability of descending it, of which the Indians discourage our expectations. It was therefore agreed that captain Clark should set off in the morning with eleven men, furnished, besides their arms, with tools for making canoes; that he should take Chaboneau and his wife to the camp of the Shoshonees, where he was to leave them, in order to hasten the collection of horses; that he was then to lead his men down to the Columbia, and if he found it navigable, and the timber in sufficient quantity, begin to build canoes. As soon as he had decided as to the propriety of proceeding down the Columbia or across the mountains, he was to send back one of the men with information of it to captain Lewis, who by that time would have brought up the whole party, and the rest of the baggage as far as the Shoshonee village.

Preparations were accordingly made this evening for such an arrangement. The sun is excessively hot in the day time, but the nights very cold, and rendered still more unpleasant from the want of any fuel except willow brush. The appearances too of game, for many days' subsistence, are not very favourable.

Sunday 18.—In order to relieve the men of captain Clark's party from the heavy weight of their arms, provisions and tools, we exposed a few articles to barter for horses, and soon obtained three very good ones, in exchange for which we gave a uniform coat, a pair of leggings, a few handkerchiefs, three knifes and some other small articles, the whole of which did not in the United States cost more than twenty dollars: a fourth was purchased by the men for an old chequered shirt, a pair of old leggings and a knife. The Indians seemed to be quite as well pleased as ourselves at the bargains they had made. We now found that the two inferior chiefs were somewhat displeased at not having received a present equal to that given to the great chief, who appeared in a dress so much finer than their own. To allay their discontent, we bestowed on them two old coats, and promised them that if they were active in assisting us across the mountains they should have an additional present. This treatment completely reconciled them, and the whole Indian party, except two men and two women, set out in perfect good humour to return home with captain Clark. After going fifteen miles through a wide level valley with no wood but willows and shrubs, he encamped in the Shoshonee cove near a narrow pass where the highlands approach within two hundred yards of each other, and the river is only ten yards wide. The Indians went on further, except the three chiefs and two young men, who assisted in eating two deer brought in by the hunters. After their departure every thing was prepared for the transportation of the baggage, which was now exposed to the air and dried. Our game was one deer and a beaver, and we saw an abundance of trout in the river for which we fixed a net in the evening.

We have now reached the extreme navigable point of the Missouri, which our observation places in latitude 43° 30′ 43″ north. It is difficult to comprise in any general description the characteristics of a river so extensive, and fed by so many streams which have their sources in a great variety of soils and climates. But the Missouri is still sufficiently powerful to give to all its waters something of a common character, which is of course decided by the nature of the country through which it passes. The bed of the river is chiefly composed of a blue mud from which the water itself derives a deep tinge. From its junction here to the place near which it leaves the mountains, its course is embarrassed by rapids and rocks which the hills on each side have thrown into its channel. From that place, its current, with the exception of the falls, is not difficult of navigation, nor is there much variation in its appearance till the mouth of the Platte. That powerful river throws out vast quantities of coarse sand which contribute to give a new face to the Missouri, which is now much more impeded by islands. The sand, as it is drifted down, adheres in time to some of the projecting points from the shore, and forms a barrier to the mud, which at length fills to the same height with the sandbar itself: as soon as it has acquired a consistency, the willow grows there the first year, and by its roots assists the solidity of the whole: as the mud and sand accumulate the cottonwood tree next appears; till the gradual excretion of soils raises the surface of the point above the highest freshets. Thus stopped in its course the water seeks a passage elsewhere, and as the soil on each side is light and yielding, what was only a peninsula, becomes gradually an island, and the river indemnifies itself for the usurpation by encroaching on the adjacent shore. In this way the Missouri like the Mississippi is constantly cutting off the projections of the shore, and leaving its ancient channel, which is then marked by the mud it has deposited and a few stagnant ponds.

The general appearance of the country as it presents itself on ascending may be thus described: From its mouth to the two Charletons, a ridge of highlands borders the river at a small distance, leaving between them fine rich meadows. From the mouth of the two Charletons the hills recede from the river, giving greater extent to the low grounds, but they again approach the river for a short distance near Grand river, and again at Snake creek. From that point they retire, nor do they come again to the neighbourhood of the river till above the Sauk prairie, where they are comparatively low and small. Thence they diverge and reappear at the Charaton Searty, after which they are scarcely if at all discernible, till they advance to the Missouri nearly opposite to the Kanzas.

The same ridge of hills extends on the south side, in almost one unbroken chain, from the mouth of the Missouri to the Kanzas, though decreasing in height beyond the Osage. As they are nearer the river than the hills on the opposite sides, the intermediate low grounds are of course narrower, but the general character of the soil is common to both sides.

In the meadows and along the shore, the tree most common is the cottonwood, which with the willow forms almost the exclusive growth of the Missouri. The hills or rather high grounds, for they do not rise higher than from one hundred and fifty to two hundred feet, are composed of a good rich black soil, which is perfectly susceptible of cultivation, though it becomes richer on the hills beyond the Platte, and are in general thinly covered with timber. Beyond these hills the country extends into high open plains, which are on both sides sufficiently fertile, but the south has the advantage of better streams of water, and may therefore be considered as preferable for settlements. The lands, however, become much better and the timber more abundant between the Osage and the Kanzas. From the Kanzas to the Nadawa the hills continue at nearly an equal distance, varying from four to eight miles from each other, except that from the little Platte to nearly opposite the ancient Kanzas village, the hills are more remote, and the meadows of course wider on the north side of the river. From the Nadawa the northern hills disappear, except at occasional intervals, where they are seen at a distance, till they return about twenty-seven miles above the Platte near the ancient village of the Ayoways. On the south the hills continue close to the river from the ancient village of the Kanzas up to Council bluff, fifty miles beyond the Platte; forming high prairie lands. On both sides the lands are good, and perhaps this distance from the Osage to the Platte may be recommended as among the best districts on the Missouri for the purposes of settlers.

From the Ayoway village the northern hills again retire from the river, to which they do not return till three hundred and twenty miles above, at Floyd's river. The hills on the south also leave the river at Council bluffs, and reappear at the Mahar village, two hundred miles up the Missouri. The country thus abandoned by the hills is more open and the timber in smaller quantities than below the Platte, so that although the plain is rich and covered with high grass, the want of wood renders it less calculated for cultivation than below that river.

The northern hills after remaining near the Missouri for a few miles at Floyd's river, recede from it at the Sioux river, the course of which they follow; and though they again visit the Missouri at Whitestone river, where they are low, yet they do not return to it till beyond James river. The highlands on the south, after continuing near the river at the Mahar villages, again disappear, and do not approach it till the Cobalt bluffs, about forty-four miles from the villages, and then from those bluffs to the Yellowstone river, a distance of about one thousand miles, they follow the banks of the river with scarcely any deviation.

From the James river, the lower grounds are confined within a narrow space by the hills on both sides, which now continue near each other up to the mountains. The space between them however varies from one to three miles as high as the Muscleshell river, from which the hills approach so high as to leave scarcely any low grounds on the river, and near the falls reach the water's edge. Beyond the falls the hills are scattered and low to the first range of mountains.

The soil during the whole length of the Missouri below the Platte is generally speaking very fine, and although the timber is scarce, there is still sufficient for the purposes of settlers. But beyond that river, although the soil is still rich, yet the almost total absence of timber, and particularly the want of good water, of which there is but a small quantity in the creeks, and even that brackish, oppose powerful obstacles to its settlement. The difficulty becomes still greater between the Muscleshell river and the falls, where besides the greater scarcity of timber, the country itself is less fertile.

The elevation of these highlands varies as they pass through this extensive tract of country. From Wood river they are about one hundred and fifty feet above the water, and continue at that height till they rise near the Osage, from which place to the ancient fortification they again diminish in size. Thence they continue higher till the Mandan village, after which they are rather lower till the neighbourhood of Muscleshell river, where they are met by the Northern hills, which have advanced at a more uniform height, varying from one hundred and fifty to two hundred or three hundred feet. From this place to the mountains the height of both is nearly the same, from three hundred to five hundred feet, and the low grounds so narrow that the traveller seems passing through a range of high country. From Maria's river to the falls, the hills descend to the height of about two or three hundred feet.

Monday 19.—The morning was cold, and the grass perfectly whitened by the frost. We were engaged in preparing packs and saddles to load the horses as soon as they should arrive. A beaver was caught in a trap, but we were disappointed in trying to catch trout in our net; we therefore made a seine of willow brush, and by hauling it procured a number of fine trout, and a species of mullet which we had not seen before: it is about sixteen inches long, the scales small; the nose long, obtusely pointed, and exceeding the under jaw; the mouth opens with folds at the sides; it has no teeth, and the tongue and palate is smooth. The colour of its back and sides is a bluish brown while the belly is white: it has the faggot bones, whence we concluded it to be of the mullet species. It is by no means so well flavoured a fish as the trout, which are the same as those we first saw at the falls, larger than the speckled trout of the mountains in the Atlantic states, and equally well flavoured. In the evening the hunters returned with two deer.

Captain Clark, in the meantime, proceeded through a wide level valley, in which the chief pointed out a spot where many of his tribe were killed in battle a year ago. The Indians accompanied him during the day, and as they had nothing to eat, he was obliged to feed them from his own stores, the hunters not being able to kill any thing. Just as he was entering the mountains, he met an Indian with two mules and a Spanish saddle, who was so polite as to offer one of them to him to ride over the hills. Being on foot, captain Clark accepted his offer and gave him a waistcoat as a reward for his civility. He encamped for the night on a small stream, and the next morning,

Tuesday, August 20, he set out at six o'clock. In passing through a continuation of the hilly broken country, he met several parties of Indians. On coming near the camp, which had been removed since we left them two miles higher up the river, Cameahwait requested that the party should halt. This was complied with: a number of Indians came out from the camp, and with great ceremony several pipes were smoked. This being over captain Clark was conducted to a large leathern lodge prepared for his party in the middle of the encampment, the Indians having only shelters of willow bushes. A few dried berries, and one salmon, the only food the whole village could contribute, were then presented to him; after which he proceeded to repeat in council, what had been already told them, the purposes of his visit; urged them to take their horses over and assist in transporting our baggage, and expressed a wish to obtain a guide to examine the river. This was explained and enforced to the whole village by Cameahwait, and an old man was pointed out who was said to know more of their geography to the north than any other person, and whom captain Clark engaged to accompany him. After explaining his views he distributed a few presents, the council was ended, and nearly half the village set out to hunt the antelope, but returned without success.

Captain Clark in the meantime made particular inquiries as to the situation of the country, and the possibility of soon reaching a navigable water. The chief began by drawing on the ground a delineation of the rivers, from which it appeared that his information was very limited. The river on which the camp is he divided into two branches just above us, which, as he indicated by the opening of the mountains, were in view: he next made it discharge itself into a larger river ten miles below, coming from the southwest: the joint stream continued one day's march to the northwest, and then inclined to the westward for two days' march farther. At that place he placed several heaps of sand on each side, which, as he explained them, represented vast mountains of rock always covered with snow, in passing through which the river was so completely hemmed in by the high rocks, that there was no possibility of travelling along the shore; that the bed of the river was obstructed by sharp-pointed rocks, and such its rapidity, that as far as the eye could reach it presented a perfect column of foam. The mountains he said were equally inaccessible, as neither man nor horse could cross them; that such being the state of the country neither he nor any of his nation had ever attempted to go beyond the mountains. Cameahwait said also that he had been informed by the Chopunnish, or pierced-nose Indians, who reside on this river west of the mountains, that it ran a great way towards the setting sun, and at length lost itself in a great lake of water which was ill-tasted, and where the white men lived. An Indian belonging to a band of Shoshonees who live to the southwest, and who happened to be at camp, was then brought in, and enquiries made of him as to the situation of the country in that direction: this he described in terms scarcely less terrible than those in which Cameahwait had represented the west. He said that his relations lived at the distance of twenty days' march from this place, on a course a little to the west of south and not far from the whites, with whom they traded for horses, mules, cloth, metal, beads, and the shells here worn as ornaments, and which are those of a species of pearl oyster. In order to reach his country we should be obliged during the first seven days to climb over steep rocky mountains where there was no game, and we should find nothing but roots for subsistence. Even for these however we should be obliged to contend with a fierce warlike people, whom he called the Broken-moccasin, or moccasin with holes, who lived like bears in holes, and fed on roots and the flesh of such horses as they could steal or plunder from those who passed through the mountains. So rough indeed was the passage, that the feet of the horses would be wounded in such a manner that many of them would be unable to proceed. The next part of the route was for ten days through a dry parched desert of sand, inhabited by no animal which would supply us with subsistence, and as the sun had now scorched up the grass and dried up the small pools of water which are sometimes scattered through this desert in the spring, both ourselves and our horses would perish for want of food and water. About the middle of this plain a large river passes from southeast to northwest, which, though navigable, afforded neither timber nor salmon. Three or four days' march beyond this plain his relations lived, in a country tolerably fertile and partially covered with timber, on another large river running in the same direction as the former; that this last discharges itself into a third large river, on which resided many numerous nations, with whom his own were at war, but whether this last emptied itself into the great or stinking lake, as they called the ocean, he did not know; that from his country to the stinking lake was a great distance, and that the route to it, taken by such of his relations as had visited it, was up the river on which they lived, and over to that on which the white people lived, and which they knew discharged itself into the ocean. This route he advised us to take, but added, that we had better defer the journey till spring, when he would himself conduct us. This account persuaded us that the streams of which he spoke were southern branches of the Columbia, heading with the Rio des Apostolos, and Rio Colorado, and that the route which he mentioned was to the gulf of California: captain Clark therefore told him that this road was too much towards the south for our purpose, and then requested to know if there was no route on the left of the river where we now are, by which we might intercept it below the mountains; but he knew of none except that through the barren plains, which he said joined the mountains on that side, and through which it was impossible to pass at this season, even if we were fortunate enough to escape the Broken-moccasin Indians. Captain Clark recompensed the Indian by a present of a knife, with which he seemed much gratified, and now inquired of Cameahwait by what route the Pierced-nose Indians, who he said lived west of the mountains, crossed over to the Missouri: this he said was towards the north, but that the road was a very bad one; that during the passage he had been told they suffered excessively from hunger, being obliged to subsist for many days on berries alone, there being no game in that part of the mountains, which were broken and rocky, and so thickly covered with timber that they could scarcely pass. Surrounded by difficulties as all the other routes are, this seems to be the most practicable of all the passages by land, since, if the Indians can pass the mountains with their women and children, no difficulties which they could encounter could be formidable to us; and if the Indians below the mountains are so numerous as they are represented to be, they must have some means of subsistence equally within our power. They tell us indeed that the nations to the westward subsist principally on fish and roots, and that their only game were a few elk, deer, and antelope, there being no buffalo west of the mountain. The first inquiry however was to ascertain the truth of their information relative to the difficulty of descending the river: for this purpose captain Clark set out at three o'clock in the afternoon, accompanied by the guide and all his men, except one whom he left with orders to purchase a horse and join him as soon as possible. At the distance of four miles he crossed the river, and eight miles from the camp halted for the night at a small stream. The road which he followed was a beaten path through a wide rich meadow, in which were several old lodges. On the route he met a number of men, women, and children, as well as horses, and one of the men who appeared to possess some consideration turned back with him, and observing a woman with three salmon obtained them from her, and presented them to the party. Captain Clark shot a mountain cock or cock of the plains, a dark brown bird larger than the dunghill fowl, with a long and pointed tail, and a fleshy protuberance about the base of the upper chop, something like that of the turkey though without the snout. In the morning,

Wednesday 21, he resumed his march early, and at the distance of five miles reached an Indian lodge of brush, inhabited by seven families of Shoshonees. They behaved with great civility, gave the whole party as much boiled salmon as they could eat, and added as a present several dried salmon and a considerable quantity of chokecherries. After smoking with them all he visited the fish weir, which was about two hundred yards distant; the river was here divided by three small islands, which occasioned the water to pass along four channels. Of these three were narrow, and stopped by means of trees which were stretched across, and supported by willow stakes, sufficiently near each other to prevent the passage of the fish. About the centre of each was placed a basket formed of willows, eighteen or twenty feet in length, of a cylindrical form, and terminating in a conic shape at its lower extremity; this was situated with its mouth upwards, opposite to an aperture in the weir. The main channel of the water was then conducted to this weir, and as the fish entered it they were so entangled with each other that they could not move, and were taken out by untying the small end of the willow basket. The weir in the main channel was formed in a manner somewhat different; there were in fact two distinct weirs formed of poles and willow sticks quite across the river, approaching each other obliquely with an aperture in each side near the angle. This is made by tying a number of poles together at the top, in

parcels of three, which were then set up in a triangular form at the base, two of the poles being
in the range desired for the weir, and the third
down the stream. To these poles two ranges of
other poles are next lashed horizontally, with willow bark and wythes, and willow sticks joined in
with these crosswise, so as to form a kind of
wicker-work from the bottom of the river to the
height of three or four feet above the surface of
the water. This is so thick as to prevent the fish
from passing, and even in some parts with the
help of a little gravel and some stone enables
them to give any direction which they wish to the
water. These two weirs being placed near to each
other, one for the purpose of catching the fish as
they ascend, the other as they go down the river,
is provided with two baskets made in the form
already described, and which are placed at the
apertures of the weir. After examining these curious objects, he returned to the lodges, and soon
passed the river to the left, where an Indian
brought him a tomahawk which he said he had
found in the grass, near the lodge where captain
Lewis had stayed on his first visit to the village.
This was a tomahawk which had been missed at
the time, and supposed to be stolen; it was however the only article which had been lost in our
intercourse with the nation, and as even that was
returned the inference is highly honourable to the
integrity of the Shoshonees. On leaving the lodges
captain Clark crossed to the left side of the river,
and despatched five men to the forks of it, in
search of the man left behind yesterday, who procured a horse and passed by another road as they
learnt, to the forks. At the distance of fourteen
miles they killed a very large salmon, two and a
half feet long, in a creek six miles below the forks:

and after travelling about twenty miles through the valley, following the course of the river, which runs nearly northwest, halted in a small meadow on the right side, under a cliff of rocks. Here they were joined by the five men who had gone in quest of Crusatte. They had been to the forks of the river, where the natives resort in great numbers for the purpose of gigging fish, of which they made our men a present of five fresh salmon. In addition to this food, one deer was killed to-day. The western branch of this river is much larger than the eastern, and after we passed the junction we found the river about one hundred yards in width, rapid and shoaly, but containing only a small quantity of timber. As captain Lewis was the first white man who visited its waters, captain Clark gave it the name of Lewis's river. The low grounds through which he had passed to-day were rich and wide, but at his camp this evening the hills begin to assume a formidable aspect. The cliff under which he lay is of a reddish brown colour, the rocks which have fallen from it are a dark brown flintstone. Near the place are gulleys of white sandstone, and quantities of a fine sand, of a snowy whiteness: the mountains on each side are high and rugged, with some pine trees scattered over them.

Thursday 22.—He soon began to perceive that the Indian accounts had not exaggerated: at the distance of a mile he passed a small creek, and the points of four mountains, which were rocky, and so high that it seemed almost impossible to cross them with horses. The road lay over the sharp fragments of rocks which had fallen from the mountains, and were strewed in heaps for miles together, yet the horses altogether unshod, travelled across them as fast as the men, and without

91

detaining them a moment. They passed two
bold-running streams, and reached the entrance of
a small river, where a few Indian families resided.
They had not been previously acquainted with the
arrival of the whites, the guide was behind, and
the wood so thick that we came upon them unobserved, till at a very short distance. As soon as
they saw us, the women and children fled in great
consternation; the men offered us every thing they
had, the fish on the scaffolds, the dried berries and
the collars of elk's tushes worn by the children.
We took only a small quantity of the food, and
gave them in return some small articles which
conduced very much to pacify them. The guide
now coming up, explained to them who we were,
and the object of our visit, which seemed to relieve the fears, but still a number of the women
and children did not recover from their fright, but
cried during our stay, which lasted about an
hour. The guide, whom we found a very intelligent friendly old man, informed us that up this
river there was a road which led over the mountains to the Missouri. On resuming his route, he
went along the steep side of a mountain about
three miles, and then reached the river near a
small island, at the lower part of which he encamped; he here attempted to gig some fish, but
could only obtain one small salmon. The river is
here shoal and rapid, with many rocks scattered
in various directions through its bed. On the
sides of the mountains are some scattered pines,
and of those on the left the tops are covered with
them; there are however but few in the low
grounds through which they passed, indeed they
have seen only a single tree fit to make a canoe,
and even that was small. The country has an
abundant growth of berries, and we met several

women and children gathering them who bestowed them upon us with great liberality. Among the woods captain Clark observed a species of woodpecker, the beak and tail of which were white, the wings black, and every other part of the body of a dark brown; its size was that of the robin, and it fed on the seeds of the pine.

Friday 23.—Captain Clark set off very early, but as his route lay along the steep side of a mountain, over irregular and broken masses of rocks, which wounded the horses' feet, he was obliged to proceed slowly. At the distance of four miles he reached the river, but the rocks here became so steep, and projected so far into the river, that there was no mode of passing, except through the water. This he did for some distance, though the river was very rapid, and so deep that they were forced to swim their horses. After following the edge of the water for about a mile under this steep cliff, he reached a small meadow, below which the whole current of the river beat against the right shore on which he was, and which was formed of a solid rock perfectly inaccessible to horses. Here too, the little track which he had been pursuing terminated. He therefore resolved to leave the horses and the greater part of the men at this place, and examine the river still further, in order to determine if there were any possibility of descending it in canoes. Having killed nothing except a single goose to-day, and the whole of our provision being consumed last evening, it was by no means advisable to remain any length of time where they were. He now directed the men to fish and hunt at this place till his return, and then with his guide and three men he proceeded, clambering over immense rocks, and along the sides of lofty precipices which bordered the river, when at about twelve miles distance he reached a small meadow, the first he had seen on the river since he left his party. A little below this meadow, a large creek twelve yards wide, and of some depth, discharges itself from the north. Here were some recent signs of an Indian encampment, and the tracks of a number of horses, who must have come along a plain Indian path, which he now saw following the course of the creek. This stream his guide said led towards a large river running to the north, and was frequented by another nation for the purpose of catching fish. He remained here two hours, and having taken some small fish, made a dinner on them with the addition of a few berries. From the place where he had left the party, to the mouth of this creek, it presents one continued rapid, in which are five shoals, neither of which could be passed with loaded canoes; and the baggage must therefore be transported for a considerable distance over the steep mountains, where it would be impossible to employ horses for the relief of the men. Even the empty canoes must be let down the rapids by means of cords, and not even in that way without great risk both to the canoes as well as to the men. At one of these shoals, indeed the rocks rise so perpendicularly from the water as to leave no hope of a passage or even a portage without great labour in removing rocks, and in some instances cutting away the earth. To surmount these difficulties would exhaust the strength of the party, and what is equally discouraging would waste our time and consume our provisions, of neither of which have we much to spare. The season is now far advanced, and the Indians tell us we shall shortly have snow: the salmon too have so far declined that the natives themselves are hastening from the country, and not an animal of any kind larger than a pheasant or a squirrel, and of even these a few only will then be seen in this part of the mountains: after which we shall be obliged to rely on our own stock of provisions, which will not support us more than ten days. These circumstances combine to render a passage by water impracticable in our present situation. To descend the course of the river on horseback is the other alternative, and scarcely a more inviting one. The river is so deep that there are only a few places where it can be forded, and the rocks approach so near the water as to render it impossible to make a route along the water's edge. In crossing the mountains themselves we should have to encounter, besides their steepness, one barren surface of broken masses of rock, down which in certain seasons the torrents sweep vast quantities of stone into the river. These rocks are of a whitish brown, and towards the base of a gray colour, and so hard, that on striking them with steel, they yield a fire like flint. This sombre appearance is in some places scarcely relieved by a single tree, though near the river and on the creeks there is more timber, among which are some tall pine: several of these might be made into canoes, and by lashing two of them together, one of tolerable size might be formed.

After dinner he continued his route, and at the distance of half a mile passed another creek about five yards wide. Here his guide informed him that by ascending the creek for some distance he would have a better road, and cut off a considerable bend of the river towards the south. He therefore pursued a well-beaten Indian track up this creek for about six miles, when leaving the creek to the right he passed over a ridge, and after walking a mile again met the river, where it flows through a meadow of about eighty acres in extent. This they passed and then ascended a high and steep point of a mountain, from which the guide now pointed out where the river broke through the mountains about twenty miles distant. Near the base of the mountains a small river falls in from the south: this view was terminated by one of the loftiest mountains captain Clark had ever seen, which was perfectly covered with snow. Towards this formidable barrier the river went directly on, and there it was, as the guide observed, that the difficulties and dangers of which he and Cameahwait had spoken commenced. After reaching the mountain, he said, the river continues its course towards the north for many miles, between high perpendicular rocks, which were scattered through its bed: it then penetrated the mountain through a narrow gap, on each side of which arose perpendicularly a rock as high as the top of the mountain before them; that the river then made a bend which concealed its future course from view, and as it was alike impossible to descend the river or clamber over that vast mountain, eternally covered with snow, neither he nor any of his nation had ever been lower than at a place where they could see the gap made by the river on entering the mountain. To that place he said he would conduct captain Clark if he desired it by the next evening. But he was in need of no further evidence to convince him of the utter impracticability of the route before him. He had already witnessed the difficulties of part of the road, yet after all these dangers his guide, whose intelligence and fidelity he could not doubt, now assured him that the difficulties were only commencing, and what he saw before him too clearly convinced him of the Indian's veracity. He therefore determined to abandon this route, and returned to the upper part of the last creek we had passed, and reaching it an hour after dark encamped for the night: on this creek he had seen in the morning an Indian road coming in from the north. Disappointed in finding a route by water, captain Clark now questioned his guide more particularly as to the direction of this road which he seemed to understand perfectly. He drew a map on the sand, and represented this road as well as that we passed yesterday on Berry creek as both leading towards two forks of the same great river, where resided a nation called Tushepaws, who having no salmon on their river, came by these roads to the fish weirs on Lewis's river. He had himself been among these Tushepaws, and having once accompanied them on a fishing party to another river he had there seen Indians who had come across the rocky mountains. After a great deal of conversation, or rather signs, and a second and more particular map from his guide, captain Clark felt persuaded that his guide knew of a road from the Shoshonee village they had left, to the great river to the north, without coming so low down as this on a route impracticable for horses. He was desirous of hastening his return, and therefore set out early,

Saturday 24, and after descending the creek to the river, stopped to breakfast on berries in the meadow above the second creek. He then went on, but unfortunately fell from a rock and injured his leg very much; he however walked on as rapidly as he could, and at four in the afternoon rejoined his men. During his absence they had killed one of the mountain cocks, a few pheasants,

and some small fish, on which with haws and serviceberries they had subsisted. Captain Clark
immediately sent forward a man on horseback
with a note to captain Lewis, apprising him of
the result of his inquiries, and late in the afternoon set out with the rest of the party and
encamped at the distance of two miles. The men
were much disheartened at the bad prospect of
escaping from the mountains, and having nothing
to eat but a few berries which have made several
of them sick, they all passed a disagreeable night,
which was rendered more uncomfortable by a
heavy dew.

Sunday 25.—The want of provisions urged captain Clark to return as soon as possible; he therefore set out early, and halted an hour in passing
the Indian camp near the fish weirs. These people
treated them with great kindness, and though
poor and dirty they willingly give what little they
possess; they gave the whole party boiled salmon
and dried berries, which were not however in
sufficient quantities to appease their hunger.
They soon resumed their old road, but as the
abstinence or strange diet had given one of the
men a very severe illness, they were detained very
much on his account, and it was not till late in
the day they reached the cliff under which they
had encamped on the twenty-first. They immediately began to fish and hunt, in order to procure
a meal. We caught several small fish, and by
means of our guide, obtained two salmon from a
small party of women and children, who, with
one man, were going below to gather berries.
This supplied us with about half a meal, but after
dark we were regaled with a beaver which one of
the hunters brought in. The other game seen in
the course of the day were one deer, and a party

of elk among the pines on the sides of the mountains.

Monday 26.—The morning was fine, and three men were despatched ahead to hunt, while the rest were detained until nine o'clock, in order to retake some horses which had strayed away during the night. They then proceeded along the route by the forks of the river, till they reached the lower Indian camp where they first were when we met them. The whole camp immediately flocked around him with great appearance of cordiality, but all the spare food of the village did not amount to more than two salmon, which they gave to captain Clark, who distributed them among his men. The hunters had not been able to kill any thing, nor had captain Clark or the greater part of the men any food during the twenty-four hours, till towards evening one of them shot a salmon in the river, and a few small fish were caught, which furnished them with a scanty meal. The only animals they had seen were a few pigeons, some very wild hares, a great number of the large black grasshopper, and a quantity of ground lizards.

Tuesday 27.—The men, who were engaged last night in mending their moccasins, all except one, went out hunting, but no game was to be procured. One of the men however killed a small salmon, and the Indians made a present of another, on which the whole party made a very slight breakfast. These Indians, to whom this life is familiar, seem contented, although they depend for subsistence on the scanty productions of the fishery. But our men who are used to hardships, but have been accustomed to have the first wants of nature regularly supplied, feel very sensibly their wretched situation; their strength is wasting

99

away; they begin to express their apprehensions of being without food in a country perfectly destitute of any means of supporting life, except a few fish. In the course of the day an Indian brought into the camp five salmon, two of which captain Clark bought, and made a supper for the party.

Wednesday 28.—There was a frost again this morning. The Indians gave the party two salmon out of several which they caught in their traps, and having purchased two more, the party was enabled to subsist on them during the day. A camp of about forty Indians from the west fork passed us to-day, on their route to the eastward. Our prospect of provisions is getting worse every day: the hunters who had ranged through the country in every direction where game might be reasonably expected, have seen nothing. The fishery is scarcely more productive, for an Indian who was out all day with his gig killed only one salmon. Besides the four fish procured from the Indians, captain Clark obtained some fishroe in exchange for three small fishhooks, the use of which he taught them, and which they very readily comprehended. All the men who are not engaged in hunting, are occupied in making pack-saddles for the horses which captain Lewis informed us he had bought.

August 20.—Two hunters were despatched early in the morning, but they returned without killing any thing, and the only game we procured was a beaver, who was caught last night in a trap which he carried off two miles before he was found. The fur of this animal is as good as any we have ever seen, nor does it in fact appear to be ever out of season on the upper branches of the Missouri. This beaver, with several dozen of fine trout, gave us a plentiful subsistence for the day.

100

The party were occupied chiefly in making pack-saddles, in the manufacture of which we supply the place of nails and boards, by substituting for the first thongs of raw hide, which answer very well; and for boards we use the handles of our oars, and the plank of some boxes, the contents of which we empty into sacks of raw hides made for the purpose. The Indians who visit us behave with the greatest decorum, and the women are busily engaged in making and mending the moccasins of the party. As we had still some superfluous baggage which would be too heavy to carry across the mountains, it became necessary to make a cache or deposit. For this purpose we selected a spot on the bank of the river, three quarters of a mile below the camp, and three men were set to dig it, with a sentinel in the neighbourhood, who was ordered if the natives were to straggle that way, to fire a signal for the workmen to desist and separate. Towards evening the cache was completed without being perceived by the Indians, and the packages prepared for deposit.

CHAPTER XVI.

Contest between Drewyer and a Shoshonee—The fidelity and honour of that tribe—The party set out on their journey—The conduct of Cameahwait reproved, and himself reconciled—The easy parturition of the Shoshonee women—History of this nation—Their terror of the Pawkees—Their government and family economy in their treatment of their women—Their complaints of Spanish treachery—Description of their weapons of warfare—Their curious mode of making a shield—The comparison of their horses—The dress of the men and of the women particularly described—Their mode of acquiring new names.

Wednesday, August 21.—The weather was very cold; the water which stood in the vessels exposed to the air being covered with ice a quarter of an inch thick: the ink freezes in the pen, and the low grounds are perfectly whitened with frost: after this the day proved excessively warm. The party were engaged in their usual occupations, and completed twenty saddles with the necessary harness, all prepared to set off as soon as the Indians should arrive. Our two hunters who were despatched early in the morning have not returned, so that we were obliged to encroach on our pork and corn, which we consider as the last resource when our casual supplies of game fail. After dark we carried our baggage to the cache, and deposited what we thought too cumbrous to carry with us: a small assortment of medicines, and all the specimens of plants, seeds, and minerals, collected since leaving the falls of the Missouri. Late at night Drewyer, one of the hunters, returned with a fawn and a considerable quantity of Indian plunder, which he had taken by way of reprisal. While hunting this morning in the Shoshonee cove, he came suddenly upon an Indian camp, at which were an old man, a young one, three women, and a boy: they showed no surprise at the sight of him, and he therefore rode up to them, and after turning his horse loose to graze sat down and began to converse with them by signs. They had just finished a repast on some roots, and in about twenty minutes one of the women spoke to the rest of the party, who immediately went out, collected their horses and began to saddle them. Having rested himself, Drewyer thought that he would continue his hunt, and rising went to catch his horse who was at a short distance, forgetting at the moment to take up his rifle. He had scarcely gone more than fifty paces when the Indians mounted their horses, the young man snatched up the rifle, and leaving all their baggage, whipped their horses, and set off at full speed towards the passes of the mountains: Drewyer instantly jumped on his horse and pursued them. After running about ten miles the horses of the women nearly gave out, and the women finding Drewyer gain on them raised dreadful cries, which induced the young man to slacken his pace, and being mounted on a very fleet horse rode round them at a short distance. Drewyer now came up with the women, and by signs persuaded them that he did not mean to hurt them: they then stopped, and as the young man came towards them Drewyer asked him for his rifle, but the only part of the answer which he understood was Pahkee, the name by which they call their enemies, the Minnetarees of fort de Prairie. While they were thus engaged in talking, Drewyer watched his opportunity, and seeing the Indian off his guard, galloped up to him and seized his rifle: the Indian struggled for some time,

103

but finding Drewyer getting too strong for him, had the presence of mind to open the pan and let the priming fall out: he then let go his hold, and giving his horse the whip escaped at full speed, leaving the women to the mercy of the conqueror. Drewyer then returned to where he had first seen them, where he found that their baggage had been left behind, and brought it to camp with him.

Thursday, 22.—This morning early two men were sent to complete the covering of the cache, which could not be so perfectly done during the night as to elude the search of the Indians. On examining the spoils which Drewyer had obtained, they were found to consist of several dressed and undressed skins; two bags wove with the bark of the silk-grass, each containing a bushel of dried serviceberries, and about the same quantity of roots; an instrument made of bone for manufacturing the flints into heads for arrows; and a number of flints themselves: these were much of the same colour and nearly as transparent as common black glass, and when cut detached itself into flakes, leaving a very sharp edge.

The roots were of three kinds, and folded separate from each in hides of buffalo made into parchment. The first is a fusiform root six inches long, and about the size of a man's finger at the largest end, with radicles larger than is usual in roots of the fusiform sort: the rind is white and thin, the body is also white, mealy, and easily reducible, by pounding, to a substance resembling flour, like which it thickens by boiling, and is of an agreeable flavour: it is eaten frequently in its raw state either green or dried. The second species was much mutilated, but appeared to be fibrous; it is of a cylindrical form about the size

104

of a small quill, hard and brittle. A part of the
rind which had not been detached in the preparation was hard and black, but the rest of the root
was perfectly white; this the Indians informed us
was always boiled before eating; and on making
the experiment we found that it became perfectly
soft, but had a bitter taste, which was nauseous
to our taste, but which the Indians seemed to
relish; for on giving the roots to them they were
very heartily swallowed.

The third species was a small nut about the size
of a nutmeg, of an irregularly rounded form,
something like the smallest of the Jerusalem arti-
chokes, which, on boiling, we found them to resemble also in flavour, and is certainly the best
root we have seen in use among the Indians. On
inquiring of the Indians from what plant these
roots were procured, they informed us that none
of them grew near this place.

The men were chiefly employed in dressing the
skins belonging to the party who accompanied
captain Clark. About eleven o'clock Chaboneau
and his wife returned with Camcahwait, accompanied by about fifty men with their women and
children. After they had encamped near us and
turned loose their horses, we called a council of all
the chiefs and warriors and addressed them in a
speech: additional presents were then distributed,
particularly to the two second chiefs, who had
agreeably to their promises exerted themselves in
our favour. The council was then adjourned, and
all the Indians were treated with an abundant
meal of boiled Indian corn and beans. The poor
wretches, who had no animal food and scarcely any
thing but a few fish, had been almost starved, and
received this new luxury with great thankfulness.
Out of compliment to the chief we gave him a few

dried squashes which we had brought from the Mandans, and he declared it was the best food he had ever tasted except sugar, a small lump of which he had received from his sister: he now declared how happy they should all be to live in a country which produced so many good things, and we told him that it would not be long before the white men would put it in their power to live below the mountains, where they might themselves cultivate all these kinds of food instead of wandering in the mountains. He appeared to be much pleased with this information, and the whole party being now in excellent temper after their repast, we began our purchase of horses. We soon obtained five very good ones on very reasonable terms; that is, by giving for each merchandise which cost us originally about six dollars. We have again to admire the perfect decency and propriety of their conduct; for although so numerous, they do not attempt to crowd round our camp or take any thing which they see lying about, and whenever they borrow knives or kettles or any other article from the men, they return them with great fidelity.

Towards evening we formed a drag of bushes, and in about two hours caught five hundred and twenty-eight very good fish most of them large trout. Among them we observed for the first time ten or twelve trout of a white or silvery colour, except on the back and head where they are of a bluish cast: in appearance and shape they resemble exactly the speckled trout, except that they are not quite so large, though the scales are much larger, and the flavour equally good. The greater part of the fish was distributed among the Indians.

Friday 23.—Our visitors seem to depend wholly

on us for food, and as the state of our provisions obliges us to be careful of our remaining stock of corn and flour, this was an additional reason for urging our departure; but Cameahwait requested us to wait till the arrival of another party of his nation who were expected to-day. Knowing that it would be in vain to oppose his wish, we consented, and two hunters were sent out with orders to go further up the southeast fork than they had hitherto been. At the same time the chief was informed of the low state of our provisions, and advised to send out his young men to hunt. This he recommended them to do, and most of them set out: we then sunk our canoes by means of stones to the bottom of the river, a situation which better than any other secured them against the effects of the high waters, and the frequent fires of the plains; the Indians having promised not to disturb them during our absence, a promise we believe the more readily, as they are almost too lazy to take the trouble of raising them for fire-wood. We were desirous of purchasing some more horses, but they declined selling any until we reached their camp in the mountains. Soon after starting the Indian hunters discovered a mule buck, and twelve of their horsemen pursued it, for four miles. We saw the chase, which was very entertaining, and at length they rode it down and killed it. This mule buck was the largest deer of any kind we have seen, being nearly as large as a doe elk. Besides this they brought in another deer and three goats; but instead of a general distribution of the meat, and such as we have hitherto seen among all tribes of Indians, we observed that some families had a large share, while others received none. On enquiring of Camcahwait the reason of this custom, he said that meat among them was scarce, that each hunter reserved what he killed for the use of himself and his own family, none of the rest having any claim on what he chose to keep. Our hunters returned soon after with two mule deer and three common deer, three of which we distributed among the families who had received none of the game of their own hunters. About three o'clock the expected party consisting of fifty men, women and children arrived. We now learnt that most of the Indians were on their way down the valley towards the buffalo country, and some anxiety to accompany them appeared to prevail among those who had promised to assist us in crossing the mountains. We ourselves were not without some apprehension that they might leave us, but as they continued to say that they would return with us nothing was said upon the subject. We were, however, resolved to move early in the morning, and therefore despatched two men to hunt in the cove and leave the game on the route we should pass to-morrow.

Saturday 24.—As the Indians who arrived yesterday had a number of spare horses, we thought it probable they might be willing to dispose of them, and desired the chief to speak to them for that purpose. They declined giving any positive answer, but requested to see the goods which we proposed to exchange. We then produced some battle-axes which we had made at fort Mandan, and a quantity of knives; with both of which they appeared very much pleased; and we were soon able to purchase three horses by giving for each an axe, a knife, a handkerchief and a little paint. To this we were obliged to add a second knife, a shirt, a handkerchief and a pair of leggings; and such is the estimation in which those animals are

held, that even at this price, which was double
that for a horse, the fellow who sold him took
upon himself great merit in having given away a
mule to us. They now said that they had no
more horses for sale, and as we had now nine of
our own, two hired horses, and a mule, we began
loading them as heavily as was prudent, and
placing the rest on the shoulders of the Indian
women, left our camp at twelve o'clock. We were
all on foot, except Sacajawea, for whom her husband had purchased a horse with some articles
which we gave him for that purpose; an Indian
however had the politeness to offer captain Lewis
one of his horses to ride, which he accepted in
order better to direct the march of the party. We
crossed the river below the forks, directing our
course towards the cove by the route already
passed, and had just reached the lower part of the
cove when an Indian rode up to captain Lewis to
inform him that one of his men was very sick,
and unable to come on. The party was immediately halted at a run which falls into the creek on
the left, and captain Lewis rode back two miles,
and found Wiser severely afflicted with the colic:
by giving him some of the essence of peppermint
and laudanum, he recovered sufficiently to ride
the horse of captain Lewis, who then rejoined the
party on foot. When he arrived he found that the
Indians who had been impatiently expecting his
return, at last unloaded their horses and turned
them loose, and had now made their camp for the
night. It would have been fruitless to remon-
strate, and not prudent to excite any irritation,
and therefore, although the sun was still high,
and we had made only six miles, we thought it
best to remain with them: after we had encamped
there fell a slight shower of rain. One of the men

caught several fine trout; but Drewyer had been sent out to hunt without having killed any thing. We therefore gave a little corn to those of the Indians who were actually engaged in carrying our baggage, and who had absolutely nothing to eat. We also advised Cameahwait, as we could not supply all his people with provisions, to recommend to all who were not assisting us, to go on before us to their camp. This he did: but in the morning,

Sunday 25, a few only followed his advice, the rest accompanying us at some distance on each side. We set out at sunrise and after going seventeen miles halted for dinner within two miles of the narrow pass in the mountains. The Indians who were on the sides of our party had started some antelopes, but were obliged after a pursuit of several hours to abandon the chase: our hunters had in the meantime brought in three deer, the greater part of which was distributed among the Indians. Whilst at dinner we learnt by means of Sacajawea, that the young men who left us this morning, carried a request from the chief, that the village would break up its encampment and meet this party to-morrow, when they would all go down the Missouri into the buffalo country. Alarmed at this new caprice of the Indians which, if not counteracted, threatened to leave ourselves and our baggage on the mountains, or even if we reached the waters of the Columbia, prevent our obtaining horses to go on further, captain Lewis immediately called the three chiefs together. After smoking a pipe he asked them if they were men of their words, and if we can rely on their promises. They readily answered in the affirmative. He then asked, if they had not agreed to assist us in carrying our baggage over the mountains. To this they also answered yes; and why then, said he, have you requested your people to meet us to-morrow, where it will be impossible for us to trade for horses, as you promised we should. If, he continued, you had not promised to help us in transporting our goods over the mountains, we should not have attempted it, but have returned down the river, after which no white men would ever have come into your country. If you wish the whites to be your friends, and to bring you arms and protect you from your enemies, you should never promise what you do not mean to perform: when I first met you, you doubted what I said, yet you afterwards saw that I told you the truth. How therefore can you doubt what I now tell you; you see that I have divided amongst you the meat which my hunters kill, and I promise to give all who assist us a share of whatever we have to eat. If therefore you intend to keep your promise, send one of the young men imme-diately to order the people to remain at the vil-lage till we arrive.

The two inferior chiefs then said, that they had wished to keep their words and to assist us; that they had not sent for the people, but on the con-trary had disapproved of the measure which was done wholly by the first chief. Cameahwait re-mained silent for some time: at last he said that he knew he had done wrong, but that seeing his people all in want of provisions, he had wished to hasten their departure for the country where their wants might be supplied. He however now de-clared, that having passed his word he would never violate it, and counter orders were immediately sent to the village by a young man, to whom we gave a handkerchief in order to ensure despatch and fidelity.

This difficulty being now adjusted, our march was resumed with an unusual degree of alacrity on the part of the Indians. We passed a spot, where six years ago the Shoshonees suffered a very severe defeat from the Minnetarees; and late in the evening we reached the upper part of the cove where the creek enters the mountains. The part of the cove on the northeast side of the creek has lately been burnt, most probably as a signal on some occasion. Here we were joined by our hunters with a single deer, which captain Lewis gave, as a proof of his sincerity, to the women and children, and remained supperless himself. As we came along we observed several large hares, some ducks, and many of the cock of the plains: in the low grounds of the cove were also considerable quantities of wild onions.

Monday 26.—The morning was excessively cold, and the ice in our vessels was nearly a quarter of an inch in thickness: we set out at sunrise, and soon reached the fountain of the Missouri, where we halted for a few minutes, and then crossing the dividing ridge reached the fine spring where captain Lewis had slept on the 12th in his first excursion to the Shoshonee camp. The grass on the hill sides is perfectly dry and parched by the sun, but near the spring was a fine green grass: we therefore halted for dinner and turned our horses to graze. To each of the Indians who were engaged in carrying our baggage was distributed a pint of corn, which they parched, then pounded, and made a sort of soup. One of the women who had been leading two of our pack horses halted at a rivulet about a mile behind, and sent on the two horses by a female friend: on inquiring of Cameahwait the cause of her detention, he answered with great appearance of unconcern, that she had just stopped to lie in, but would soon overtake us. In fact, we were astonished to see her in about an hour's time come on with her new born infant and pass us on her way to the camp, apparently in perfect health.

This wonderful facility with which the Indian women bring forth their children, seems rather some benevolent gift of nature, in exempting them from pains which their savage state would render doubly grievous, than any result of habit. If, as has been imagined, a pure dry air or a cold and elevated country are obstacles to easy delivery, every difficulty incident to that operation might be expected in this part of the continent: nor can another reason, the habit of carrying heavy burdens during pregnancy, be at all applicable to the Shoshonee women, who rarely carry any burdens, since their nation possesses an abundance of horses. We have indeed been several times informed by those conversant with Indian manners, and who asserted their knowledge of the fact, that Indian women pregnant by white men experience more difficulty in child-birth than when the father is an Indian. If this account be true, it may contribute to strengthen the belief, that the easy delivery of the Indian women is wholly constitutional.

The tops of the high irregular mountains to the westward are still entirely covered with snow; and the coolness which the air acquires in passing them, is a very agreeable relief from the heat, which has dried up the herbage on the sides of the hills. While we stopped, the women were busily employed in collecting the root of a plant with which they feed their children, who like their mothers are nearly half starved and in a wretched condition. It is a species of fennel which grows in the moist grounds; the radix is of the knob kind, of a long ovate form, terminating in a single radicle, the whole being three or four inches long, and the thickest part about the size of a man's little finger: when fresh, it is white, firm, and crisp; and when dried and pounded makes a fine white meal. Its flavour is not unlike that of aniseed, though less pungent. From one to four of these knobbed roots are attached to a single stem which rises to the height of three or four feet, and is jointed, smooth, cylindric, and has several small peduncles, one at each joint above the sheathing leaf. Its colour is a deep green, as is also that of the leaf, which is sheathing, sessile, and *polipartite*, the divisions being long and narrow. The flowers, which are now in bloom, are small and numerous, with white and umbelliferous petals: there are no root leaves. As soon as the seeds have matured, the roots of the present year as well as the stem decline, and are renewed in the succeeding spring from the little knot which unites the roots. The sunflower is also abundant here, and the seeds, which are now ripe, are gathered in considerable quantities, and after being pounded and rubbed between smooth stones, form a kind of meal, which is a favourite dish among the Indians.

After dinner we continued our route and were soon met by a party of young men on horseback, who turned with us and went to the village. As soon as we were within sight of it, Cameahwait requested that we would discharge our guns; the men were therefore drawn up in a single rank, and gave a running fire of two rounds, to the great satisfaction of the Indians. We then proceeded to the encampment where we arrived about six o'clock, and were conducted to the leathern

114

lodge in the centre of thirty-two others made of brush. The baggage was arranged near this tent, which captain Lewis occupied, and surrounded by those of the men so as to secure it from pillage. This camp was in a beautiful smooth meadow near the river, and about three miles above their camp when we first visited the Indians. We here found Colter, who had been sent by captain Clark with a note apprising us that there were no hopes of a passage by water, and that the most practicable route seemed to be that mentioned by his guide, towards the north. Whatever road we meant to take, it was now necessary to provide ourselves with horses; we therefore informed Cameahwait of our intention of going to the great river beyond the mountains, and that we would wish to purchase twenty more horses: he said the Minnetarees had stolen a great number of their horses this spring, but he still hoped they could spare us that number. In order not to lose the present favourable moment, and to keep the Indians as cheerful as possible, the violins were brought out and our men danced to the great diversion of the Indians. This mirth was the more welcome because our situation was not precisely that which would most dispose us for gaiety, for we have only a little parched corn to eat, and our means of subsistence or of success, depend on the wavering temper of the natives, who may change their minds to-morrow.

The Shoshonees are a small tribe of the nation called Snake Indians, a vague denomination, which embraces at once the inhabitants of the southern parts of the Rocky mountains and of the plains on each side. The Shoshonees with whom we now are, amount to about one hundred warriors, and three times that number of women and children. Within their own recollection they formerly lived in the plains, but they have been driven into the mountains by the Pawkees, or the roving Indians of the Sascatchawain, and are now obliged to visit occasionally, and by stealth, the country of their ancestors. Their lives are indeed migratory. From the middle of May to the beginning of September, they reside on the waters of the Columbia, where they consider themselves perfectly secure from the Pawkees who have never yet found their way to that retreat. During this time they subsist chiefly on salmon, and as that fish disappears on the approach of autumn, they are obliged to seek subsistence elsewhere. They then cross the ridge to the waters of the Missouri, down which they proceed slowly and cautiously, till they are joined near the three forks by other bands, either of their own nation or of the Flatheads, with whom they associate against the common enemy. Being now strong in numbers, they venture to hunt buffalo in the plains eastward of the mountains, near which they spend the winter, till the return of the salmon invites them to the Columbia. But such is their terror of the Pawkees, that as long as they can obtain the scantiest subsistence, they do not leave the interior of the mountains; and as soon as they collect a large stock of dried meat, they again retreat, and thus alternately obtaining their food at the hazard of their lives, and hiding themselves to consume it. In this loose and wandering existence they suffer the extremes of want; for two-thirds of the year they are forced to live in the mountains, passing whole weeks without meat, and with nothing to eat but a few fish and roots. Nor can any thing be imagined more wretched than their condition at the present time, when the salmon is fast retiring, when roots are becoming scarce, and they have not yet acquired strength to hazard an encounter with their enemies. So insensible are they however to these calamities, that the Shoshonees are not only cheerful but even gay; and their character, which is more interesting than that of any Indians we have seen, has in it much of the dignity of misfortune. In their intercourse with strangers they are frank and communicative, in their dealings perfectly fair, nor have we had during our stay with them, any reason to suspect that the display of all our new and valuable wealth, has tempted them into a single act of dishonesty. While they have generally shared with us the little they possess, they have always abstained from begging any thing from us. With their liveliness of temper, they are fond of gaudy dresses, and of all sorts of amusements, particularly to games of hazard; and like most Indians fond of boasting of their own warlike exploits, whether real or fictitious. In their conduct towards ourselves, they were kind and obliging, and though on one occasion they seemed willing to neglect us, yet we scarcely knew how to blame the treatment by which we suffered, when we recollected how few civilised chiefs would have hazarded the comforts or the subsistence of their people for the sake of a few strangers. This manliness of character may cause or it may be formed by the nature of their government, which is perfectly free from any restraint. Each individual is his own master, and the only control to which his conduct is subjected, is the advice of a chief supported by his influence over the opinions of the rest of the tribe. The chief himself is in fact no more than the most confidential person among the warriors, a rank neither distinguished by any

117

external honor, nor invested by any ceremony, but gradually acquired from the good wishes of his companions and by superior merit. Such an officer has therefore strictly no power; he may recommend or advise or influence, but his commands have no effect on those who incline to disobey, and who may at any time withdraw from their voluntary allegiance. His shadowy authority which cannot survive the confidence which supports it, often decays with the personal vigour of the chief, or is transferred to some more fortunate or favourite hero.

In their domestic economy, the man is equally sovereign. The man is the sole proprietor of his wives and daughters, and can barter them away, or dispose of them in any manner he may think proper. The children are seldom corrected; the boys, particularly, soon become their own masters; they are never whipped, for they say that it breaks their spirit, and that after being flogged they never recover their independence of mind, even when they grow to manhood. A plurality of wives is very common; but these are not generally sisters, as among the Minnetarees and Mandans, but are purchased of different fathers. The infant daughters are often betrothed by the father to men who are grown, either for themselves or for their sons, for whom they are desirous of providing wives. The compensation to the father is usually made in horses or mules; and the girl remains with her parents till the age of puberty, which is thirteen or fourteen, when she is surrendered to her husband. At the same time the father often makes a present to the husband equal to what he had formerly received as the price of his daughter, though this return is optional with her parent. Sacajawea had been contracted in this way before she was taken prisoner, and when we brought her back, her betrothed was still living. Although he was double the age of Sacajawea, and had two other wives, he claimed her, but on finding that she had a child by her new husband, Chaboneau, he relinquished his pretensions and said he did not want her.

The chastity of the women does not appear to be held in much estimation. The husband will for a trifling present lend his wife for a night to a stranger, and the loan may be protracted by increasing the value of the present. Yet strange as it may seem, notwithstanding this facility, any connection of this kind not authorised by the husband, is considered highly offensive and quite as disgraceful to his character as the same licentiousness in civilised societies. The Shoshonees are not so importunate in volunteering the services of their wives as we found the Sioux were; and indeed we observed among them some women who appeared to be held in more respect than those of any nation we had seen. But the mass of the females are condemned, as among all savage nations, to the lowest and most laborious drudgery. When the tribe is stationary, they collect the roots, and cook; they build the huts, dress the skins and make clothing; collect the wood, and assist in taking care of the horses on the route; they load the horses and have the charge of all the baggage. The only business of the man is to fight; he therefore takes on himself the care of his horse, the companion of his warfare; but he will descend to no other labour than to hunt and to fish. He would consider himself degraded by being compelled to walk any distance; and were he so poor as to possess only two horses, he would ride the best of them, and leave the other for his wives and children and their baggage; and if he has too many wives or too much baggage for the horse, the wives have no alternative but to follow him on foot; they are not however often reduced to those extremities, for their stock of horses is very ample. Notwithstanding their losses this spring they still have at least seven hundred, among which are about forty colts, and half that number of mules. There are no horses here which can be considered as wild; we have seen two only on this side of the Muscleshell river which were without owners, and even those although shy, showed every mark of having been once in the possession of man. The original stock was procured from the Spaniards, but they now raise their own. The horses are generally very fine, of a good size, vigorous and patient of fatigue as well as hunger. Each warrior has one or two tied to a stake near his hut both day and night, so as to be always prepared for action. The mules are obtained in the course of trade from the Spaniards, with whose brands several of them are marked, or stolen from them by the frontier Indians. They are the finest animals of that kind we have ever seen, and at this distance from the Spanish colonies are very highly valued. The worst are considered as worth the price of two horses, and a good mule cannot be obtained for less than three and sometimes four horses.

We also saw a bridle bit, stirrups and several other articles which, like the mules, came from the Spanish colonies. The Shoshonees say that they can reach those settlements in ten days' march by the route of the Yellowstone river; but we readily perceive that the Spaniards are by no means favourites. They complain that the Spaniards refuse to let them have fire arms under pretence that these dangerous weapons will only induce them to kill each other. In the meantime, say the Shoshonees, we are left to the mercy of the Minnetarees, who having arms, plunder them of their horses, and put them to death without mercy. "But this should not be," said Cameahwait fiercely, "if we had guns, instead of hiding ourselves in the mountains and living like the bears on roots and berries, we would then go down and live in the buffalo country in spite of our enemies, whom we never fear when we meet on equal terms."

As war is the chief occupation, bravery is the first virtue among the Shoshonees. None can hope to be distinguished without having given proofs of it, nor can there be any preferment, or influence among the nation, without some warlike achievement. Those important events which give reputation to a warrior, and which entitle him to a new name, are killing a white bear, stealing individually the horses of the enemy, leading out a party who happen to be successful either in plundering horses or destroying the enemy, and lastly scalping a warrior. These acts seem of nearly equal dignity, but the last, that of taking an enemy's scalp, is an honour quite independent of the act of vanquishing him. To kill your adversary is of no importance unless the scalp is brought from the field of battle, and were a warrior to slay any number of his enemies in action, and others were to obtain the scalps or first touch the dead, they would have all the honours, since they have borne off the trophy.

Although thus oppressed by the Minnetarees, the Shoshonees are still a very military people. Their cold and rugged country inures them to fatigue; their long abstinence makes them support

121

the dangers of mountain warfare, and worn down as we saw them, by want of sustenance, have a look of fierce and adventurous courage. The Shoshonee warrior always fights on horseback; he possesses a few bad guns, which are reserved exclusively for war, but his common arms are the bow and arrow, a shield, a lance and a weapon called by the Chippeways, by whom it was formerly used, the poggamoggon. The bow is made of cedar or pine covered on the outer side with sinews and glue. It is about two and a half feet long, and does not differ in shape from those used by the Sioux, Mandans and Minnetarees. Sometimes, however, the bow is made of a single piece of the horn of an elk, covered on the back like those of wood with sinews and glue, and occasionally ornamented by a strand wrought of porcupine quills and sinews, which is wrapped round the horn near its two ends. The bows made of the horns of the bighorn, are still more prized, and are formed by cementing with glue flat pieces of the horn together, covering the back with sinews and glue, and loading the whole with an unusual quantity of ornaments. The arrows resemble those of the other Indians except in being more slender than any we have seen. They are contained, with the implements for striking fire, in a narrow quiver formed of different kinds of skin, though that of the otter seems to be preferred. It is just long enough to protect the arrows from the weather, and is worn on the back by means of a strap passing over the right shoulder and under the left arm. The shield is a circular piece of buffalo hide about two feet four or five inches in diameter, ornamented with feathers, and a fringe round it of dressed leather, and adorned or deformed with paintings of strange figures. The buffalo hide is perfectly proof against any arrow, but in the minds of the Shoshonees, its power to protect them is chiefly derived from the virtues which are communicated to it by the old men and jugglers. To make a shield is indeed one of their most important ceremonies: it begins by a feast to which all the warriors, old men and jugglers are invited. After the repast a hole is dug in the ground about eighteen inches in depth and of the same diameter as the intended shield: into this hole red hot stones are thrown and water poured over them, till they emit a very strong hot steam. The buffalo skin, which must be the entire hide of a male two years old, and never suffered to dry since it was taken from the animal, is now laid across the hole, with the fleshy side to the ground, and stretched in every direction by as many as can take hold of it. As the skin becomes heated, the hair separates and is taken off by the hand; till at last the skin is contracted into the compass designed for the shield. It is then taken off and placed on a hide prepared into parchment, and then pounded during the rest of the festival by the bare heels of those who are invited to it. This operation sometimes continues for several days, after which it is delivered to the proprietor, and declared by the old men and jugglers to be a security against arrows; and provided the feast has been satisfactory, against even the bullets of their enemies. Such is the delusion, that many of the Indians implicitly believe that this ceremony has given to the shield supernatural powers, and that they have no longer to fear any weapons of their enemies.

The paggamoggon is an instrument, consisting of a handle twenty-two inches long, made of wood, covered with dressed leather about the size of a whip-handle: at one end is a thong of two inches in length, which is tied to a round stone weighing two pounds and held in a cover of leather: at the other end is a loop of the same material, which is passed round the wrist so as to secure the hold of the instrument, with which they strike a very severe blow.

Besides these, they have a kind of armour something like a coat of mail, which is formed by a great many folds of dressed antelope skins, united by means of a mixture of glue and sand. With this they cover their own bodies and those of their horses, and find it impervious to the arrow.

The caparison of their horses is a halter and a saddle: the first is either a rope of six or seven strands of buffalo hair plaited or twisted together, about the size of a man's finger and of great strength; or merely a thong of raw hide, made pliant by pounding and rubbing; though the first kind is much preferred. The halter is very long, and is never taken from the neck of the horse when in constant use. One end of it is first tied round the neck in a knot and then brought down to the under jaw, round which it is formed into a simple noose, passing through the mouth: it is then drawn up on the right side and held by the rider in his left hand, while the rest trails after him to some distance. At other times the knot is formed at a little distance from one of the ends, so as to let that end serve as a bridle, while the other trails on the ground. With these cords dangling along side of them the horse is put to his full speed without fear of falling, and when he is turned to graze the noose is merely taken from his mouth. The saddle is formed like the pack-saddles used by the French and Spaniards, of two flat thin boards which fit the sides of the horse, and are kept together by two cross pieces, one before and the other behind, which rise to a considerable height, ending sometimes in a flat point extending outwards, and always making the saddle deep and narrow. Under this a piece of buffalo skin, with the hair on, is placed so as to prevent the rubbing of the boards, and when they mount they throw a piece of skin or robe over the saddle, which has no permanent cover. When stirrups are used, they consist of wood covered with leather; but stirrups and saddles are conveniences reserved for old men and women. The young warriors rarely use any thing except a small leather pad stuffed with hair, and secured by a girth made of a leathern thong. In this way they ride with great expertness, and they have a particular dexterity in catching the horse when he is running at large. If he will not immediately submit when they wish to take him, they make a noose in the rope, and although the horse may be at a distance, or even running, rarely fail to fix it on his neck; and such is the docility of the animal, that however unruly he may seem, he surrenders as soon as he feels the rope on him. This cord is so useful in this way that it is never dispensed with, even when they use the Spanish bridle, which they prefer, and always procure when they have it in their power. The horse becomes almost an object of attachment: a favourite is frequently painted and his ears cut into various shapes: the mane and tail, which are never drawn nor trimmed, are decorated with feathers of birds, and sometimes a warrior suspends at the breast of his horse the finest ornaments he possesses.

Thus armed and mounted the Shoshonee is a formidable enemy, even with the feeble weapons which he is still obliged to use. When they attack

125

at full speed they bend forward and cover their bodies with the shield, while with the right hand they shoot under the horses neck.

The only articles of metal which the Shoshonees possess are a few bad knives, some brass kettles, some bracelets or armbands of iron and brass, a few buttons worn as ornaments in their hair, one or two spears about a foot in length, and some heads for arrows made of iron and brass. All these they had obtained in trading with the Crow or Rocky mountain Indians, who live on the Yellowstone. The few bridle-bits and stirrups they procured from the Spanish colonies.

The instrument which supplies the place of a knife among them, is a piece of flint with no regular form, and the sharp part of it not more than one or two inches long: the edge of this is renewed, and the flint itself is formed into heads for arrows, by means of the point of a deer or elk horn, an instrument which they use with great art and ingenuity. There are no axes or hatchets; all the wood being cut with flint or elk-horn, the latter of which is always used as a wedge in splitting wood. Their utensils consist, besides the brass kettles, of pots in the form of a jar, made either of earth, or of a stone found in the hills between Madison and Jefferson rivers, which, though soft and white in its natural state, becomes very hard and black after exposure to the fire. The horns of the buffalo and the bighorn supply them with spoons.

The fire is always kindled by means of a blunt arrow, and a piece of well-seasoned wood of a soft spongy kind, such as the willow or cottonwood.

The Shoshonees are of a diminutive stature, with thick flat feet and ankles, crooked legs, and

are, generally speaking, worse formed than any
nation of Indians we have seen. Their complexion
resembles that of the Sioux, and is darker than
that of the Minnetarees, Mandans, or Shawnees.
The hair in both sexes is suffered to fall loosely
over the face and down the shoulders: some men,
however, divide it by means of thongs of dressed
leather or otter skin into two equal queues, which
hang over the ears and are drawn in front of the
body; but at the present moment, when the nation is afflicted by the loss of so many relations
killed in war, most of them have the hair cut
quite short in the neck, and Cameahwait has the
hair cut short all over his head, this being the
customary mourning for a deceased kindred.

The dress of the men consists of a robe, a tippet,
a shirt, long leggings and moccasins. The robe is
formed most commonly of the skins of antelope,
bighorn, or deer, though when it can be procured,
the buffalo hide is preferred. Sometimes too they
are made of beaver, moonax, and small wolves,
and frequently during the summer of elk skin.
These are dressed with the hair on, and reach
about as low as the middle of the leg. They are
worn loosely over the shoulders, the sides being
at pleasure either left open or drawn together by
the hand, and in cold weather kept close by a
girdle round the waist. This robe answers the
purpose of a cloak during the day, and at night
is their only covering.

The tippet is the most elegant article of Indian
dress we have ever seen. The neck or collar of it
is a strip about four or five inches wide, cut from
the back of the otter skin, the nose and eyes forming one extremity, and the tail another. This
being dressed with the fur on, they attach to one
edge of it from one hundred to two hundred and fifty

127

little rolls of ermine skin, beginning at the ear, and proceeding towards the tail. These ermine skins are the same kind of narrow strips from the back of that animal, which are sewed round a small cord of twisted silkgrass thick enough to make the skin taper towards the tail which hangs from the end, and are generally about the size of a large quill. These are tied at the head into little bundles, of two, three or more according to the caprice of the wearer, and then suspended from the collar, and a broad fringe of ermine skin is fixed so as to cover the parts where they unite, which might have a coarse appearance. Little tassels of fringe of the same materials are also fastened to the extremities of the tail, so as to show its black colour to greater advantage. The centre of the collar is further ornamented with the shells of the pearl oyster. Thus adorned, the collar is worn close round the neck, and the little rolls fall down over the shoulders nearly to the waist, so as to form a sort of short cloak, which has a very handsome appearance. These tippets are very highly esteemed, and are given or disposed of on important occasions only. The ermine is the fur known to the northwest traders by the name of the white weasel, but is the genuine ermine; and by encouraging the Indians to take them, might no doubt be rendered a valuable branch of trade. These animals must be very abundant, for the tippets are in great numbers, and the construction of each requires at least one hundred skins.

The shirt is a covering of dressed skin without the hair, and formed of the hide of the antelope, deer, bighorn, or elk, though the last is more rarely used than any other for this purpose. It fits the body loosely, and reaches half way down the

128

thigh. The aperture at the top is wide enough to admit the head, and has no collar, but is either left square, or most frequently terminates in the tail of the animal, which is left entire, so as to fold outwards, though sometimes the edges are cut into a fringe, and ornamented with quills of the porcupine. The seams of the shirt are on the sides, and are richly fringed and adorned with porcupine quills, till within five or six inches of the sleeve, where it is left open, as is also the under side of the sleeve from the shoulder to the elbow, where it fits closely round the arm as low as the wrist, and has no fringe like the sides, and the under part of the sleeve above the elbow. It is kept up by wide shoulder straps, on which the manufacturer displays his taste by the variety of figures wrought with porcupine quills of different colours, and sometimes by beads when they can be obtained. The lower end of the shirt retains the natural shape of the fore legs and neck of the skin, with the addition of a slight fringe; the hair too is left on the tail and near the hoofs, part of which last is retained and split into a fringe.

The leggings are generally made of antelope skins, dressed without the hair, and with the legs, tail and neck hanging to them. Each legging is formed of a skin nearly entire, and reaches from the ankle to the upper part of the thigh, and the legs of the skin are tucked before and behind under a girdle round the waist. It fits closely to the leg, the tail being worn upwards, and the neck highly ornamented with fringe and porcupine quills, drags on the ground behind the heels. As the legs of the animal are tied round the girdle, the wide part of the skin is drawn so high as to conceal the parts usually kept from view, in which respect their dress is much more decent than that of any nation of Indians on the Missouri. The seams of the leggings down the sides, are also fringed and ornamented, and occasionally decorated with tufts of hair taken from enemies whom they have slain. In making all these dresses, their only thread is the sinew taken from the backs and loins of deer, elk, buffalo, or any other animal.

The moccasin is of the deer, elk, or buffalo skin, dressed without the hair, though in winter they use the buffalo skin with the hairy side inward, as do most of the Indians who inhabit the buffalo country. Like the Mandan moccasin, it is made with a single seam on the outer edge, and sewed up behind, a hole being left at the instep to admit the foot. It is variously ornamented with figures wrought with porcupine quills, and sometimes the young men most fond of dress cover it with the skin of a polecat, and trail at their heels the tail of the animal.

The dress of the women consists of the same articles as that of their husbands. The robe though smaller is worn in the same way: the moccasins are precisely similar. The shirt or chemise reaches half way down the leg, is in the same form, except that there is no shoulder-strap, the seam coming quite up to the shoulder; though for women who give suck both sides are open, almost down to the waist. It is also ornamented in the same way with the addition of little patches of red cloth, edged round with beads at the skirts. The chief ornament is over the breast, where there are curious figures made with the usual luxury of porcupine quills. Like the men they have a girdle round the waist, and when either sex wishes to disengage the arm, it is drawn up through the hole near the shoulder, and the lower part of the sleeve thrown behind the body.

Children alone wear beads round their necks; grown persons of both sexes prefer them suspended in little bunches from the ear, and sometimes intermixed with triangular pieces of the shell of the pearl oyster. Sometimes the men tie them in the same way to the hair of the forepart of the head, and increase the beauty of it by adding the wings and tails of birds, and particularly the feathers of the great eagle or calumet bird, of which they are extremely fond. The collars are formed either of sea shells procured from their relations to the southwest, or of the sweet-scented grass which grows in the neighbourhood, and which they twist or plait together, to the thickness of a man's finger, and then cover with porcupine quills of various colours. The first of these is worn indiscriminately by both sexes, the second principally confined to the men, while a string of elk's tusks is a collar almost peculiar to the women and children. Another collar worn by the men is a string of round bones like the joints of a fish's back, but the collar most preferred, because most honourable, is one of the claws of the brown bear. To kill one of these animals is as distinguished an achievement as to have put to death an enemy, and in fact with their weapons is a more dangerous trial of courage. These claws are suspended on a thong of dressed leather, and being ornamented with beads, are worn round the neck by the warriors with great pride. The men also frequently wear the skin of a fox, or a strip of otter skin round the head in the form of a bandeau.

In short, the dress of the Shoshonees is as convenient and decent as that of any Indians we have seen.

They have many more children than might have

been expected, considering their precarious means of support and their wandering life. This inconvenience is however balanced by the wonderful facility with which their females undergo the operations of child-birth. In the most advanced state of pregnancy they continue their usual occupations, which are scarcely interrupted longer than the mere time of bringing the child into the world.

The old men are few in number, and do not appear to be treated with much tenderness or respect.

The tobacco used by the Shoshonees is not cultivated among them, but obtained from the Indians of the Rocky mountains, and from some of the bands of their own nation who live south of them: it is the same plant which is in use among the Minnetarees, Mandans, and Ricaras.

Their chief intercourse with other nations seems to consist in their association with other Snake Indians, and with the Flatheads when they go eastward to hunt buffalo, and in the occasional visits made by the Flatheads to the waters of the Columbia for the purpose of fishing. Their intercourse with the Spaniards is much more rare, and it furnishes them with a few articles, such as mules, and some bridles, and other ornaments for horses, which, as well as some of their kitchen utensils, are also furnished by the bands of Snake Indians from the Yellowstone. The pearl ornaments which they esteem so highly come from other bands, whom they represent as their friends and relations, living to the southwest beyond the barren plains on the other side of the mountains: these relations they say inhabit a good country, abounding with elk, deer, bear, and antelope, where horses and mules are much more abundant than they are here, or to use their own expression, as numerous as the grass of the plains.

The names of the Indians varies in the course of their life: originally given in childhood, from the mere necessity of distinguishing objects, or from some accidental resemblance to external objects, the young warrior is impatient to change it by some achievement of his own. Any important event, the stealing of horses, the scalping an enemy, or killing a brown bear, entitles him at once to a new name which he then selects for himself, and it is confirmed by the nation. Sometimes the two names subsist together: thus, the chief Cameahwait, which means, "one who never walks," has the war name of Tooettecone, or "black gun," which he acquired when he first signalised himself. As each new action gives a warrior a right to change his name, many of them have had several in the course of their lives. To give to a friend his own name is an act of high courtesy, and a pledge like that of pulling off the moccasin of sincerity and hospitality. The chief in this way gave his name to captain Clark when he first arrived, and he was afterwards known among the Shoshonees by the name of Cameahwait.

The diseases incident to this state of life may be supposed to be few, and chiefly the result of accidents. We were particularly anxious to ascertain whether they had any knowledge of the venereal disorder. After inquiring by means of the interpreter and his wife, we learnt that they sometimes suffered from it, and that they most usually die with it; nor could we discover what was their remedy. It is possible that this disease may have reached them in their circuitous communications with the whites through the intermediate Indians;

but the situation of the Shoshonees is so insulated, that it is not probable that it could have reached them in that way, and the existence of such a disorder among the Rocky mountains seems rather a proof of its being aboriginal.

CHAPTER XVII.

The party, after procuring horses from the Shoshonees, proceed on their journey through the mountains—The difficulties and dangers of the route—A council held with another band of the Shoshonees, of whom some account is given—They are reduced to the necessity of killing their horses for food—Captain Clark with a small party precedes the main body in quest of food, and is hospitably received by the Pierced-nose Indians—Arrival of the main body amongst this tribe, with whom a council is held—They resolve to perform the remainder of their journey in canoes—Sickness of the party—They descend the Kooskooskee to its junction with Lewis river, after passing several dangerous rapids—Short description of the manners and dress of the Pierced-nose Indians.

August 27.—We were now occupied in determining our route and procuring horses from the Indians. The old guide who had been sent on by captain Clark, now confirmed, by means of our interpreter, what he had already asserted, of a road up Berry creek which would lead to Indian establishments on another branch of the Columbia: his reports however were contradicted by all the Shoshonees. This representation we ascribed to a wish on their part to keep us with them during the winter, as well for the protection we might afford against their enemies, as for the purpose of consuming our merchandise amongst them; and as the old man promised to conduct us himself, that route seemed to be the most eligible. We were able to procure some horses, though not enough for all our purposes. This traffic, and our inquiries and councils with the Indians, consumed the remainder of the day.

August 28.—The purchase of horses was resumed, and our stock raised to twenty-two.

135

Having now crossed more than once the country which separates the head waters of the Missouri from those of the Columbia, we can designate the easiest and most expeditious route for a portage: it is as follows:

From the forks of the river north 60° west, five miles to the point of a hill on the right: then south 80° west, ten miles to a spot where the creek is ten miles wide, and the highlands approach within two hundred yards; southwest five miles to a narrow part of the bottom; then turning south 70° west, two miles to a creek on the right: thence south 80 west, three miles to a rocky point opposite to a thicket of pines on the left: from that place west, three miles to the gap where is the fountain of the Missouri: on leaving this fountain south 80° west, six miles across the dividing ridge, to a run from the right passing several small streams north 80° west, four miles over hilly ground to the east fork of Lewis's river, which is here forty yards wide.

Thursday 29.—Captain Clark joined us this morning, and we continued our bargains for horses. The late misfortunes of the Shoshonees make the price higher than common, so that one horse cost a pistol, one hundred balls, some powder and a knife; another was changed for a musket, and in this way we obtained twenty-nine. The horses themselves are young and vigorous, but they are very poor, and most of them have sore backs in consequence of the roughness of the Shoshonee saddle. We are therefore afraid of loading them too heavily and are anxious to obtain one at least for each man, to carry the baggage, or the man himself, or in the last resource to serve as food; but with all our exertions we could not provide all our men with horses. We have, however, been fortunate in obtaining for the last three days a sufficient supply of flesh, our hunters having killed two or three deer every day.

Friday 30.—The weather was fine, and having now made all our purchases, we loaded our horses, and prepared to start. The greater part of the band who had delayed their journey on our account, were also ready to depart. We then took our leave of the Shoshonees, who set out on their visit to the Missouri at the same time that we accompanied by the old guide, his four sons, and another Indian, began the descent of the river, along the same road which captain Clark had previously pursued. After riding twelve miles we encamped on the south bank of the river, and as the hunters had brought in three deer early in the morning we did not feel the want of provisions.

Saturday 31.—At sunrise we resumed our journey, and halted for three hours on Salmon creek to let the horses graze. We then proceeded to the stream called Berry creek eighteen miles from the camp of last night: as we passed along, the valleys and prairies were on fire in several places, in order to collect the bands of the Shoshonees and the Flatheads, for their journey to the Missouri. The weather was warm and sultry, but the only inconvenience which we apprehend is a dearth of food, of which we had to-day an abundance, having procured a deer, a goose, one duck, and a prairie fowl. On reaching Tower creek we left the former track of captain Clark, and began to explore the new route, which is our last hope of getting out of the mountains. For four miles the road, which is tolerably plain, led us along Berry creek to some old Indian lodges where we encamped for the night; the next day,

Sunday, September 1, 1805, we followed the same road which here left the creek and turned to the northwest across the hills. During all day we were riding over these hills, from which are many drains and small streams running into the river to the left, and at the distance of eighteen miles, came to a large creek called Fish creek emptying into the Columbia which is about six miles from us. It had rained in the course of the day, and commenced raining again towards evening. We therefore determined not to leave the low grounds to night, and after going up Fish creek four miles formed our encampment. The country over which we passed is well watered, but poor and rugged or stony, except the bottoms of Fish creek, and even these are narrow. Two men were sent to purchase fish of the Indians at the mouth of the creek, and with the dried fish which they obtained, and a deer and a few salmon killed by the party, we were still well supplied. Two bear also were wounded but we could procure neither of them.

Monday 2.—This morning all the Indians left us, except the old guide, who now conducted us up Fish creek: at one mile and a half we passed a branch of the river coming in through a low ground covered with pine on the left, and two and a half miles further is a second branch from the right; after continuing our route along the hills covered with pine, and a low ground of the same growth, we arrived at the distance of three and a half miles at the forks of the creek. The road which we were following now turned up the east side of these forks, and as our guide informed us led to the Missouri. We were therefore left without any track; but as no time was to be lost we began to cut our road up the west branch of the creek. This we effected with much difficulty; the thickets of trees and brush through which we were obliged to cut our way required great labour; the road itself was over the steep and rocky sides of the hills where the horses could not move without danger of slipping down, while their feet were bruised by the rocks and stumps of trees. Accustomed as these animals were to this kind of life they suffered severely, several of them fell to some distance down the sides of the hills, some turned over with the baggage, one was crippled, and two gave out exhausted with fatigue. After crossing the creek several times we at last made five miles, with great fatigue and labour, and encamped on the left side of the creek in a small stony low ground. It was not, however, till after dark that the whole party was collected, and then, as it rained, and we killed nothing, we passed an uncomfortable night. The party had been too busily occupied with the horses to make any hunting excursion, and though as we came along Fish creek we saw many beaver dams we saw none of the animals themselves. In the morning,

Tuesday 3, the horses were very stiff and weary. We sent back two men for the load of the horse which had been crippled yesterday, and which we had been forced to leave two miles behind. On their return we set out at eight o'clock, and proceeded up the creek, making a passage through the brush and timber along its borders. The country is generally supplied with pine, and in the low grounds is a great abundance of fir trees, and under bushes. The mountains are high and rugged, and those to the east of us, covered with snow. With all our precautions the horses were very much injured in passing over the ridges and steep points of the hills, and to add to the difficulty, at the distance of eleven miles, the high mountains closed the creek, so that we were obliged to leave the creek to the right, and cross the mountain abruptly. The ascent was here so steep, that several of the horses slipped and hurt themselves, but at last we succeeded in crossing the mountain, and encamped on a small branch of Fish creek. We had now made fourteen miles in a direction nearly north from the river; but this distance, though short, was very fatiguing, and rendered still more disagreeable by the rain which began at three o'clock. At dusk it commenced snowing, and continued till the ground was covered to the depth of two inches, when it changed into a sleet. We here met with a serious misfortune the last of our thermometers being broken by accident. After making a scanty supper on a little corn and a few pheasants killed in the course of the day, we laid down to sleep, and next morning,

Wednesday 4, found every thing frozen, and the ground covered with snow. We were obliged to wait some time in order to thaw the covers of the baggage, after which we began our journey at eight o'clock. We crossed a high mountain which forms the dividing ridge between the waters of the creek we had been ascending, and those running to the north and west. We had not gone more than six miles over the snow, when we reached the head of a stream from the right, which directed its course more to the westward. We descended the steep sides of the hills along its border, and at the distance of three miles found a small branch coming in from the eastward. We saw several of the argalia, but they were too shy to be killed, and we therefore made a dinner from a deer shot by one of the hunters. Then we pursued the course of the stream for three miles, till it emptied itself into a river from the east. In the wide valley at their junction, we discovered a large encampment of Indians: when we had reached them and alighted from our horses, we were received with great cordiality. A council was immediately assembled, white robes were thrown over our shoulders, and the pipe of peace introduced. After this ceremony, as it was too late to go any further, we encamped, and continued smoking and conversing with the chiefs till a late hour. The next morning,

Thursday 5, we assembled the chiefs and warriors, and informed them who we were, and the purpose for which we visited their country. All this was however conveyed to them through so many different languages, that it was not comprehended without difficulty. We therefore proceeded to the more intelligible language of presents, and made four chiefs by giving a medal and a small quantity of tobacco to each. We received in turn from the principal chief, a present consisting of the skins of a braro, an otter, and two antelopes, and were treated by the women to some dried roots and berries. We then began to traffic for horses, and succeeded in exchanging seven, purchasing eleven, for which we gave a few articles of merchandise.

This encampment consists of thirty-three tents, in which were about four hundred souls, among whom eighty were men. They are called Ootla-shoots, and represent themselves as one band of a nation called Tushepaws, a numerous people of four hundred and fifty tents, residing on the heads of the Missouri and Columbia rivers, and some of them lower down the latter river. In person these Indians are stout, and their complexion lighter

141

than that common among Indians. The hair of the men is worn in queues of otter skin, falling in front over the shoulders. A shirt of dressed skin covers the body to the knee, and on this is worn occasionally a robe. To these were added leggings and moccasins. The women suffer their hair to fall in disorder over the face and shoulders, and their chief article of covering is a long shirt of skin, reaching down to the ankles, and tied round the waist. In other respects, as also in the few ornaments which they possess, their appearance is similar to that of the Shoshonees; there is however a difference between the language of these people which is still farther increased by the very extraordinary pronunciation of the Ootlashoots. Their words have all a remarkably guttural sound, and there is nothing which seems to represent the tone of their speaking more exactly than the clucking of a fowl, or the noise of a parrot. This peculiarity renders their voices scarcely audible, except at a short distance, and when many of them are talking, forms a strange confusion of sounds. The common conversation we overheard, consisted of low guttural sounds occasionally broken by a loud word or two, after which it would relapse and scarcely be distinguished. They seem kind and friendly and willingly shared with us berries and roots, which formed their only stock of provisions. Their only wealth is their horses, which are very fine, and so numerous that this party had with them at least five hundred.

Friday 6.—We continued this morning with the Ootlashoots, from whom we purchased two more horses, and procured a vocabulary of their language. The Ootlashoots set off about two o'clock to join the different bands who were collecting at the three forks of the Missouri. We ourselves pro-

ceeded at the same time, and taking a direction
N. 30 W. crossed within the distance of one mile
and a half, a small river from the right, and a
creek coming in from the north. This river is the
main stream, and when it reaches the end of the
valley, where the mountains close in upon it, is
joined by the river on which we encamped last
evening, as well as by the creek just mentioned.
To the river thus formed we gave the name of
captain Clark, he being the first white man who
had ever visited its waters. At the end of five
miles on this course we had crossed the valley,
and reached the top of a mountain covered with
pine; this we descended along the steep sides and
ravines for a mile and a half, when we came to a
spot on the river, where the Ootlashoots had encamped a few days before. We then followed the
course of the river, which is from twenty-five to
thirty yards wide, shallow, stony, and the low
grounds on its borders narrow. Within the distance of three and a half miles, we crossed it
several times, and after passing a run on each
side, encamped on its right bank, after making ten
miles during the afternoon. The horses were
turned out to graze, but those we had lately
bought were secured and watched, lest they
should escape, or be stolen by their former owners.
Our stock of flour was now exhausted, and we
had but little corn, and as our hunters had killed
nothing except two pheasants, our supper consisted chiefly of berries.

Saturday, 7.—The greater part of the day the
weather was dark and rainy: we continued
through the narrow low grounds along the river,
till at the distance of six miles we came to a large
creek from the left, after which the bottoms widen.
Four miles lower is another creek on the same

side, and the valley now extends from one to three miles, the mountains on the left being high and bald, with snow on the summits, while the country to the right is open and hilly. Four miles beyond this is a creek running from the snow-top'd mountains, and several runs on both sides of the river. Two miles from this last is another creek on the left. The afternoon was now far advanced, but not being able to find a fit place to encamp we continued six miles further till after dark, when we halted for the night. The river here is still shallow and stony, but is increased to the width of fifty yards. The valley through which we passed is of a poor soil, and its fertility injured by the quantity of stone scattered over it. We met two horses which had strayed from the Indians and were now quite wild. No fish was to be seen in the river, but we obtained a very agreeable supply of two deer, two cranes, and two pheasants.

Sunday 8.—We set out early: the snow-top'd hills on the left approach the river near our camp, but we soon reached a valley four or five miles wide, through which we followed the course of the river in a direction due north. We passed three creeks on the right, and several runs emptying themselves into the opposite side of the river. At the distance of eleven miles the river turned more towards the west: we pursued it for twelve miles, and encamped near a large creek coming in from the right, which, from its being divided into four different channels, we called Scattering creek. The valley continues to be a poor stony land, with scarcely any timber, except some pine trees along the waters and partially scattered on the hills to the right, which, as well as those on the left, have snow on them. The plant which forces itself most

144

on our attention is a species of prickly pear very common on this part of the river: it grows in clusters, in an oval form about the size of a pigeon's egg, and its thorns are so strong and bearded, that when it penetrates our feet it brings away the pear itself. We saw two mares and a colt, which, like the horses seen yesterday, seemed to have lost themselves and become wild. Our game to-day consisted of two deer, an elk, and a prairie fowl.

Monday, 9.—We resumed our journey through the valley, and leaving the road on our right crossed the Scattering creek, and halted at the distance of twelve miles on a small run from the east, where we breakfasted on the remains of yesterday's hunt: we here took a meridian altitude, which gave the latitude of 46° 41′ 38″ 9: we then continued, and at the distance of four miles passed over to the left bank of the river, where we found a large road through the valley. At this place is a handsome stream of very clear water, a hundred yards wide with low banks, and a bed formed entirely of gravel: it has every appearance of being navigable, but as it contains no salmon, we presume there must be some fall below which obstructs their passage. Our guide could not inform us where this river discharged its waters; he said that as far as he knew its course it ran along the mountains to the north, and that not far from our present position it was joined by another stream nearly as large as itself, which rises in the mountains to the east near the Missouri, and flows through an extensive valley or open prairie. Through this prairie is the great Indian road to the waters of the Missouri; and so direct is the route, that in four days' journey from this place we might reach the Missouri about thirty miles above what we called the Gates of the Rocky mountains, or the spot where the valley of that river widens into an extensive plain on entering the chain of mountains. At ten miles from our camp is a small creek falling in from the eastward, five miles below which we halted at a large stream which empties itself on the west side of the river. It is a fine bold creek of clear water about twenty yards wide, and we called it *Traveller's-rest* creek; for as our guide told us that we should here leave the river, we determined to remain for the purpose of making celestial observations and collecting some food, as the country through which we are to pass has no game for a great distance.

The valley of the river through which we have been passing is generally a prairie from five to six miles in width, and with a cold gravelly white soil. The timber which it possesses is almost exclusively pine, chiefly of the long-leafed kind, with some spruce, and a species of fir resembling the Scotch fir: near the water courses are also seen a few narrow-leafed cottonwood trees, and the only underbrush is the redwood, honeysuckle, and rose-bushes. Our game was four deer, three geese, four ducks, and three prairie fowls: one of the hunters brought in a red-headed woodpecker of the large kind common in the United States, but the first of the kind we have seen since leaving the Illinois.

Tuesday, 10.—The morning being fair all the hunters were sent out, and the rest of the party employed in repairing their clothes: two of them were sent to the junction of the river from the east, along which the Indians go to the Missouri: it is about seven miles below Traveller's-rest creek; the country at the forks is seven or eight miles wide, level and open, but with little timber:

its course is to the north, and we incline to believe that this is the river which the Minnetarees
had described to us as running from south to
north along the west side of the Rocky mountains, not far from the sources of Medicine river:
there is moreover reason to suppose, that after
going as far northward as the head-waters of
that river it turns to the westward and joins the
Tacootchetessee. Towards evening one of the
hunters returned with three Indians, whom he had
met in his excursion up Traveller's-rest creek: as
soon as they saw him they prepared to attack
him with arrows, but he quieted them by laying
down his gun and advancing towards them, and
soon persuaded them to come to the camp. Our
Shoshonee guide could not speak the language of
these people, but by the universal language of
signs and gesticulations, which is perfectly intelligible among the Indians, he found that these were
three Tushepaw Flatheads in pursuit of two men,
supposed to be Shoshonees, who had stolen
twenty-three of their horses: we gave them some
boiled venison and a few presents; such as a fish-
hook, a steel to strike fire, and a little powder;
but they seemed better pleased with a piece of
ribbon which we tied in the hair of each of them.
They were however in such haste, lest their horses
should be carried off, that two of them set off
after sunset in quest of the robbers: the third
however was persuaded to remain with us and
conduct us to his relations: these he said were
numerous, and resided on the Columbia in the
plain below the mountains. From that place he
added, the river was navigable to the ocean; that
some of his relations had been there last fall and
seen an old white man who resided there by himself, and who gave them some handkerchiefs like

147

those we have. The distance from this place is five sleeps or days' journey. When our hunters had all joined us we found our provisions consisted of four deer, a beaver, and three grouse.

The observation of to-day gave 46° 48′ 28″ as the latitude of Traveller's-rest creek.

Wednesday 11.—Two of our horses having strayed away we were detained all the morning before they were caught. In the meantime our Tushepaw Indian became impatient of the delay, and set out to return home alone. As usual we had despatched four of our best hunters ahead, and as we hoped with their aid and our present stock of provisions to subsist on the route, we proceeded at three o'clock up the right side of the creek, and encamped under some old Indian huts at the distance of seven miles. The road was plain and good: the valley is however narrower than that which we left and bordered by high and rugged hills to the right, while the mountains on the left were covered with snow. The day was fair and warm, the wind from the northwest.

Thursday 12.—There was a white frost this morning. We proceeded at seven o'clock and soon passed a stream falling in on the right, near which was an old Indian camp with a bath or sweating-house covered with earth. At two miles distance we ascended a high, and thence continued through a hilly and thickly timbered country for nine miles, when we came to the forks of the creek, where the road branches up each fork. We followed the western route, and finding that the creek made a considerable bend at the distance of four miles, crossed a high mountain in order to avoid the circuit. The road had been very bad during the first part of the day, but the passage of the mountain, which was eight miles across, was very painful to the horses, as we were obliged to go over steep stony sides of hills and along the hollows and ravines, rendered more disagreeable by the fallen timber, chiefly pine, spruce pine and fir. We at length reached the creek, having made twenty-three miles of a route so difficult that some of the party did not join us before ten o'clock. We found the account of the scantiness of game but too true, as we were not able to procure any thing during the whole of yesterday, and to-day we killed only a single pheasant. Along the road we observed many of the pine trees peeled off, which is done by the Indians to procure the inner bark for food in the spring.

Friday 13.—Two of the horses strayed away during the night, and one of them being captain Lewis's, he remained with four men to search for them while we proceeded up the creek: at the distance of two miles we came to several springs issuing from large rocks of a coarse hard grit, and nearly boiling hot. These seem to be much frequented as there are several paths made by elk, deer and other animals, and near one of the springs a hole or Indian bath, and roads leading in different directions. These embarrassed our guide, who mistaking the road took us three miles out of the proper course over an exceedingly bad route. We then fell into the right road, and proceeded on very well, when having made five miles we stopped to refresh the horses. Captain Lewis here joined us, but not having been able to find his horse, two men were sent back to continue the search. We then proceeded along the same kind of country which we passed yesterday, and after crossing a mountain and leaving the sources of the Traveller's-rest creek on the left, reached after five miles riding a small creek which also came in

149

from the left hand, passing through open glades, some of which were half a mile wide. The road which had been as usual rugged and stony, became firm, plain and level after quitting the head of Traveller's-rest. We followed the course of this new creek for two miles and encamped at a spot where the mountains close on each side. Other mountains covered with snow are in view to the southeast and southwest. We were somewhat more fortunate to-day in killing a deer and several pheasants which were of the common species, except that the tail was black.

Saturday 14.—The day was very cloudy with rain and hail in the valleys, while on the top of the mountains some snow fell. We proceeded early, and continuing along the right side of Glade creek crossed a high mountain, and at the distance of six miles reached the place where it is joined by another branch of equal size from the right. Near the forks the Tushepaws have had an encampment which is but recently abandoned, for the grass is entirely destroyed by horses, and two fish weirs across the creek are still remaining; no fish were however to be seen. We here passed over to the left side of the creek and began the ascent of a very high and steep mountain nine miles across. On reaching the other side we found a large branch from the left, which seems to rise in the snowy mountains to the south and southeast. We continued along the creek two miles further, when night coming on we encamped opposite a small island at the mouth of a branch on the right side of the river. The mountains which we crossed to-day were much more difficult than those of yesterday; the last was particularly fatiguing, being steep and stony, broken by fallen timber, and thickly overgrown by pine, spruce, fir, hackmatack and tamarack. Although we had made only seventeen miles we were all very weary. The whole stock of animal food was now exhausted, and we therefore killed a colt, on which we made a hearty supper. From this incident we called the last creek we had passed from the south Colt-killed creek. The river itself is eighty yards wide, with a swift current, and a stony channel. Its Indian name is Kooskooskee.

Sunday 15.—At an early hour we proceeded along the right side of the Kooskooskee over steep rocky points of land, till at the distance of four miles we reached an old Indian fishing place: the road here turned to the right of the water, and began to ascend a mountain: but the fire and wind had prostrated or dried almost all the timber on the south side, and the ascents were so steep that we were forced to wind in every direction round the high knobs which constantly impeded our progress. Several of the horses lost their foot-hold and slipped: one of them which was loaded with a desk and small trunk, rolled over and over for forty yards, till his fall was stopped by a tree. The desk was broken; but the poor animal escaped without much injury. After clambering in this way for four miles, we came to a high snowy part of the mountain where was a spring of water, at which we halted two hours to refresh our horses.

On leaving the spring the road continued as bad as it was below, and the timber more abundant. At four miles we reached the top of the mountain, and foreseeing no chance of meeting with water, we encamped on the northern side of the mountain, near an old bank of snow, three feet deep. Some of this we melted, and supped on the remains of the colt killed yesterday. Our only game

151

to-day was two pheasants, and the horses on which we calculated as a last resource begin to fail us, for two of them were so poor, and worn out with fatigue, that we were obliged to leave them behind. All around us are high rugged mountains, among which is a lofty range from southeast to northwest, whose tops are without timber, and in some places covered with snow. The night was cloudy and very cold, and three hours before daybreak,

Monday 16, it began to snow, and continued all day, so that by evening it was six or eight inches deep. This covered the track so completely, that we were obliged constantly to halt and examine, lest we should lose the route. In many places we had nothing to guide us except the branches of the trees which, being low, have been rubbed by the burdens of the Indian horses. The road was, like that of yesterday, along steep hill sides, obstructed with fallen timber, and a growth of eight different species of pine, so thickly strewed that the snow falls from them as we pass, and keeps us continually wet to the skin, and so cold, that we are anxious lest our feet should be frozen, as we have only thin moccasins to defend them.

At noon we halted to let the horses feed on some long grass on the south side of the mountains, and endeavoured by making fires to keep ourselves warm. As soon as the horses were refreshed, captain Clark went ahead with one man, and at the distance of six miles reached a stream from the right, and prepared fires by the time of our arrival at dusk. We here encamped in a piece of low ground, thickly timbered, but scarcely large enough to permit us to lie level. We had now made thirteen miles. We were all very wet, cold, and hungry: but although before setting out this morning, we had seen four deer, yet we could not procure any of them, and were obliged to kill a second colt for our supper.

Tuesday 17.—Our horses became so much scattered during the night, that we were detained till one o'clock before they were all collected. We then continued our route over high rough knobs, and several drains and springs, and along a ridge of country separating the waters of two small rivers. The road was still difficult, and several of the horses fell and injured themselves very much, so that we were unable to advance more than ten miles to a small stream, on which we encamped.

We had killed a few pheasants, but these being insufficient for our subsistence, we killed another of the colts. This want of provisions, and the extreme fatigue to which we were subjected, and the dreary prospects before us, began to dispirit the men. It was therefore agreed that captain Clark should go on ahead with six hunters, and endeavour to kill something for the support of the party. He therefore set out,

Wednesday 18, early in the morning in hopes of finding a level country from which he might send back some game. His route lay S. 85° W. along the same high dividing ridge, and the road was still very bad; but he moved on rapidly, and at the distance of twenty miles was rejoiced on discovering far off an extensive plain towards the west and southwest, bounded by a high mountain. He halted an hour to let the horses eat a little grass on the hill sides, and then went on twelve and a half miles till he reached a bold creek, running to the left, on which he encamped. To this stream he gave the very appropriate name of Hungry creek; for having procured no game, they had nothing to eat.

In the meantime we were detained till after eight o'clock by the loss of one of our horses which had strayed away and could not be found. We then proceeded, but having soon finished the remainder of the colt killed yesterday, felt the want of provisions, which was more sensible from our meeting with no water, till towards nightfall we found some in a ravine among the hills. By pushing on our horses almost to their utmost strength, we made eighteen miles.

We then melted some snow, and supped on a little portable soup, a few canisters of which, with about twenty weight of bear's oil, are our only remaining means of subsistence. Our guns are scarcely of any service, for there is no living creature in these mountains, except a few small pheasants, a small species of gray squirrel, and a blue bird of the vulture kind about the size of a turtle dove or jay, and even these are difficult to shoot.

Thursday 19.—Captain Clark proceeded up the creek, along which the road was more steep and stony than any he had yet passed. At six miles distance he reached a small plain, in which he fortunately found a horse, on which he breakfasted, and hung the rest on a tree for the party in the rear. Two miles beyond this he left the creek, and crossed three high mountains, rendered almost impassable from the steepness of the ascent and the quantity of fallen timber. After clambering over these ridges and mountains, and passing the heads of some branches of Hungry creek, he came to a large creek running westward. This he followed for four miles, then turned to the right down the mountain, till he came to a small creek to the left. Here he halted, having made twenty-two miles on his course, south eighty degrees

154

west, though the winding route over the mountains almost doubled the distance. On descending the last mountain, the heat became much more sensible after the extreme cold he had experienced for several days past. Besides the breakfast in the morning, two pheasants were their only food during the day, and the only kinds of birds they saw were the blue jay, a small white-headed hawk, a larger hawk, crows, and ravens.

We followed soon after sunrise. At six miles the ridge terminated and we had before us the cheering prospect of the large plain to the southwest. On leaving the ridge we again ascended and went down several mountains, and six miles further came to Hungry creek where it was fifteen yards wide, and received the waters of a branch from the north. We went up it on a course nearly due west, and at three miles crossed a second branch flowing from the same quarter. The country is thickly covered with pine timber, of which we have enumerated eight distinct species. Three miles beyond this last branch of Hungry creek we encamped, after a fatiguing route of eighteen miles. The road along the creek is a narrow rocky path near the borders of very high precipices, from which a fall seems almost inevitable destruction. One of our horses slipped and rolling over with his load down the hill side, which was nearly perpendicular and strewed with large irregular rocks, nearly a hundred yards, and did not stop till he fell into the creek: we all expected he was killed, but to our astonishment, on taking off his load, he rose, and seemed but little injured, and in twenty minutes proceeded with his load. Having no other provision we took some portable soup, our only refreshment during the day. This abstinence, joined with fatigue, has a visible effect on our health. The men are growing weak and losing their flesh very fast: several are afflicted with the dysentery, and eruptions of the skin are very common.

Friday 20.—Captain Clark went on through a country as rugged as usual, till on passing a low mountain he came at the distance of four miles to the forks of a large creek. Down this he kept on a course south 60° west for two miles, then turning to the right, continued over a dividing ridge where were the heads of several little streams, and at twelve miles distance descended the last of the rocky mountains and reached the level country. A beautiful open plain partially supplied with pine now presented itself. He continued for five miles when he discovered three Indian boys, who, on observing the party, ran off and hid themselves in the grass. Captain Clark immediately alighted, and giving his horse and gun to one of the men went after the boys. He soon relieved their apprehensions and sent them forward to the village about a mile off with presents of small pieces of ribbon. Soon after the boys had reached home, a man came out to meet the party, with great caution, but he conducted them to a large tent in the village, and all the inhabitants gathered round to view with a mixture of fear and pleasure these wonderful strangers. The conductor now informed captain Clark by signs, that the spacious tent was the residence of the great chief, who had set out three days ago with all the warriors to attack some of their enemies towards the southwest; that he would not return before fifteen or eighteen days, and that in the meantime there were only a few men left to guard the women and children. They now set before them a small piece of buffalo meat, some dried salmon, berries, and

156

several kinds of roots. Among these last is one which is round and much like an onion in appearance and sweet to the taste: it is called quamash, and is eaten either in its natural state, or boiled into a kind of soup or made into a cake, which is then called pasheco. After the long abstinence this was a sumptuous treat; we returned the kindness of the people by a few small presents, and then went on in company with one of the chiefs to a second village in the same plain, at the distance of two miles. Here the party was treated with great kindness and passed the night. The hunters were sent out, but though they saw some tracks of deer were not able to procure any thing.

We were detained till ten o'clock before we could collect our scattered horses; we then proceeded for two miles, when to our great joy we found the horse which captain Clark had killed, and a note apprising us of his intention of going to the plains towards the southwest, and collect provisions by the time we reached him. At one o'clock we halted on a small stream, and made a hearty meal of horse flesh. On examination it now appeared that one of the horses was missing, and the man in whose charge he had been, was directed to return and search for him. He came back in about two hours without having been able to find the horse; but as the load was too valuable to be lost, two of the best woodsmen were directed to continue the search while we proceeded. Our general course was south 25° west through a thick forest of large pine, which has fallen in many places, and very much obstructs the road. After making about fifteen miles we encamped on a ridge where we could find but little grass and no water. We succeeded, however, in procuring a little from a distance, and supped on the remainder of the horse.

On descending the heights of the mountains the soil becomes gradually more fertile, and the land through which we passed this evening, is of an excellent quality. It has a dark gray soil, though very broken, and with large masses of gray free-stone above the ground in many places. Among the vegetable productions we distinguished the alder, honeysuckle, and huckleberry, common in the United States, and a species of honeysuckle, known only westward of the Rocky mountains, which rises to the height of about four feet, and bears a white berry. There is also a plant resembling the chokecherry, which grows in thick clumps eight or ten feet high, and bears a black berry with a single stone of a sweetish taste. The arbor vitae too, is very common, and grows to a great size, being from two to six feet in diameter.

Saturday 21.—The free use of food, to which he had not been accustomed, made captain Clark very sick both yesterday evening and during the whole of to-day. He therefore sent out all the hunters and remained himself at the village, as well on account of his sickness as for the purpose of avoiding suspicion and collecting information from the Indians as to the route.

The two villages consist of about thirty double tents, and the inhabitants call themselves Chopun-nish or Pierced-nose. The chief drew a chart of the river, and explained, that a greater chief than himself, who governed this village and was called the Twisted-hair, was now fishing at the distance of half a day's ride down the river: his chart made the Kooskooskee fork a little below his camp, a second fork below, still further on a large branch flowed in on each side, below which the river passed the mountains: here was a great fall of water, near which lived white people, from whom were procured the white beads and brass ornaments worn by the women.

A chief of another band made a visit this morning, and smoked with captain Clark. The hunters returned without having been able to kill any thing; captain Clark purchased as much dried salmon, roots and berries as he could, with the few articles he chanced to have in his pockets, and having sent them by one of the men and a hired Indian back to captain Lewis, he went on towards the camp of the Twisted-hair. It was four o'clock before he set out, and the night soon came on; but having met an Indian coming from the river, they engaged him by a present of a neckcloth, to guide them to the Twisted-hair's camp. For twelve miles they proceeded through the plain before they reached the river hills, which are very high and steep. The whole valley from these hills to the Rocky mountain is a beautiful level country, with a rich soil covered with grass: there is however, but little timber, and the ground is badly watered: the plain is so much lower than the surrounding hills, or so much sheltered by them, that the weather is quite warm, while the cold of the mountains was extreme. From the top of the river hills they proceeded down for three miles till they reached the water side, between eleven and twelve o'clock at night: here we found a small camp of five squaws and three children, the chief himself being encamped, with two others, on a small island in the river: the guide called to him and he soon came over. Captain Clark gave him a medal, and they smoked together till one o'clock.

We could not set out till eleven o'clock, because being obliged in the evening to loosen our horses to enable them to find subsistence, it is always difficult to collect them in the morning. At that hour we continued along the ridge on which we had slept, and at a mile and a half reached a large creek running to our left, just above its junction with one of its branches. We proceeded down the low grounds of this creek, which are level, wide, and heavily timbered, but turned to the right at the distance of two and a half miles, and began to pass the broken and hilly country; but the thick timber had fallen in so many places that we could scarcely make our way. After going five miles we passed the creek on which captain Clark had encamped during the night of the 19th, and continued five miles further over the same kind of road, till we came to the forks of a large creek. We crossed the northern branch of this stream, and proceeded down it on the west side for a mile: here we found a small plain where there was tolerable grass for the horses, and therefore remained during the night, having made fifteen miles on a course S. 30° W.

The arbor vitae increases in size and quantity as we advance: some of the trees we passed to-day being capable of forming periogues at least forty-five feet in length. We were so fortunate also as to kill a few pheasants and a prairie wolf, which, with the remainder of the horse, supplied us with one meal, the last of our provisions, our food for the morrow being wholly dependent on the chance of our guns.

Sunday, 22.—Captain Clark passed over to the island with the Twisted-hair, who seemed to be cheerful and sincere in his conduct. The river at this place is about one hundred and sixty yards wide, but interrupted by shoals, and the low grounds on its borders are narrow. The hunters brought in three deer; after which captain Clark left his party, and accompanied by the Twisted-hair and his son, rode back to the village, where he arrived about sunset: they then walked up together to the second village, where we had just arrived. We had intended to set out early, but one of the men having neglected to hobble his horse he strayed away, and we were obliged to wait till nearly twelve o'clock. We then proceeded on a western course for two and a half miles, when we met the hunters sent by captain Clark from the village, seven and a half miles distant, with provisions. This supply was most seasonable, as we had tasted nothing since last night, and the fish, and roots, and berries, in addition to a crow which we killed on the route, completely satisfied our hunger. After this refreshment we proceeded in much better spirits, and at a few miles were overtaken by the two men who had been sent back after a horse on the 20th. They were perfectly exhausted with the fatigue of walking and the want of food; but as we had two spare horses they were mounted and brought on to the village.

They had set out about three o'clock in the afternoon of the 20th with one horse between them: after crossing the mountain they came to the place where we had eaten the horse. Here they encamped, and having no food made a fire and roasted the head of the horse, which even our appetites had spared, and supped on the ears, skin, lips, &c. of the animal. The next morning, 21st, they found the track of the horse, and pursuing it recovered the saddle-bags, and at length about eleven o'clock, the horse himself. Being now both mounted, they set out to return and slept at a small stream: during the day they had nothing at all except two pheasants, which were so torn to pieces by the shot, that the head and legs were the only parts fit for food. In this situation they found the next morning, 22d, that during the night their horses had run away from them or been stolen by the Indians. They searched for them until nine o'clock, when seeing that they could not recover them and fearful of starving if they remained where they were, they set out on foot to join us, carrying the saddle-bags alternately. They walked as fast as they could during the day, till they reached us in a deplorable state of weakness and inanition.

As we approached the village, most of the women, though apprised of our being expected, fled with their children into the neighbouring woods. The men, however, received us without any apprehension, and gave us a plentiful supply of provisions. The plains were now crowded with Indians, who came to see the persons of the whites, and the strange things they brought with them: but as our guide was perfectly a stranger to their language we could converse by signs only. Our inquiries were chiefly directed to the situation of the country, the courses of the rivers, and the Indian villages, of all which we received information from several of the Indians, and as their accounts varied but little from each other, we were induced to place confidence in them. Among others, the Twisted-hair drew a chart of the river on a white elk skin. According to this, the Kooskooskee forks a few miles from this place; two days towards the south is another and larger fork on which the Shoshonee or Snake Indians fish: five days' journey further is a large river from the northwest into which Clark's river empties itself: from the mouth of that river to the falls is five days' journey further: on all the forks as well as on the main river great numbers of Indians reside, and at the falls are establishments of whites. This was the story of the Twisted-hair.

Monday 23.—The chiefs and warriors were all assembled this morning, and we explained to them where we came from, the objects of our visiting them, and our pacific intentions towards all the Indians. This being conveyed by signs, might not have been perfectly comprehended, but appeared to give perfect satisfaction. We now gave a medal to two of the chiefs, a shirt in addition to the medal already received by the Twisted-hair, and delivered a flag and a handkerchief for the grand chief on his return. To these were added a knife, a handkerchief and a small piece of tobacco for each chief. The inhabitants did not give us any provisions gratuitously. We therefore purchased a quantity of fish, berries (chiefly red haws) and roots; and in the afternoon went on to the second village. The Twisted-hair introduced us into his own tent, which consisted however of nothing more than pine bushes and bark, and gave us some dried salmon boiled. We continued our purchases, and obtained as much provision as our horses could carry in their present weak condition as far as the river. The men exchanged a few old canisters for dressed elk skins, of which they made shirts: great crowds of the natives are round us all night, but we have not yet missed any thing except a knife and a few other articles stolen yesterday from a shot pouch. At dark we had a hard wind from the southwest accompanied with rain which lasted half an hour, but in the morning,

Tuesday 24, the weather was fair. We sent back Colter in search of the horses lost in the mountains, and having collected the rest set out at ten o'clock along the same route already passed by captain Clark towards the river. All round the village the women are busily employed in gathering and dressing the pasheco root, of which large quantities are heaped up in piles over the plain. We now felt severely the consequence of eating heartily after our late privations: captain Lewis and two of the men were taken very ill last evening, and to-day he could scarcely sit on his horse, while others were obliged to be put on horseback, and some from extreme weakness and pain, were forced to lie down along side of the road for some time. At sunset we reached the island where the hunters had been left on the 22d. They had been unsuccessful, having killed only two deer since that time, and two of them are very sick. A little below this island is a larger one on which we encamped, and administered Rush's pills to the sick.

Wednesday 25.—The weather was very hot, and oppressive to the party, most of whom are now complaining of sickness. Our situation indeed, rendered it necessary to husband our remaining strength, and it was determined to proceed down the river in canoes. Captain Clark therefore set out with the Twisted-hair and two young men, in quest of timber for canoes. As he went down the river he crossed at the distance of a mile a creek from the right, which from the rocks that obstructed its passage, he called Rockdam river. The hills along the river are high and steep: the low grounds are narrow, and the navigation of the river embarrassed by two rapids. At the distance of three miles further he reached two nearly equal forks of the river, one of which flowed in from the north. Here he rested for an hour, and cooked a few salmon which one of the Indians caught with a gig. Here too, he was joined by two canoes of Indians from below: they were long, steady, and loaded with the furniture and provisions of two families. He now crossed the south fork, and returned to the camp on the south side, through a narrow pine bottom the greater part of the way, in which was found much fine timber for canoes. One of the Indian boats with two men, set out at the same time, and such was their dexterity in managing the pole, that they reached camp within fifteen minutes after him, although they had to drag the canoe over three rapids. He found captain Lewis, and several of the men still very sick; and distributed to such as were in need of it, salts and tartar emetic.

Thursday 26.—Having resolved to go down to some spot calculated for building canoes, we set out early this morning and proceeded five miles, and encamped on low ground on the south, opposite the forks of the river. But so weak were the men that several were taken sick in coming down; the weather being oppressively hot. Two chiefs and their families followed us, and encamped with a great number of horses near us: and soon after our arrival we were joined by two Indians, who came down the north fork on a raft. We purchased some fresh salmon, and having distributed axes, and portioned off the labour of the party, began,

Friday 27, at an early hour, the preparations for making five canoes. But few of the men, however, were able to work, and of these several were soon taken ill, as the day proved very hot. The hunters too, returned without any game, and seriously indisposed, so that nearly the whole party was now ill. We procured some fresh salmon; and Colter, who now returned with one of the horses, brought half a deer, which was very nourishing to the invalids: several Indians from a camp below, came up to see us.

Saturday 28.—The men continue ill, though some of those first attacked are recovering. Their general complaint is a heaviness at the stomach, and a lax, which is rendered more painful by the heat of the weather, and the diet of fish and roots, to which they are confined, as no game is to be procured. A number of Indians collect about us in the course of the day to gaze at the strange appearance of every thing belonging to us.

Sunday 29.—The morning was cool, the wind from the southwest; but in the afternoon the heat returned. The men continue ill; but all those who are able to work are occupied at the canoes. The spirits of the party were much recruited by three deer brought in by the hunters; and the next day,

Monday 30th, the sick began to recruit their strength, the morning being fair and pleasant. The Indians pass in great numbers up and down the river, and we observe large quantities of small duck going down this morning.

Tuesday, October 1, 1805.—The morning was cool, the wind easterly, but the latter part of the day was warm. We were visited by several Indians from the tribes below, and others from the main south fork. To two of the most distinguished men we made presents of a ring and brooch, and to five others a piece of ribbon, a little tobacco, and the fifth part of a neckcloth. We now dried our clothes and other articles, and selected some articles such as the Indians admire, in order to purchase some provisions, as we have

nothing left except a little dried fish, which oper-
ates as a complete purgative.

Wednesday 2.—The day is very warm. Two
men were sent to the village with a quantity of
these articles to purchase food. We are now reduced to roots, which produce violent pains in the
stomach. Our work continued as usual, and
many of the party are convalescent. The hunters
returned in the afternoon with nothing but a
small prairie-wolf, so that our provisions being
exhausted, we killed one of the horses to eat, and
provide soup for the sick.

Thursday 3.—The fine cool morning and easterly wind had an agreeable effect upon the party,
most of whom are now able to work. The Indians from below left us, and we were visited by
others from different quarters.

Friday 4.—Again we had a cool east wind from
the mountains. The men were now much better,
and captain Lewis himself so far recovered as to
walk about a little. Three Indians arrived to-day
from the Great river to the south. The two men
also returned from the village with roots and
fish, and as the flesh of the horse killed yesterday
was exhausted, we were confined to that diet,
although unwholesome as well as unpleasant.
The afternoon was warm.

Saturday 5.—The wind easterly, and the
weather cool. The canoes being nearly finished it
became necessary to dispose of our horses. They
were therefore collected to the number of thirty-
eight, and being branded and marked were delivered to three Indians, the two brothers and the
son of a chief, who promises to accompany us
down the river. To each of these men we gave a
knife and some small articles, and they agreed to
take good care of the horses till our return. The

hunters with all their diligence are unable to kill any thing, the hills being high and rugged, and the woods too dry to hunt deer, which is the only game in the country. We therefore continue to eat dried fish and roots, which are purchased from the squaws, by means of small presents, but chiefly white beads, of which they are extravagantly fond. Some of these roots seem to possess very active properties, for after supping on them this evening, we were swelled to such a degree as to be scarcely able to breathe for several hours. Towards night we launched two canoes which proved to be very good.

Sunday 6.—This morning is again cool, and the wind easterly. The general course of the winds seems to resemble that which we observed on the east side of the mountain. While on the head waters of the Missouri, we had every morning a cool wind from the west. At this place a cool breeze springs up during the latter part of the night, or near daybreak, and continues till seven or eight o'clock, when it subsides, and the latter part of the day is warm. Captain Lewis is not so well as he was, and captain Clark was also taken ill. We had all our saddles buried in a cache near the river, about half a mile below, and deposited at the same time a canister of powder, and a bag of balls. The time which could be spared from our labours on the canoes, was devoted to some astronomical observations. The latitude of our camp as deduced from the mean of two observations is 46° 34′ 56″ 3 north.

Monday 7.—This morning all the canoes were put in the water and loaded, the oars fixed, and every preparation made for setting out, but when we were all ready, the two chiefs who had promised to accompany us, were not to be found, and

at the same time we missed a pipe tomahawk.
We therefore proceeded without them. Below the
forks this river is called the Kooskooskee, and is
a clear rapid stream, with a number of shoals and
difficult places. For some miles the hills are steep,
the low grounds narrow, but then succeeds an
open country with a few trees scattered along the
river. At the distance of nine miles is a small
creek on the left. We passed in the course of the
day ten rapids, in descending which, one of the
canoes struck a rock, and sprung a leak: we however continued for nineteen miles, and encamped
on the left side of the river, opposite to the mouth
of a small run. Here the canoe was unloaded and
repaired, and two lead canisters of powder deposited; several camps of Indians were on the
sides of the river, but we had little intercourse
with any of them.

Tuesday 8.—We set out at nine o'clock. At
eight and a half miles we passed an island: four
and a half miles lower a second island, opposite a
small creek on the left side of the river. Five
miles lower is another island on the left: a mile
and a half below which is a fourth. At a short
distance from this is a large creek from the right,
to which we gave the name of Colter's creek,
from Colter one of the men. We had left this
creek about a mile and a half, and were passing
the last of fifteen rapids which we had been fortunate enough to escape, when one of the canoes
struck, and a hole being made in her side, she
immediately filled and sunk. The men, several of
whom could not swim, clung to the boat till one
of our canoes could be unloaded, and with the
assistance of an Indian boat, they were all
brought to shore. All the goods were so much
wet, that we were obliged to halt for the night,

and spread them out to dry. While all this was exhibited, it was necessary to place two sentinels over the merchandise, for we found that the Indians, though kind and disposed to give us every aid during our distress, could not resist the temptation of pilfering some of the small articles. We passed during our route of twenty miles to-day, several encampments of Indians on the islands, and near the rapids, which places are chosen as most convenient for taking salmon. At one of these camps we found our two chiefs, who after promising to descend the river with us, had left us; they however willingly came on board after we had gone through the ceremony of smoking.

Wednesday 9.—The morning was as usual, cool; but as the weather both yesterday and to-day was cloudy, our merchandise dried but slowly. The boat, though much injured, was repaired by ten o'clock so as to be perfectly fit for service; but we were obliged to remain during the day till the articles were sufficiently dry to be reloaded: the interval we employed in purchasing fish for the voyage and conversing with the Indians. In the afternoon we were surprised at hearing that our old Shoshonee guide and his son had left us, and been seen running up the river several miles above. As he had never given any notice of his intention, nor had even received his pay for guiding us, we could not imagine the cause of his desertion, nor did he ever return to explain his conduct. We requested the chief to send a horseman after him to request that he would return and receive what we owed him. From this however he dissuaded us, and said very frankly, that his nation, the Chopunnish, would take from the old man any presents that he might have on passing their camp.

The Indians came about our camp at night, and were very gay and good-humoured with the men. Among other exhibitions was that of a squaw who appeared to be crazy: she sang in a wild incoherent manner, and would offer to the spectators all the little articles she possessed, scarifying herself in a horrid manner if any one refused her present: she seemed to be an object of pity among the Indians, who suffered her to do as she pleased without interruption.

Thursday, 10.—A fine morning. We loaded the canoes and set off at seven o'clock. At the distance of two and a half miles we had passed three islands, the last of which is opposite to a small stream on the right. Within the following three and a half miles is another island and a creek on the left, with wide low grounds, containing willow and cottonwood trees, on which were three tents of Indians. Two miles lower is the head of a large island, and six and a half miles further we halted at an encampment of eight lodges on the left, in order to view a rapid before us: we had already passed eight, and some of them difficult; but this was worse than any of them, being a very hazardous ripple strewed with rocks: we here purchased roots and dined with the Indians. Among them was a man from the falls, who says that he saw white people at that place, and is very desirous of going down with us; an offer which however we declined. Just above this camp we had passed a tent, near which was an Indian bathing himself in a small pond or hole of water, warmed by throwing in hot stones. After finishing our meal we descended the rapid with no injury, except to one of our boats which ran against a rock, but in the course of an hour was brought off with only a small split in her side.

This ripple, from its appearance and difficulty, we named the Rugged rapid. We went on over five other rapids of a less dangerous kind, and at the distance of five miles reached a large fork of the river from the south; and after coming twenty miles, halted below the junction on the right side of the river: our arrival soon attracted the attention of the Indians, who flocked in all directions to see us. In the evening the Indian from the falls, whom we had seen at the Rugged rapid, joined us with his son in a small canoe, and insisted on accompanying us to the falls. Being again reduced to fish and roots we made an experiment to vary our food by purchasing a few dogs, and after having been accustomed to horse-flesh, felt no disrelish to this new dish. The Chopunnish have great numbers of dogs which they employ for domestic purposes, but never eat; and our using the flesh of that animal soon brought us into ridicule as dog-eaters.

The country at the junction of the two rivers is an open plain on all sides, broken towards the left by a distant ridge of highland, thinly covered with timber: this is the only body of timber which the country possesses; for at the forks there is not a tree to be seen, and during almost the whole descent of sixty miles down the Kooskooskee from its forks there are very few. This southern branch is in fact the main stream of Lewis's river on which we encamped when among the Shoshonees. The Indians inform us that it is navigable for sixty miles; that not far from its mouth it receives a branch from the south; and a second and larger branch, two days' march up, and nearly parallel to the first Chopunnish villages, we met near the mountains. This branch is called Pawnashte, and is the residence of a chief, who, according to their expression, has more horses than he can count. The river has many rapids, near which are situated many fishing camps; there being ten establishments of this before reaching the first southern branch; one on that stream, five between that and the Pawnashte; one on that river, and two above it; besides many other Indians who reside high up on the more distant waters of this river. All these Indians belong to the Chopunnish nation, and live in tents of an oblong form, covered with flat roofs.

At its mouth Lewis's river is about two hundred and fifty yards wide, and its water is of a greenish blue colour. The Kooskooskee, whose waters are clear as crystal, one hundred and fifty yards in width, and after the union the river enlarges to the space of three hundred yards: at the point of the union is an Indian cabin, and in Lewis's river a small island.

The Chopunnish or Pierced-nose nation, who reside on the Kooskooskee and Lewis's rivers, are in person stout, portly, well-looking men: the women are small, with good features, and generally handsome, though the complexion of both sexes is darker than that of the Tushepaws. In dress they resemble that nation, being fond of displaying their ornaments. The buffalo or elk-skin robe decorated with beads, sea-shells, chiefly mother-of-pearl, attached to an otter-skin collar and hung in the hair, which falls in front in two queues; feathers, paints of different kinds, principally white, green, and light blue, all of which they find in their own country: these are the chief ornaments they use. In the winter they wear a short shirt of dressed skins, long painted leggings and moccasins, and a plait of twisted grass round the neck.

173

The dress of the women is more simple, consisting of a long shirt of argalia or ibex skin, reaching down to the ankles without a girdle: to this are tied little pieces of brass and shells and other small articles; but the head is not at all ornamented. The dress of the female is indeed more modest, and more studiously so than any we have observed, though the other sex is careless of the indelicacy of exposure.

The Chopunnish have very few amusements, for their life is painful and laborious; and all their exertions are necessary to earn even their precarious subsistence. During the summer and autumn they are busily occupied in fishing for salmon, and collecting their winter store of roots. In the winter they hunt the deer on snow shoes over the plains, and towards spring cross the mountains to the Missouri for the purpose of trafficking for buffalo robes. The inconveniences of that comfortless life are increased by frequent encounters with their enemies from the west, who drive them over the mountains with the loss of their horses, and sometimes the lives of many of the nation. Though originally the same people, their dialect varies very perceptibly from that of the Tushepaws: their treatment to us differed much from the kind and disinterested services of the Shoshonees: they are indeed selfish and avaricious; they part very reluctantly with every article of food or clothing; and while they expect a recompense for every service however small, do not concern themselves about reciprocating any presents we may give them.

They are generally healthy—the only disorders which we have had occasion to remark being of a scrofulous kind, and for these, as well as for the amusement of those who are in good health, hot and cold bathing is very commonly used.

The soil of these prairies is of a light yellow clay intermixed with small smooth grass: it is barren, and produces little more than a bearded grass about three inches high, and a prickly pear, of which we now found three species: the first is of the broad-leafed kind, common to the Missouri. The second has the leaf of a globular form, and is also frequent on the upper part of the Missouri, particularly after it enters the Rocky mountains. The third is peculiar to this country, and is much more inconvenient than the other two: it consists of small thick leaves of a circular form, which grow from the margin of each other as in the broad-leafed pear of the Missouri: these leaves are armed with a greater number of thorns, which are stronger, and appear to be barbed; and as the leaf itself is very slightly attached to the stem, as soon as one thorn touches the moccasin it adheres and brings with it the leaf, which is accompanied by a reinforcement of thorns.

CHAPTER XVIII.

The party proceed in canoes—Description of an Indian sweating bath and burial place—Many dangerous rapids passed—Narrow escape of one of the canoes—In the passage down they are visited by several Indians, all of whom manifest pacific dispositions—Description of the Sokulk tribe—Their dress, and manner of building houses—Their pacific character—Their habits of living—Their mode of boiling salmon—Vast quantities of salmon amongst the Sokulk—Council held with this tribe—The terror and consternation excited by captain Clark, concerning which an interesting cause is related—Some account of the Pisquitpaws—Their mode of burying the dead.

Friday, October 11, 1805.—This morning the wind was from the east, and the weather cloudy. We set out early, and at the distance of a mile and a half reached a point of rocks in a bend of the river towards the left, near to which was an old Indian house, and a meadow on the opposite bank. Here the hills came down towards the water, and formed by the rocks, which have fallen from their sides, a rapid over which we dragged the canoes. We passed, a mile and a half further, two Indian lodges in a bend towards the right, and at six miles from our camp of last evening reached the mouth of a brook on the left. Just above this stream we stopped for breakfast at a large encampment of Indians on the same side: we soon began to trade with them for a stock of provisions, and were so fortunate as to purchase seven dogs and all the fish they would spare: while this traffic was going on, we observed a vapour bath or sweating house in a different form from that used on the frontiers of the United States, or in the Rocky mountains, It was a hol-

low square of six or eight feet deep, formed in the
river bank by damming up with mud the other
three sides, and covering the whole completely
except an aperture about two feet wide at the
top. The bathers descend by this hole, taking
with them a number of heated stones, and jugs of
water; and after being seated round the room,
throw the water on the stones till the steam becomes of a temperature sufficiently high for their
purposes. The baths of the Indians in the Rocky
mountains is of different sizes, the most common
being made of mud and sticks like an oven, but
the mode of raising the steam is exactly the same.
Among both these nations it is very uncommon
for a man to bathe alone, he is generally accompanied by one or sometimes several of his acquaintances; indeed it is so essentially a social
amusement, that to decline going in to bathe
when invited by a friend is one of the highest in-
dignities which can be offered to him. The Indians on the frontiers generally use a bath which
will accommodate only one person, and is formed
of a wickered work of willows about four feet
high, arched at the top, and covered with skins.
In this the patient sits till by means of the heated
stones and water he has perspired sufficiently.
Almost universally these baths are in the neighbourhood of running water, into which the Indians plunge immediately on coming out of the
vapour bath, and sometimes return again, and
subject themselves to a second perspiration. This
practice is, however, less frequent among our
neighbouring nations than those to the westward.
This bath is employed either for pleasure or for
health, and is used indiscriminately for rheuma-
tism, venereal, or in short for all kinds of diseases.

On leaving this encampment we passed two

more rapids, and some swift water, and at the
distance of four and a half miles reached one
which was much more difficult to pass. Three
miles beyond this rapid, are three huts of Indians
on the right, where we stopped and obtained in
exchange for a few trifles some pasheco roots,
five dogs and a small quantity of dried fish. We
made our dinner of part of each of these articles,
and then proceeded on without any obstruction,
till after making twelve and a half miles we came
to a stony island on the right side of the river,
opposite to which is a rapid, and a second at its
lower point. About three and a half miles beyond
the island is a small brook which empties itself
into a bend on the right, where we encamped at
two Indian huts, which are now inhabited. Here
we met two Indians belonging to a nation who
reside at the mouth of this river. We had made
thirty-one miles to-day, although the weather was
warm, and we found the current obstructed by
nine different rapids, more or less difficult to pass.
All these rapids are fishing places of great resort
in the season, and as we passed we observed near
them slabs and pieces of split timber raised from
the ground, and some entire houses which are
vacant at present, but will be occupied as soon as
the Indians return from the plains on both sides
of the river, where our chief informs us they are
now hunting the antelope. Near each of these
houses is a small collection of graves, the burial
places of those who frequent these establishments.
The dead are wrapped up in robes of skins, and
deposited in graves, which are covered over with
earth and marked or secured by little pickets or
pieces of wood, stuck promiscuously over and
around it. The country on both sides, after
mounting a steep ascent of about two hundred

feet, becomes an open, level and fertile plain, which is, however, as well as the borders of the river itself, perfectly destitute of any kind of timber; and the chief growth which we observed consisted of a few low blackberries. We killed some geese and ducks. The wind in the after part of the day changed to the southwest and became high, but in the morning,

Saturday 12, it shifted to the east, and we had a fair cool morning. After purchasing all the provisions these Indians would spare, which amounted to only three dogs and a few fish, we proceeded. We soon reached a small island, and in the course of three miles passed three other islands nearly opposite to each other, and a bad rapid on the left in the neighbourhood of them. Within the following seven miles we passed a small rapid, and an island on the left, another stony island and a rapid on the right, just below which a brook comes in on the same side, and came to a bend towards the right opposite to a small island. From this place we saw some Indians on the hills, but they were too far off for us to have any intercourse, and showed no disposition to approach us. After going on two miles to a bend towards the left, we found the plains, which till now had formed rugged cliffs over the river, leaving small and narrow bottoms, become much lower on both sides, and the river itself widens to the space of four hundred yards, and continues for the same width, the country rising by a gentle ascent towards the high plains. At two and a half miles is a small creek on the left opposite to an island. For the three following miles, the country is low and open on both sides, after which it gradually rises till we reached a bend of the river towards the right, three and a

half miles further, in the course of which we
passed a rapid and an island. The wind now
changed to the southwest, and became violent.
We passed an island at the distance of four miles,
another one mile beyond it, where the water was
swift and shallow, and two miles further, a rapid
at the upper point of a small stony island. We
went along this island by the mouth of a brook
on the right, and encamped on the same side
opposite to a small island close under the left
shore. Our day's journey had been thirty miles,
and we might have gone still further, but as the
evening was coming on we halted at the head of
a rapid, which the Indians represented as dangerous to pass, for the purpose of examining it before
we set out in the morning. The country has
much the same appearance as that we passed
yesterday, consisting of open plains, which when
they approach the water are faced with a dark-
coloured rugged stone. The river is as usual
much obstructed by islands and rapids, some of
which are difficult to pass. Neither the plains nor
the borders of the river possess any timber, except
a few hackberry bushes and willows, and as there
is not much driftwood, fuel is very scarce.

Sunday 13.—The morning was windy and dark,
and the rain which began before daylight, continued till near twelve o'clock. Having viewed
very accurately the whole of this rapid we set
out, the Indians going on before us to pilot the
canoes. We found it, as had been reported, a very
dangerous rapid, about two miles in length, and
strewed with rocks in every direction, so as to
require great dexterity to avoid running against
them. We however passed through the channel,
which is towards the left, and about the centre of
the rapid, without meeting with any accident.

Two miles below it we had another bad rapid, a mile beyond which is a large creek in a bend to the left. This we called Kimooenim creek.

On leaving it the river soon became crowded with rough black rocks, till at the distance of a mile it forms a rapid which continues for four miles, and during the latter part of it for a mile and a half, the whole river is compressed into a narrow channel, not more than twenty-five yards wide. The water happened to be low as we passed, but during the high waters, the navigation must be very difficult. Immediately at the end of this rapid, is a large stream in a bend to the right, which we called Drewyer's river, after George Drewyer one of the party. A little below the mouth of this river is a large fishing establishment, where there are the scaffolds and timbers of several houses piled up against each other, and the meadow adjoining contains a number of holes, which seem to have been used as places of deposits for fish for a great length of time. There were no entire houses standing, and we saw only two Indians who had visited the narrows, but we were overtaken by two others, who accompanied us on horseback down the river, informing us that they meant to proceed by land down to the great river. Nine and a half miles below Drewyer's river, we passed another rapid, and three and a half miles farther reached some high cliffs in a bend to the left. Here after passing the timbers of a house, which were preserved on forks, we encamped on the right side, near a collection of graves, such as we had seen above. The country was still an open plain without timber, and our day's journey had no variety, except the fishing houses which are scattered near the situations convenient for fishing, but are now empty. Our two Indian companions spent the night with us.

Monday 14.—The wind was high from the southwest during the evening, and this morning it changed to the west, and the weather became very cold until about twelve o'clock, when it shifted to the southwest, and continued in that quarter during the rest of the day. We set out early, and after passing some swift water, reached at two and a half miles a rock of a very singular appearance. It was situated on a point to the left, at some distance from the ascending country, very high and large, and resembling in its shape the hull of a ship. At five miles we passed a rapid; at eight another rapid, and a small island on the right, and at ten and a half a small island on the right. We halted a mile and a half below for the purpose of examining a much larger and more dangerous rapid than those we had yet passed. It is three miles in length, and very difficult to navigate. We had scarcely set out, when three of the canoes stuck fast in endeavouring to avoid the rocks in the channel; soon after in passing two small rocky islands, one of the canoes struck a rock, but was prevented from upsetting, and fortunately we all arrived safe at the lower end of the rapid. Here we dined, and then proceeded, and soon reached another rapid on both sides of the river, which was divided by an island.

As we were descending it one of the boats was driven crosswise against a rock in the middle of the current. The crew attempted to get her off, but the waves dashed over her, and she soon filled; they got out on the rock and held her above water with great exertion, till another canoe was unloaded and sent to her relief; but they could not prevent a great deal of her baggage from floating down the stream. As soon as she was lightened, she was hurried down the channel leaving the crew on the rock. They were brought off by the rest of the party, and the canoe itself, and nearly all that had been washed overboard was recovered. The chief loss was the bedding of two of the men, a tomahawk, and some small articles. But all the rest were wet, and though by drying we were able to save the powder, all the loose packages of which were in this boat, yet we lost all the roots and other provisions, which are spoilt by the water. In order to diminish the loss as far as was in our power, we halted for the night on an island, and exposed every thing to dry. On landing we found some split timber for houses which the Indians had very securely covered with stone, and also a place where they had deposited their fish. We have hitherto abstained scrupulously from taking any thing belonging to the Indians; but on this occasion we were compelled to depart from this rule; and as there was no other timber to be found in any direction for firewood, and no owner appeared from whom it could be purchased, we used a part of these split planks, bearing in mind our obligation to repay the proprietor whenever we should discover him. The only game which we observed were geese and ducks, of the latter we killed some, and a few of the blue-winged teal. Our journey was fifteen miles in length.

Tuesday 15.—The morning was fair, and being obliged to remain for the purpose of drying the baggage, we sent out the hunters to the plains, but they returned at ten o'clock, without having seen even the tracks of any large game, but brought in three geese and two ducks. The plains are waving, and as we walked in them, we could

plainly discover a range of mountains bearing
southeast and northwest, becoming higher as they
advanced towards the north, the nearest point
bearing south about sixty miles from us. Our
stores being sufficiently dry to be reloaded, and as
we shall be obliged to stop for the purpose of
making some celestial observations at the mouth
of the river, which cannot be at a great distance,
we concluded to embark and complete the drying
at that place: we therefore set out at two o'clock.
For the first four miles we passed three islands, at
the lower points of which were the same number
of rapids, besides a fourth at a distance from
them. During the next ten miles we passed eight
islands and three more rapids, and reached a
point of rocks on the left side. The islands were
of various sizes, but were all composed of round
stone and sand: the rapids were in many places
difficult and dangerous to pass. About this place
the country becomes lower than usual, the ground
over the river not being higher than ninety or a
hundred feet, and extending back into a waving
plain. Soon after leaving this point of rocks, we
entered a narrow channel formed by the projecting
cliffs of the bank, which rise nearly perpendicular
from the water. The river is not however rapid,
but gentle and smooth during its confinement,
which lasts for three miles, when it falls, or rather
widens into a kind of basin nearly round, and
without any perceptible current. After passing
through this basin, we were joined by the three
Indians who had piloted us through the rapids
since we left the forks, and who in company with
our two chiefs had gone before us. They had now
halted here to warn us of a dangerous rapid,
which begins at the lower point of the basin. As
the day was too far spent to descend it, we de-

termined to examine before we attempted it, and therefore landed near an island at the head of the rapid, and studied particularly all its narrow and difficult parts. The spot where we landed was an old fishing establishment, of which there yet remained the timbers of a house carefully raised on scaffolds to protect them against the spring tide. Not being able to procure any other fuel, and the night being cold, we were again obliged to use the property of the Indians, who still remain in the plains hunting the antelope. Our progress was only twenty miles in consequence of the difficulty of passing the rapids. Our game consisted of two teal.

Wednesday, 16.—Having examined the rapids, which we found more difficult than the report of the Indians had induced us to believe, we set out early, and putting our Indian guide in front, our smallest canoe next, and the rest in succession, began the descent: the passage proved to be very disagreeable; as there is a continuation of shoals extending from bank to bank for the distance of three miles, during which the channel is narrow and crooked, and obstructed by large rocks in every direction, so as to require great dexterity to avoid being dashed on them. We got through the rapids with no injury to any of the boats except the hindmost, which ran on a rock; but by the assistance of the other boats, and of the Indians who were very alert, she escaped, though the baggage she contained was wet. Within three miles after leaving the rapid we passed three small islands, on one of which were the parts of a house put on scaffolds as usual, and soon after came to a rapid at the lower extremity of three small islands; and a second at the distance of a mile and a half below them; reaching six miles below

185

the great rapid a point of rocks at a rapid opposite to the upper point of a small island on the
left. Three miles further is another rapid; and
two miles beyond this a very bad rapid, or rather
a fall of the river: this, on examination, proved so
difficult to pass, that we thought it imprudent to
attempt, and therefore unloaded the canoes and
made a portage of three quarters of a mile. The
rapid, which is of about the same extent, is much
broken by rocks and shoals, and has a small
island in it on the right side. After crossing by
land we halted for dinner, and whilst we were
eating were visited by five Indians, who came up
the river on foot in great haste: we received them
kindly, smoked with them, and gave them a piece
of tobacco to smoke with their tribe: on receiving
the present they set out to return, and continued
running as fast as they could while they remained
in sight. Their curiosity had been excited by the
accounts of our two chiefs, who had gone on in
order to apprise the tribes of our approach and of
our friendly dispositions towards them. After
dinner we reloaded the canoes and proceeded: we
soon passed a rapid opposite to the upper point
of a sandy island on the left, which has a smaller
island near it. At three miles is a gravelly bar in
the river: four miles beyond this the Kimooenim
empties itself into the Columbia, and at its mouth
has an island just below a small rapid. We halted
above the point of junction on the Kimooenim to
confer with the Indians, who had collected in
great numbers to receive us. On landing we were
met by our two chiefs, to whose good offices we
were indebted for this reception, and also the two
Indians who had passed us a few days since on
horseback; one of whom appeared to be a man of
influence, and harangued the Indians on our ar-

rival. After smoking with the Indians, we formed a camp at the point where the two rivers unite, near to which we found some driftwood, and were supplied by our two old chiefs with the stalks of willows and some small bushes for fuel. We had scarcely fixed the camp and got the fires prepared, when a chief came from the Indian camp about a quarter of a mile up the Columbia, at the head of nearly two hundred men: they formed a regular procession, keeping time to the noise, rather the music of their drums, which they accompanied with their voices. As they advanced they formed a semicircle round us, and continued singing for some time: we then smoked with them all, and communicated, as well as we could by signs, our friendly intentions towards all nations, and our joy at finding ourselves surrounded by our children: we then proceeded to distribute presents to them, giving the principal chief a large medal, a shirt and handkerchief; to the second chief, a medal of a smaller size, and to a third chief who came down from some of the upper villages, a small medal and a handkerchief. This ceremony being concluded they left us; but in the course of the afternoon several of them returned and remained with us till a late hour. After they had dispersed we proceeded to purchase provisions, and were enabled to collect seven dogs, to which some of the Indians added small presents of fish, and one of them gave us twenty pounds of fat dried horseflesh.

Thursday, October 17.—The day being fair we were occupied in making the necessary observations for determining our longitude, and obtained a meridian altitude, from which it appeared that we were in latitude 46° 15′ 13″ 9. We also measured the two rivers by angles, and found that at the junction the Columbia is nine hundred and sixty yards wide, and Lewis's river five hundred and seventy-five; but soon after they unite, the former widens to the space of from one to three miles, including the islands. From the point of junction the country is a continued plain, which is low near the water, from which it rises gradually, and the only elevation to be seen is a range of high country running from the northeast towards the southwest, where it joins a range of mountains from the southwest, and is on the opposite side about two miles from the Columbia. There is through this plain no tree and scarcely any shrub, except a few willow bushes; and even of smaller plants there is not much more than the prickly pear, which is in great abundance, and is even more thorny and troublesome than any we have yet seen. During this time the principal chief came down with several of his warriors and smoked with us: we were also visited by several men and women, who offered dogs and fish for sale, but as the fish was out of season, and at present abundant in the river, we contented ourselves with purchasing all the dogs we could obtain. The nation among which we now are call themselves Sokulks; and with them are united a few of another nation, who reside on a western branch, emptying itself into the Columbia a few miles above the mouth of the latter river, and whose name is Chimnapum. The language of both these nations, of each of which we obtained a vocabulary, differs but little from each other, or from that of the Chopunnish who inhabit the Kooskooskee and Lewis's river. In their dress and general appearance also they resemble much those nations; the men wearing a robe of deer or antelope skin, under which a few of them have a

188

short leathern shirt. The most striking difference between them is among the females, the Sokulk women being more inclined to corpulency than any we have yet seen: their stature is low, their faces broad, and their heads flattened in such a manner that the forehead is in a straight line from the nose to the crown of the head: their eyes are of a dirty sable, their hair too is coarse and black, and braided as above without ornament of any kind: instead of wearing, as do the Chopunnish, long leathern shirts, highly decorated with beads and shells, the Sokulk females have no other covering but a truss or piece of leather tied round the hips and then drawn tight between the legs. The ornaments usually worn by both sexes are large blue or white beads, either pendent from their ears, or round the necks, wrists, and arms: they have likewise bracelets of brass, copper, and horn, and some trinkets of shells, fish bones, and curious feathers. The houses of the Sokulks are made of large mats of rushes, and are generally of a square or oblong form, varying in length from fifteen to sixty feet, and supported in the inside by poles or forks about six feet high: the top is covered with mats, leaving a space of twelve or fifteen inches the whole length of the house, for the purpose of admitting the light and suffering the smoke to pass through: the roof is nearly flat, which seems to indicate that rains are not common in this open country, and the house is not divided into apartments, the fire being in the middle of the large room, and immediately under the hole in the roof: the rooms are ornamented with their nets, gigs, and other fishing tackle, as well as the bow for each inhabitant, and a large quiver of arrows, which are headed with flint stones.

The Sokulks seem to be of a mild and peaceable disposition, and live in a state of comparative happiness. The men like those on the Kimooenim, are said to content themselves with a single wife, with whom we observe the husband shares the labours of procuring subsistence much more than is usual among savages. What may be considered as an unequivocal proof of their good disposition, is the great respect which was shown to old age. Among other marks of it, we observed in one of the houses an old woman perfectly blind, and who we were informed had lived more than a hundred winters. In this state of decrepitude, she occupied the best position in the house, seemed to be treated with great kindness, and whatever she said was listened to with much attention. They are by no means intrusive, and as their fisheries supply them with a competent, if not an abundant subsistence, although they receive thankfully whatever we choose to give, they do not importune us by begging. The fish is, indeed, their chief food, except the roots, and the casual supplies of the antelope, which to those who have only bows and arrows, must be very scanty. This diet may be the direct or the remote cause of the chief disorder which prevails among them, as well as among the Flatheads, on the Kooskooskee and Lewis's river. With all these Indians a bad soreness of the eyes is a very common disorder, which is suffered to ripen by neglect, till many are deprived of one of their eyes, and some have totally lost the use of both. This dreadful calamity may reasonably, we think, be imputed to the constant reflection of the sun on the waters where they are constantly fishing in the spring, summer and fall, and during the rest of the year on the snows of a country which affords no object to relieve the sight. Among the Sokulks too, and indeed among all the tribes whose chief subsistence is fish, we have observed that bad teeth are very general: some have the teeth, particularly those of the upper jaw, worn down to the gums, and many of both sexes, and even of middle age, have lost them almost entirely. This decay of the teeth is a circumstance very unusual among the Indians, either of the mountains or the plains, and seems peculiar to the inhabitants of the Columbia. We cannot avoid regarding as one principal cause of it, the manner in which they eat their food. The roots are swallowed as they are dug from the ground, frequently nearly covered with a gritty sand: so little idea have they that this is offensive, that all the roots they offer us for sale are in the same condition. A second and a principal cause may be their great use of the dried salmon, the bad effects of which are most probably increased by their mode of cooking it, which is simply to warm, and then swallow the rind, scales and flesh without any preparation. The Sokulks possess but few horses, the greater part of their labours being performed in canoes. Their amusements are similar to those of the Missouri Indians.

In the course of the day captain Clark, in a small canoe with two men, ascended the Columbia. At the distance of five miles he passed an island in the middle of the river, at the head of which is a small and not a dangerous rapid. On the left bank of the river opposite to this river is a fishing place, consisting of three mat houses. Here were great quantities of salmon drying on scaffolds: and indeed from the mouth of the river upwards he saw immense numbers of dead salmon strewed along the shore or floating on the surface of the water, which is so clear that the salmon

191

may be seen swimming in the water at the depth of fifteen or twenty feet. The Indians who had collected on the banks to view him, now joined him in eighteen canoes, and accompanied him up the river. A mile above the rapids he came to the lower point of an island where the course of the river, which had been from its mouth north 83° west, now became due west. He proceeded in that direction, when observing three houses of mats at a short distance he landed to visit them. On entering one of the houses he found it crowded with men, women and children, who immediately provided a mat for him to sit on, and one of the party undertook to prepare something to eat. He began by bringing in a piece of pine wood that had drifted down the river, which he split into small pieces, with a wedge made of the elks' horn, by means of a mallet of stone curiously carved. The pieces were then laid on the fire, and several round stones placed upon them: one of the squaws now brought a bucket of water, in which was a large salmon about half dried, and as the stones became heated, they were put into the bucket till the salmon was sufficiently boiled for use. It was then taken out, put on a platter of rushes neatly made, and laid before captain Clark, and another was boiled for each of his men. During these preparations he smoked with those about him who would accept of tobacco, but very few were desirous of smoking, a custom which is not general among them, and chiefly used as a matter of form in great ceremonies. After eating the fish, which was of an excellent flavour, captain Clark set out, and at the distance of four miles from the last island, came to the lower point of another near the left shore, where he halted at two large mat houses. Here as at the three houses below, the inhabitants were occupied in splitting and drying salmon. The multitudes of this fish are almost inconceivable. The water is so clear that they can readily be seen at the depth of fifteen or twenty feet, but at this season they float in such quantities down the stream, and are drifted ashore, that the Indians have only to collect, split and dry them on the scaffolds. Where they procure the timber of which these scaffolds are composed he could not learn, but as there are nothing but willow bushes to be seen for a great distance from the place, it rendered very probable, what the Indians assured him by signs, that they often used dried fish as fuel for the common occasions of cooking. From this island they showed him the entrance of a western branch of the Columbia, called the *Tapteal*, which as far as could be seen bears nearly west, and empties itself about eight miles above into the Columbia; the general course of which is northwest: towards the southwest a range of highland runs parallel to the river, at the distance of two miles on the left, while on the right side the country is low and covered with the prickly pear, and a weed or plant two or three feet high resembling whins. To the eastward is a range of mountains about fifty or sixty miles distant, which bear north and south; but neither in the low grounds, nor in the highlands is any timber to be seen. The evening coming on he determined not to proceed further than the island, and therefore returned to camp, accompanied by three canoes, which contained twenty Indians. In the course of his excursion he shot several grouse and ducks, and received some presents of fish, for which he gave in return small pieces of ribbon. He also killed a prairie cock, an animal of the pheasant kind, but about the size of a small turkey. It measured from the beak to the end of the toe two feet six inches and three-quarters, from the extremity of the wings three feet six inches, and the feathers of the tail were thirteen inches long. This bird we have seen nowhere except on this river. Its chief food is the grasshopper, and the seed of the wild plant which is peculiar to this river and the upper parts of the Missouri.

The men availed themselves of this day's rest to mend their clothes, dressing skins, and putting their arms in complete order, an object always of primary concern, but particularly at a moment when we are surrounded by so many strangers.

Friday 18.—We were visited this morning by several canoes of Indians, who joined those who were already with us, and soon opened a numerous council. We informed them as we had done all the other Indian nations of our friendship for them, and of our desire to promote peace among all our red children in this country. This was conveyed by signs through the means of our two chiefs, and seemed to be perfectly understood. We then made a second chief, and gave to all the chiefs a string of wampum, in remembrance of what we had said. Whilst the conference was going on four men came in a canoe from a large encampment on an island about eight miles below, but after staying a few minutes returned without saying a word to us. We now procured from the principal chief and one of the Cuimnapum nation a sketch of the Columbia, and the tribes of his nation living along its banks and those of the Tapteet. They drew it with a piece of coal on a robe, and as we afterwards transferred to paper, it exhibited a valuable specimen of Indian delineation.

Having completed the purposes of our stay, we now began to lay in our stores, and fish being out of season, purchased forty dogs, for which we gave small articles, such as bells, thimbles, knitting-needles, brass wire, and a few beads, an exchange with which they all seemed perfectly satisfied. These dogs, with six prairie cocks killed this morning, formed a plentiful supply for the present. We here left our guide and the two young men who had accompanied him, two of the three not being willing to go any further, and the third could be of no use as he was not acquainted with the river below. We therefore took no Indians but our two chiefs, and resumed our journey in the presence of many of the Sokulks, who came to witness our departure. The morning was cool and fair, and the wind from the southeast. Soon after proceeding,

We passed the island in the mouth of Lewis river, and at eight miles reached a larger island, which extends three miles in length. On going down by this island there is another on the right, which commences about the middle of it, and continues for three and a half miles. While they continue parallel to each other, they occasion a rapid near the lower extremity of the first island, opposite to which on the second island are nine lodges built of mats, and intended for the accommodation of the fishermen, of whom we saw great numbers, and vast quantities of dried fish on their scaffolds.

On reaching the lower point of the island, we landed to examine a bad rapid, and then undertook the passage which is very difficult, as the channel lies between two small islands, with two others still smaller near the left side of the river. Here are two Indian houses, the inhabitants of

which were as usual drying fish. We passed the
rapid without injury, and fourteen and a half
miles from the mouth of Lewis's river, came to an
island near the right shore, on which were two
other houses of Indians, pursuing the customary
occupation. One mile and a half beyond this
place, is a mouth of a small brook under a high
hill on the left. It seems to run during its whole
course through the high country, which at this
place begins, and rising to the height of two hundred feet forms cliffs of rugged black rocks which
project a considerable distance into the river. At
this place too we observed a mountain to the
S. W. the form of which is conical, and its top
covered with snow. We followed the river as it
entered these highlands, and at the distance of
two miles reached three islands, one on each side
of the river, and a third in the middle, on which
were two houses, where the Indians were drying
fish opposite a small rapid. Near these a fourth
island begins, close to the right shore, where were
nine lodges of Indians, all employed with their
fish. As we passed they called to us to land, but
as night was coming on, and there was no appearance of wood in the neighbourhood, we went
on about a mile further, till observing a log that
had drifted down the river, we landed near it on
the left side, and formed our camp under a high
hill, after having made twenty miles to-day. Directly opposite to us are five houses of Indians,
who were drying fish on the same island where we
had passed the nine lodges, and on the other side
of the river we saw a number of horses feeding.
Soon after landing, we were informed by our
chiefs that the large camp of nine houses, belonged to the first chief of all the tribes in this
quarter, and that he had called to request us to

196

land and pass the night with him as he had plenty of wood for us. This intelligence would have been very acceptable if it had been explained sooner, for we were obliged to use dried willows for fuel to cook with, not being able to burn the drift-log which had tempted us to land. We now sent the two chiefs along the left side of the river to invite the great chief down to spend the night with us. He came at a late hour, accompanied by twenty men, bringing a basket of mashed berries which he left as a present for us, and formed a camp at a short distance from us. The next morning,

Saturday 19, the great chief with two of his inferior chiefs, and a third belonging to a band on the river below, made us a visit at a very early hour. The first of these is called Yelleppit, a handsome well proportioned man, about five feet eight inches high, and thirty-five years of age, with a bold and dignified countenance; the rest were not distinguished in their appearance. We smoked with them, and after making a speech gave a medal, a handkerchief, and a string of wampum to Yelleppit, and a string of wampum only to the inferior chiefs. He requested us to remain till the middle of the day, in order that all his nation might come and see us, but we excused ourselves by telling him that on our return we would spend two or three days with him. This conference detained us till nine o'clock, by which time great numbers of the Indians had come down to visit us. On leaving them, we went on for eight miles, when we came to an island near the left shore which continued six miles in length. At the lower extremity of it is a small island on which are five houses, at present vacant, though the scaffolds of fish are as usual abundant. A

197

short distance below, are two more islands, one of them near the middle of the river. On this there were seven houses; but as soon as the Indians, who were drying fish, saw us, they fled to their houses, and not one of them appeared till we had passed, when they came out in greater numbers than is usual for houses of that size, which induced us to think that the inhabitants of the five lodges had been alarmed at our approach and taken refuge with them. We were very desirous of landing in order to relieve their apprehensions, but as there was a bad rapid along the island, all our care was necessary to prevent injury to the canoes. At the foot of this rapid is a rock, on the left shore, which is fourteen miles from our camp of last night, and resembles a hat in its shape.

Four miles beyond this island we came to a rapid, from the appearance of which it was judged prudent to examine it. After landing for that purpose on the left side, we began to enter the channel which is close under the opposite shore. It is a very dangerous rapid, strewed with high rocks and rocky islands, and in many places obstructed by shoals, over which the canoes were to be hauled, so that we were more than two hours in passing through the rapids, which extend for the same number of miles. The rapid has several small islands, and banks of muscleshells are spread along the river in several places. In order to lighten the boats, captain Clark, with the two chiefs, the interpreter, and his wife, had walked across the low grounds on the left to the foot of the rapids. On the way, captain Clark ascended a cliff about two hundred feet above the water, from which he saw that the country on both sides of the river immediately from its cliffs, was low, and spreads itself into a level plain, extending for a great distance on all sides. To the west at the distance of about one hundred and fifty miles, is a very high mountain covered with snow, and from its direction and appearance, he supposed to be the mount St. Helens, laid down by Vancouver, as visible from the mouth of the Columbia: there is also another mountain of a conical form, whose top is covered with snow, in a southwest direction. As captain Clark arrived at the lower end of the rapid before any, except one of the small canoes, he sat down on a rock to wait for them, and seeing a crane fly across the river, shot it, and it fell near him. Several Indians had been before this passing on the opposite side towards the rapids, and some few who had been nearly in front of him, being either alarmed at his appearance or the report of the gun, fled to their houses. Captain Clark was afraid that these people had not yet heard that white men were coming, and therefore, in order to allay their uneasiness before the whole party should arrive, he got into the small canoe with three men and rowed over towards the houses, and while crossing, shot a duck, which fell into the water. As he approached, no person was to be seen except three men in the plains, and they too fled as he came near the shore. He landed before five houses close to each other, but no one appeared, and the doors, which were of mat, were closed. He went towards one of them with a pipe in his hand, and pushing aside the mat entered the lodge, where he found thirty-two persons, chiefly men and women, with a few children, all in the greatest consternation; some hanging down their heads, others crying and wringing their hands. He went up to them all and shook hands with them in the most friendly manner; but their apprehensions, which had for a

199

moment subsided, revived on his taking out a burning-glass, as there was no roof to the house, and lighting his pipe: he then offered it to several of the men, and distributed among the women and children some small trinkets which he carried about with him, and gradually restored some tranquillity among them. He then left this house, and directing each of the men to go into a house, went himself to a second: here he found the inhabitants more terrified than those he had first seen; but he succeeded in pacifying them, and then visited the other houses, where the men had been equally successful. After leaving the houses he went out to sit on a rock, and beckoned to some of the men to come and smoke with him; but none of them ventured to join him till the canoes arrived with the two chiefs, who immediately explained our pacific intentions towards them. Soon after the interpreter's wife landed, and her presence dissipated all doubts of our being well-disposed, since in this country, no woman ever accompanies a war party: they therefore all came out and seemed perfectly reconciled; nor could we indeed blame them for their terrors, which were perfectly natural. They told the two chiefs that they knew we were not men, for they had seen us fall from the clouds: in fact, unperceived by them, captain Clark had shot the white crane, which they had seen fall just before he appeared to their eyes; the duck which he had killed also fell close by him, and as there were a few clouds flying over at the moment, they connected the fall of the birds and his sudden appearance, and believed that he had himself dropped from the clouds; the noise of the rifle, which they had never heard before, being considered merely as the sound to announce so extraordinary an event. This belief

200

was strengthened, when on entering the room he brought down fire from the heavens by means of his burning-glass: we soon convinced them satisfactorily that we were only mortals, and after one of our chiefs had explained our history and objects, we all smoked together in great harmony. These people do not speak precisely the same language as the Indians above, but understand them in conversation. In a short time we were joined by many of the inhabitants from below, several of them on horseback, and all pleased to see us, and to exchange their fish and berries for a few trinkets. We remained here to dine, and then proceeded. At half a mile the hilly country on the right side of the river ceased: at eleven miles we found a small rapid, and a mile further came to a small island on the left, where there are some willows. Since we had left the five lodges, we passed twenty more, dispersed along the river at different parts of the valley on the right; but as they were now apprised of our coming they showed no signs of alarm. On leaving the island we passed three miles further along a country which is low on both sides of the river, and encamped under some willow trees on the left, having made thirty-six miles to-day. Immediately opposite to us is an island close to the left shore, and another in the middle of the river, on which are twenty-four houses of Indians, all engaged in drying fish. We had scarcely landed before about a hundred of them came over in their boats to visit us, bringing with them a present of some wood, which was very acceptable: we received them in as kind a manner as we could—smoked with all of them, and gave the principal chief a string of wampum; but the highest satisfaction they enjoyed was the music of two of our violins, with which they seemed much delighted: they remained all night at our fires. This tribe is a branch of the nation called Pishquitpaws, and can raise about three hundred and fifty men. In dress they resemble the Indians near the forks of the Columbia, except that their robes are smaller and do not reach lower than the waist; indeed, three-fourths of them have scarcely any robes at all. The dress of the females is equally scanty; for they wear only a small piece of a robe which covers their shoulders and neck, and reaches down the back to the waist, where it is attached by a piece of leather tied tight round the body: their breasts, which are thus exposed to view, are large, ill-shaped, and are suffered to hang down very low: their cheek-bones high, their heads flattened, and their persons in general adorned with scarcely any ornaments. Both sexes are employed in curing fish, of which they have great quantities on their scaffolds.

Sunday 20.—The morning was cool, the wind from the southwest. Our appearance had excited the curiosity of the neighbourhood so much, that before we set out about two hundred Indians had collected to see us, and as we were desirous of conciliating their friendship, we remained to smoke and confer with them till breakfast. We then took our repast, which consisted wholly of dog-flesh, and proceeded. We passed three vacant houses near our camp, and at six miles reached the head of a rapid, on descending which we soon came to another, very difficult and dangerous. It is formed by a chain of large black rocks, stretching from the right side of the river, and with several small islands on the left, nearly choking the channel of the river. To this place we gave the name of the Pelican rapid, from seeing a number of peli-

cans and black cormorants about it. Just below
it is a small island near the right shore, where
are four houses of Indians, all busy in drying
fish. At sixteen miles from our camp we reached
a bend to the left opposite to a large island, and
at one o'clock halted for dinner on the lower
point of an island on the right side of the channel. Close to this was a larger island on the
same side, and on the left bank of the river a
small one, a little below. We landed near some
Indian huts, and counted on this cluster of three
islands, seventeen of their houses filled with inhabitants, resembling in every respect those higher
up the river; like the inhabitants, they were busy
in preparing fish. We purchased of them some
dried fish, which were not good, and a few berries, on which we dined, and then walked to the
head of the island for the purpose of examining a
vault, which we had marked in coming along.
This place, in which the dead are deposited, is a
building about sixty feet long and twelve feet
wide, and is formed by placing in the ground
poles or forks six feet high, across which a long
pole is extended the whole length of the structure.
Against this ridge-pole are placed broad boards,
and pieces of canoes, in a slanting direction, so as
to form a shed. It stands east and west, and
neither of the extremities are closed. On entering
the western end we observed a number of bodies
wrapped carefully in leather robes, and arranged
in rows on boards, which were then covered with
a mat. This was the part destined for those who
had recently died: a little farther on, the bones
half decayed were scattered about, and in the
centre of the building was a large pile of them
heaped promiscuously on each other. At the
eastern extremity was a mat, on which twenty-

one sculls were placed in a circular form, the mode of interment being first to wrap the body in robes, and as it decays the bones are thrown into the heap, and the sculls placed together. From the different boards and pieces of canoes which form the vault, were suspended on the inside fishing-nets, baskets, wooden-bowls, robes, skins, trenchers, and trinkets of various kinds, obviously intended as offerings of affection to deceased relatives. On the outside of the vault were the skeletons of several horses, and great quantities of bones in the neighbourhood, which induced us to believe that these animals were most probably sacrificed at the funeral rites of their masters. Having dined we proceeded past a small island, where were four huts of Indians, and at the lower extremity a bad rapid. Half a mile beyond this, and at the distance of twenty-four from our camp, we came to the commencement of the highlands on the right, which are the first we have seen on that side since near the Muscleshell rapids, leaving a valley forty miles in extent. Eight miles lower we passed a large island in the middle of the river, below which are eleven small islands, five on the right, the same number on the left and one in the middle of the stream. A brook falls in on the right side, and a small rivulet empties itself behind one of the islands. The country on the right consists of high and rugged hills; the left is a low plain with no timber on either side, except a few small willow-bushes along the banks; though a few miles after leaving these islands the country on the left rises to the same height with that opposite to it, and becomes an undulating plain. Two miles after passing a small rapid we reached a point of highland in a bend towards the right, and encamped for the evening, after a journey of forty-two miles. The river has been about a quarter of a mile in width, with a current much more uniform than it was during the last two days. We killed two speckled gulls, and several ducks of a delicious flavour.

CHAPTER XIX.

Monday 21.—The morning was cool, and the
wind from the southwest. At five and a half
miles we passed a small island, and one mile and
a half further, another in the middle of the river,
which has some rapid water near its head, and
opposite to its lower extremity are eight cabins of
Indians on the right side. We landed near them
to breakfast; but such is the scarcity of wood,
that last evening we had not been able to collect
any thing except dry willows, and of these not
more than barely sufficient to cook our supper,
and this morning we could not find enough even
to prepare breakfast. The Indians received us
with great kindness, and examined every thing
they saw with much attention. In their appearance and employments, as well as in their language, they do not differ from those higher up the
river. The dress too is nearly the same; that of
the men consisting of nothing but a short robe of
deer or goat skin; while the women wear only a
piece of dressed skin, falling from the neck so as to
cover the front of the body as low as the waist;

a bandage tied round the body and passing between the legs; and over this a short robe of deer and antelope skin is occasionally thrown. Here we saw two blankets of scarlet, and one of blue cloth, and also a sailor's round jacket; but we obtained only a few pounded roots, and some fish, for which we of course paid them. Among other things we observed some acorns, the fruit of the white oak. These they use as food either raw or roasted, and on enquiry informed us that they were procured from the Indians who live near the great falls. This place they designate by a name very commonly applied to it by the Indians, and highly expressive, the word *Timm*, which they pronounce so as to make it perfectly represent the sound of a distant cataract. After breakfast we resumed our journey, and in the course of three miles passed a rapid where large rocks were strewed across the river, and at the head of which on the right shore were two huts of Indians. We stopped here for the purpose of examining it, as we always do whenever any danger is to be apprehended, and send round by land all those who cannot swim. Five miles further is another rapid, formed by large rocks projecting from each side, above which were five huts of Indians on the right side, occupied like those we had already seen, in drying fish. One mile below this is the lower point of an island close to the right side, opposite to which on that shore, are two Indian huts.

On the left side of the river at this place, are immense piles of rocks, which seem to have slipped from the cliffs under which they lie; they continue till spreading still farther into the river, at the distance of a mile from the island, they occasion a very dangerous rapid; a little below which on the right side are five huts. For many miles the river is now narrow and obstructed with very large rocks thrown into its channel; the hills continue high and covered, as is very rarely the case, with a few low pine trees on their tops. Between three and four miles below the last rapid occurs a second, which is also difficult, and three miles below it is a small river, which seems to rise in the open plains to the southeast, and falls in on the left. It is forty yards wide at its mouth; but discharges only a small quantity of water at present: we gave it the name of Lepage's river from Lepage one of our company. Near this little river and immediately below it, we had to encounter a new rapid. The river is crowded in every direction, with large rocks and small rocky islands; the passage crooked and difficult, and for two miles we were obliged to wind with great care along the narrow channels and between the huge rocks. At the end of this rapid are four huts of Indians on the right, and two miles below five more huts on the same side. Here we landed and passed the night, after making thirty-three miles. The inhabitants of these huts explained to us that they were the relations of those who live at the great falls. They appear to be of the same nation with those we have seen above, whom, indeed, they resemble in every thing except that their language, although the same, has some words different. They have all pierced noses, and the men when in full dress wear a long tapering piece of shell or bead put through the nose. These people did not, however, receive us with the same cordiality to which we have been accustomed. They are poor; but we were able to purchase from them some wood to make a fire for supper, of which they have but little, and which they say they bring from the great falls. The hills in this neighbourhood are high and rugged, and a few scattered trees, either small pine or scrubby white oak, are occasionally seen on them. From the last rapids we also observed the conical mountain towards the southwest, which the Indians say is not far to the left of the great falls. From its vicinity to that place we called it the Timm or Falls mountain. The country through which we passed is furnished with several fine springs, which rise either high up the sides of the hills or else in the river meadows, and discharge themselves into the Columbia. We could not help remarking that almost universally the fishing establishments of the Indians, both on the Columbia and the waters of Lewis's river, are on the right bank. On enquiry we were led to believe that the reason may be found in their fear of the Snake Indians; between whom and themselves, considering the warlike temper of that people, and the peaceful habits of the river tribes, it is very natural that the latter should be anxious to interpose so good a barrier. These Indians are described as residing on a great river to the south, and always at war with the people of this neighbourhood. One of our chiefs pointed out to-day a spot on the left where, not many years ago, a great battle was fought, in which numbers of both nations were killed. We were agreeably surprised this evening by a present of some very good beer, made out of the remains of the bread, composed of the Pashe-coquamash, part of the stores we had laid in at the head of the Kooskooskee, and which by frequent exposure becomes sour and moulded.

Tuesday 22.—The morning was fair and calm. We left our camp at nine o'clock, and after going on for six miles came to the head of an island, and a very bad rapid, where the rocks are scat-

tered nearly across the river. Just above this and
on the right side are six huts of Indians. At the
distance of two miles below, are five more huts;
the inhabitants of which are all engaged in drying
fish, and some of them in their canoes killing fish
with gigs; opposite to this establishment is a
small island in a bend towards the right, on which
there were such quantities of fish that we counted
twenty stacks of dried and pounded salmon. This
small island is at the upper point of one much
larger, the sides of which are high uneven rocks,
jutting over the water: here there is a bad rapid.
The island continues for four miles, and at the
middle of it is a large river, which appears to
come from the southeast, and empties itself on the
left. We landed just above its mouth in order to
examine it, and soon found the route intercepted
by a deep, narrow channel, running into the
Columbia above the large entrance, so as to form
a dry and rich island about 400 yards wide and
eight hundred long. Here as along the grounds of
the river, the natives had been digging large
quantities of roots, as the soil was turned up in
many places. We reached the river about a quarter of a mile above its mouth, at a place where a
large body of water is compressed within a channel of about two hundred yards in width, where
it foams over rocks, many of which are above the
surface of the water. These narrows are the end
of a rapid which extends two miles back, where
the river is closely confined between two high
hills, below which it is divided by numbers of
large rocks and small islands, covered with a low
growth of timber. This river, which is called by
the Indians Towahnahiooks, is two hundred
yards wide at its mouth, has a very rapid current, and contributes about one fourth as much

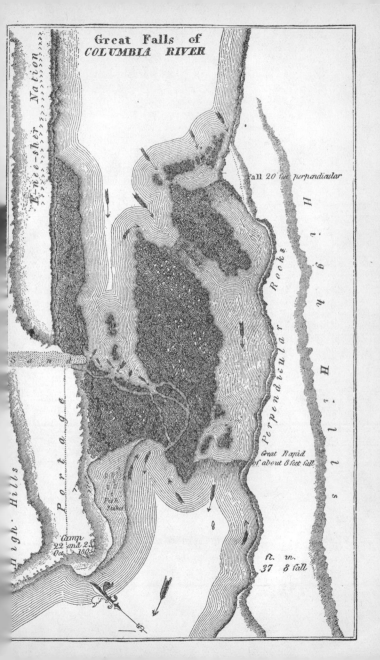

Great Falls of
COLUMBIA RIVER

E-nee-sher Nation

Fall 20 feet perpendicular

Perpendicular Rocks

High Hills

Portage

High Hills

Fish Stacks

Great Rapid
of about 8 feet fall

Camp
22 and 23
Oct. 1805

ft. in.
37 8 fall

water as the Columbia possesses before the junction. Immediately at the entrance are three sand islands, and near it the head of an island which runs parallel to the large rocky island. We now returned to our boats, and passing the mouth of the Towahnahiooks went between the islands. At the distance of two miles we reached the lower end of this rocky island, where were eight huts of Indians. Here too, we saw some large logs of wood, which were most probably rafted down the Towahnahiooks; and a mile below, on the right bank, were sixteen lodges of Indians, with whom we stopped to smoke. Then at the distance of about a mile passed six more huts on the same side, nearly opposite the lower extremity of the island, which has its upper end in the mouth of the Towahnahiooks. Two miles below we came to seventeen huts on the right side of the river, situated at the commencement of the pitch which includes the great falls. Here we halted, and immediately on landing walked down, accompanied by an old Indian from the huts, in order to examine the falls, and ascertain on which side we could make a portage most easily. We soon discovered that the nearest route was on the right side, and therefore dropped down to the head of the rapid, unloaded the canoes and took all the baggage over by land to the foot of the rapid. The distance is twelve hundred yards. On setting out we crossed a solid rock, about one third of the whole distance; then reached a space of two hundred yards wide, which forms a hollow, where the loose sand from the low grounds has been driven by the winds, and is steep and loose, and therefore disagreeable to pass; the rest of the route is over firm and solid ground. The labour of crossing would have been very inconvenient, if the Indians had not assisted us in carrying some of the heavy articles on their horses; but for this service they repaid themselves so adroitly, that on reaching the foot of the ravine we formed a camp in a position which might secure us from the pilfering of the natives, which we apprehend much more than we do their hostilities. Near our camp are five large huts of Indians engaged in drying fish and preparing it for the market. The manner of doing this, is by first opening the fish and exposing it to the sun on their scaffolds. When it is sufficiently dried it is pounded fine between two stones till it is pulverised, and is then placed in a basket about two feet long and one in diameter, neatly made of grass and rushes, and lined with the skin of a salmon stretched and dried for the purpose. Here they are pressed down as hard as possible, and the top covered with skins of fish which are secured by cords through the holes of the basket. These baskets are then placed in some dry situation, the corded part upwards, seven being usually placed as close as they can be put together, and five on the top of them. The whole is then wrapped up in mats, and made fast by cords, over which mats are again thrown. Twelve of these baskets, each of which contains from ninety to a hundred pounds, form a stack, which is now left exposed till it is sent to market; the fish thus preserved are kept sound and sweet for several years, and great quantities of it, they inform us, are sent to the Indians who live below the falls, whence it finds its way to the whites who visit the mouth of the Columbia. We observe both near the lodges and on the rocks in the river, great numbers of stacks of these pounded fish.

Besides fish, these people supplied us with fil-

212

berts and berries, and we purchased a dog for supper; but it was with much difficulty that we were able to buy wood enough to cook it. In the course of the day we were visited by many Indians, from whom we learnt that the principal chiefs of the bands, residing in this neighbourhood, are now hunting in the mountains towards the southwest. On that side of the river none of the Indians have any permanent habitations, and on enquiry we were confirmed in our belief that it was for fear of attacks from the Snake Indians with whom they are at war. This nation they represent as very numerous, and residing in a great number of villages on the Towahnahiooks, where they live principally on salmon. That river they add is not obstructed by rapids above its mouth, but there becomes large and reaches to a considerable distance: the first villages of the Snake Indians on that river being twelve days' journey on a course about southeast from this place.

Wednesday 23.—Having ascertained from the Indians, and by actual examination, the best mode of bringing down the canoes, it was found necessary, as the river was divided into several narrow channels, by rocks and islands, to follow the route adopted by the Indians themselves. This operation captain Clark began this morning, and after crossing to the other side of the river, hauled the canoes over a point of land, so as to avoid a perpendicular fall of twenty feet. At the distance of four hundred and fifty-seven yards we reached the water, and embarked at a place where a long rocky island compresses the channel of the river within the space of a hundred and fifty yards, so as to form nearly a semicircle. On leaving this rocky island the channel is somewhat wider, but a second and much larger island of hard black rock, still divides it from the main stream, while on the left shore it is closely bordered by perpendicular rocks. Having descended in this way for a mile, we reached a pitch of the river, which being divided by two large rocks, descends with great rapidity down a fall eight feet in height: as the boats could not be navigated down this steep descent, we were obliged to land and let them down as slowly as possible by strong ropes of elk skin, which we had prepared for the purpose. They all passed in safety except one, which being loosed by the breaking of the ropes, was driven down, but was recovered by the Indians below. With this rapid ends the first pitch of the great falls, which is not great in point of height, and remarkable only for the singular manner in which the rocks have divided its channel. From the marks every where perceivable at the falls, it is obvious that in high floods, which must be in the spring, the water below the falls rises nearly to a level with that above them. Of this rise, which is occasioned by some obstructions which we do not as yet know, the salmon must avail themselves to pass up the river in such multitudes, that that fish is almost the only one caught in great abundance above the falls; but below that place, we observe the salmon trout, and the heads of a species of trout smaller than the salmon trout, which is in great quantities, and which they are now burying to be used as their winter food. A hole of any size being dug, the sides and bottom are lined with straw, over which skins are laid: on these the fish, after being well dried, is laid, covered with other skins, and the hole closed with a layer of earth twelve or fifteen inc es deep. About three o'clock we reached the lower camp, but our joy at having accomplished this object was somewhat diminished, by the persecution of a new acquaintance. On reaching the upper point of the portage, we found that the Indians had been encamped there not long since, and had left behind them multitudes of fleas. These sagacious animals were so pleased to exchange the straw and fish skins, in which they had been living, for some better residence, that we were soon covered with them, and during the portage the men were obliged to strip to the skin, in order to brush them from their bodies. They were not, however, so easily dislodged from our clothes, and accompanied us in great numbers to our camp.

We saw no game except a sea otter, which was shot in the narrow channel as we came down, but we could not get it. Having therefore scarcely any provisions, we purchased eight small fat dogs, a food to which we are now compelled to have recourse, for the Indians are very unwilling to sell us any of their good fish, which they reserve for the market below. Fortunately, however, the habit of using this animal has completely overcome the repugnance hich we felt at first, and the dog, if not a favourite dish, is always an acceptable one. The meridian altitude of to-day gives 45° 42′ 57″ 3-10 north, as the latitude of our camp.

On the beach near the Indian huts, we observed two canoes of a different shape and size from any which we had hitherto seen: one of these we got in exchange for our smallest canoe, giving a hatchet and a few trinkets to the owner, who said he had purchased it from a white man below the falls, by giving him a horse. These canoes are very beautifully made; they are wide in the middle and tapering towards each end, with curious figures carved on the bow. They are thin, but being strengthened by cross bars, about an inch in diameter, which are tied with strong pieces of bark through holes in the sides, are able to bear very heavy burdens, and seem calculated to live in the roughest water.

A great number of Indians both from above and below the falls visited us to-day, and towards evening we were informed by one of the chiefs who had accompanied us, that he had overheard that the Indians below intended to attack us as we went down the river: being at all times ready for any attempt of that sort, we were not under greater apprehensions than usual at this intelligence: we, therefore, only reexamined our arms and increased the ammunition to one hundred rounds. Our chiefs, who had not the same motives of confidence, were by no means so much at their ease, and when at night they saw the Indians leave us earlier than usual, their suspicions of an intended attack were confirmed, and they were very much alarmed. The next morning,

Thursday 24, the Indians approached us with apparent caution, and behaved with more than usual reserve. Our two chiefs, by whom these circumstances were not unobserved, now told us that they wished to return home; that they could be no longer of any service to us, and they could not understand the language of the people below the falls; that those people formed a different nation from their own; that the two people had been at war with each other, and as the Indians had expressed a resolution to attack us, they would certainly kill them. We endeavoured to quiet their fears, and requested them to stay two nights longer, in which time we would see the

Indians below, and make a peace between the two nations. They replied that they were anxious to return and see their horses; we however insisted on their remaining with us, not only in hopes of bringing about an accommodation between them and their enemies, but because they might be able to detect any hostile designs against us, and also assist us in passing the next falls, which are not far off, and represented as very difficult: they at length, agreed to stay with us two nights longer. About nine o'clock we proceeded, and on leaving our camp near the lower fall, found the river about four hundred yards wide, with a current more rapid than usual, though with no perceptible descent. At the distance of two and a half miles, the river widened into a large bend or basin on the right, at the beginning of which are three huts of Indians. At the extremity of this basin stands a high black rock, which, rising perpendicularly from the right shore, seems to run wholly across the river; so totally indeed does it appear to stop the passage, that we could not see where the water escaped, except that the current appeared to be drawn with more than usual velocity to the left of the rock, where was a great roaring. We landed at the huts of the Indians, who went with us to the top of this rock, from which we saw all the difficulties of the channel. We were no longer at a loss to account for the rising of the river at the falls, for this tremendous rock stretches across the river, to meet the high hills of the left shore, leaving a channel of only forty-five yards wide, through which the whole body of the Columbia must press its way. The water thus forced into so narrow a channel, is thrown into whirls, and swells and boils in every part with the wildest agitation. But the alternative of carrying the boats over this high rock was almost impossible in our present situation, and as the chief danger seemed to be not from any rocks in the channel, but from the great waves and whirlpools, we resolved to try the passage in our boats, in hopes of being able by dexterous steering to escape. This we attempted, and with great care were able to get through, to the astonishment of all the Indians of the huts we had just passed, who now collected to see us from the top of the rock. The channel continues thus confined within a space of about half a mile, when the rock ceased. We passed a single Indian hut at the foot of it, where the river again enlarges itself to the width of two hundred yards, and at the distance of a mile and a half stopped to view a very bad rapid; this is formed by two rocky islands which divide the channel, the lower and larger of which is in the middle of the river. The appearance of this place was so unpromising, that we unloaded all the most valuable articles, such as guns, ammunition, our papers, &c. and sent them by land with all the men that could not swim to the extremity of the rapids. We then descended with the canoes two at a time, and though the canoes took in some water, we all went through safely; after which we made two miles, and stopped in a deep bend of the river towards the right, and encamped a little above a large village of twenty-one houses. Here we landed, and as it was late before all the canoes joined us, we were obliged to remain here this evening, the difficulties of the navigation having permitted us to make only six miles. This village is situated at the extremity of a deep bend towards the right, and immediately above a ledge of high rocks, twenty feet above the marks of the highest flood, but broken in several places, so as to form channels which are at present dry, extending nearly across the river; this forms the second fall, or the place most probably which the Indians indicate by the word Timm. While the canoes were coming on, captain Clark walked with two men down to examine these channels. On these rocks the Indians are accustomed to dry fish, and as the season for that purpose is now over, the poles which they use are tied up very securely in bundles, and placed on the scaffolds. The stock of fish dried and pounded were so abundant that he counted one hundred and seven of them making more than ten thousand pounds of that provision. After examining the narrows as well as the lateness of the hour would permit, he returned to the village though a rocky open country, infested with polecats. This village, the residence of a tribe called the Echeloots, consists of twenty-one houses, scattered promiscuously over an elevated situation, near a mound about thirty feet above the common level, which has some remains of houses on it, and bears every appearance of being artificial.

The houses, which are the first wooden buildings we have seen since leaving the Illinois country, are nearly equal in size, and exhibit a very singular appearance. A large hole, twenty feet wide and thirty in length, is dug to the depth of six feet. The sides are then lined with split pieces of timber, rising just above the surface of the ground, which are smoothed to the same width by burning, or shaved with small iron axes. These timbers are secured in their erect position by a pole, stretched along the side of the building near the eaves, and supported on a strong post fixed at each corner. The timbers at the gable ends rise gradually higher, the middle pieces being the broadest. At the top of these is a sort of semi-circle, made to receive a ridge-pole, the whole length of the house, propped by an additional post in the middle, and forming the top of the roof. From this ridge-pole to the eaves of the house, are placed a number of small poles or rafters, secured at each end by fibres of the cedar. On these poles, which are connected by small transverse bars of wood, is laid a covering of the white cedar, or arbor vitae, kept on by the strands of the cedar fibres: but a small distance along the whole length of the ridge-pole is left uncovered for the purpose of light, and permitting the smoke to pass through. The roof thus formed has a descent about equal to that common amongst us, and near the eaves is perforated with a number of small holes, made most probably to discharge their arrows in case of an attack. The only entrance is by a small door at the gable end, cut out of the middle piece of timber, twenty-nine and a half inches high, and fourteen inches broad, and reaching only eighteen inches above the earth. Before this hole is hung a mat, and on pushing it aside and crawling through, the descent is by a small wooden ladder, made in the form of those used amongst us. One half of the inside is used as a place of deposit for their dried fish, of which there are large quantities stored away, and with a few baskets of berries form the only family provisions; the other half adjoining the door, remains for the accommodation of the family. On each side are arranged near the walls, small beds of mats placed on little scaffolds or bedsteads, raised from eighteen inches to three feet from the ground, and in the middle of the vacant space is the fire, or sometimes two or three fires, when, as is indeed usually the case, the house contains three families.

The inhabitants received us with great kindness —invited us to their houses, and in the evening, after our camp had been formed, came in great numbers to see us: accompanying them was a principal chief, and several of the warriors of the nation below the great narrows. We made use of this opportunity to attempt a reconciliation between them and our two chiefs, and to put an end to the war which had disturbed the two nations. By representing to the chiefs the evils which the war inflicted on them, and the wants and privations to which it subjects them, they soon became disposed to conciliate with each other, and we had some reason to be satisfied with the sincerity of the mutual professions that the war should no longer continue, and that in future they would live in peace with each other. On concluding this negotiation we proceeded to invest the chief with the insignia of command, a medal and some small articles of clothing; after which the violin was produced, and our men danced to the great delight of the Indians, who remained with us till a late hour.

Friday, 25.—We walked down with several of the Indians to view the part of the narrows which they represented as most dangerous: we found it very difficult, but, as with our large canoes the portage was impracticable, we concluded on carrying our most valuable articles by land, and then hazarding the passage. We therefore returned to the village, and after sending some of the party with our best stores to make a portage, and fixed others on the rock to assist with ropes the canoes that might meet with any difficulty, we began the descent, in the presence of great numbers of Indians who had collected to witness this exploit. The channel for three miles is worn through a hard rough black rock from fifty to one hundred yards wide, in which the water swells and boils in a tremendous manner. The three first canoes escaped very well; the fourth, however, had nearly filled with water; the fifth passed through with only a small quantity of water over her. At half a mile we had got through the worst part, and having reloaded our canoes went on very well for two and a half miles, except that one of the boats was nearly lost by running against a rock. At the end of this channel of three miles, in which the Indians inform us they catch as many salmon as they wish, we reached a deep basin or bend of the river towards the right, near the entrance of which are two rocks. We crossed the basin, which has a quiet and gentle current, and at the distance of a mile from its commencement, and a little below where the river resumes its channel, reached a rock which divides it. At this place we met our old chiefs, who, when we began the portage, had walked down to a village below to smoke a pipe of friendship on the renewal of peace. Just after our meeting we saw a chief of the village above, with a party who had been out hunting, and were then crossing the river with their horses on their way home. We landed to smoke with this chief, whom we found a bold looking man of a pleasing appearance, about fifty years of age, and dressed in a war jacket, a cap, leggings and moccasins: we presented him with a medal and other small articles, and he gave us some meat, of which he had been able to procure but little; for on his route he had met with a war party of Indians from the Towahnahiooks, between whom there was a battle. We here smoked a parting pipe with our two faithful friends, the chiefs, who had accompanied us from the heads of the river, and who now had each bought a horse, intending to go home by land. On leaving this rock the river is gentle, but strewed with a great number of rocks for a few miles, when it becomes a beautiful still stream about half a mile wide. At five miles from the large bend we came to the mouth of a creek twenty yards wide, heading in the range of mountains which run S. S. W. and S. W. for a long distance, and discharging a considerable quantity of water: it is called by the Indians Quenett. We halted below it under a high point of rocks on the left; and as it was necessary to make some celestial observations, we formed a camp on the top of these rocks. This situation is perfectly well calculated for defence in case the Indians should incline to attack us, for the rocks form a sort of natural fortification with the aid of the river and creek, and is convenient to hunt along the foot of the mountains to the west and southwest, where there are several species of timber which form fine coverts for game. From this rock, the pinnacle of the round mountain covered with snow, which we had seen a short distance below the forks of the Columbia, and which we had called the Falls or Timm mountain, is south 43° west, and about thirty-seven miles distant. The face of the country on both sides of the river above and below the falls is steep, rugged, and rocky, with a very small proportion of herbage, and no timber, except a few bushes: the hills, however, to the west, have some scattered pine, white oak and other kinds of trees. All the timber used by the people at the upper falls is rafted down the Towahnahiooks; and those who live at the head of the narrows we have just passed, bring their wood in the same way from this creek to the lower part of the narrows, from which it is carried three miles by land to their habitations.

Both above and below, as well as in the narrows, we saw a great number of sea-otter or seals, and this evening one deer was killed, and great signs of that animal seen near the camp. In the creek we shot a goose, and saw much appearance of beaver, and one of the party also saw a fish, which he took to be a drum-fish. Among the willows we found several snares, set by the natives for the purpose of catching wolves.

Saturday, 26.—The morning was fine: we sent six men to hunt and to collect resin to pitch the canoes, which, by being frequently hauled over rocks, have become very leaky. The canoes were also brought out to dry, and on examination it was found that many of the articles had become spoiled by being repeatedly wet. We were occupied with the observations necessary to determine our longitude, and with conferences among the Indians, many of whom came on horseback to the opposite shore in the forepart of the day, and showed some anxiety to cross over to us: we did not however think it proper to send for them, but towards evening two chiefs with fifteen men came over in a small canoe: they proved to be the two principal chiefs of the tribes at and above the falls, who had been absent on a hunting excursion as we passed their residence: each of them on their arrival made us a present of deer's flesh, and small white cakes made of roots. Being anxious to ingratiate ourselves in their favour so as to ensure a friendly reception on our return, we treated them with all the kindness we could show: we acknowledge the chiefs, gave a medal of the small size, a red silk handkerchief, an armband, a knife, and a piece of paint to each chief, and small presents to several of the party, and half a deer: these attentions were not lost on the Indians, who appeared very well pleased with them. At night a fire was made in the middle of our camp, and as the Indians sat round it our men danced to the music of the violin, which so delighted them that several resolved to remain with us all night: the rest crossed the river. All the tribes in this neighbourhood are at war with the Snake Indians, whom they all describe as living on the Towahnahiooks, and whose nearest town is said to be four days' march from this place, and in a direction nearly southwest: there has lately been a battle between these tribes, but we could not ascertain the loss on either side. The water rose to-day eight inches, a rise which we could only ascribe to the circumstance of the wind's having been up the river for the last twenty-four hours, since the influence of the tide cannot be sensible here on account of the falls below. The hunters returned in the evening; they had seen the tracks of elk and bear in the mountains, and killed five deer, four very large gray squirrels, and a grouse: they inform us that the country off the river is broken, stony, and thinly timbered with pine and white oak; besides these delicacies one of the men killed with a gig a salmon trout, which, being fried in some bear's oil, which had been given to us by the chief whom we had met this morning below the narrows, furnished a dish of a very delightful flavour. A number of white cranes were also seen flying in different directions, but at such a height that we could not procure any of them.

The fleas, with whom we had contracted an intimacy at the falls, are so unwilling to leave us, that the men are obliged to throw off all their clothes, in order to relieve themselves from their persecution.

Sunday 27.—The wind was high from the westward during last night and this morning, but the weather being fair we continued our celestial observations. The two chiefs who remained with us, were joined by seven Indians, who came in a canoe from below. To these men we were very particular in our attentions; we smoked and eat with them; but some of them who were tempted by the sight of our goods exposed to dry, wished to take liberties with them; to which we were under the necessity of putting an immediate check; this restraint displeased them so much, that they returned down the river in a very ill humour. The two chiefs however remained with us till the evening, when they crossed the river to their party. Before they went we procured from them a vocabulary of the Echeloot, their native language, and on comparison were surprised at its difference from that of the Eneeshur tongue. In fact although the Echeloots, who live at the great narrows, are not more than six miles from the Eneeshurs or residents at and above the great falls, the two people are separated by a broad distinction of language. The Eneeshurs are understood by all the tribes residing on the Columbia, above the falls; but at that place they meet with the unintelligible language of the Echeloots, which then descends the river to a considerable distance. Yet the variation may possibly be rather a deep shade of dialect than a radical difference, since among both many words are the same, and the identity cannot be accounted for by supposing that their neighbourhood has interwoven them into their daily conversations, because the same words are equally familiar among all the Flathead bands which we have passed. To all these tribes too the strange clucking or guttural noise which first struck us is common. They also flatten the heads of the children in nearly the same manner, but we now begin to observe that the heads of the males, as well as of the other sex, are subjected to this operation, whereas among the mountains the custom has confined it almost to the females. The hunters brought home four deer, one grouse, and a squirrel.

Monday 28.—The morning was again cool and windy. Having dried our goods, we were about setting out, when three canoes came from above to visit us, and at the same time two others from below arrived for the same purpose. Among these last was an Indian who wore his hair in a queue, and had on a round hat and a sailor's jacket, which he said he had obtained from the people below the great rapids, who bought them from the whites. This interview detained us till nine o'clock, when we proceeded down the river, which is now bordered with cliffs of loose dark coloured rocks about ninety feet high, with a thin covering of pine and other small trees. At the distance of four miles we reached a small village of eight houses under some high rocks on the right, with a small creek on the opposite side of the river. We landed and found the houses similar to those we had seen at the great narrows: on entering one of them we saw a British musket, a cutlass, and several brass teakettles, of which they seemed to be very fond. There were figures of men, birds, and different animals, which were cut and painted on the boards which form the sides of the room, and though the workmanship of these uncouth figures was very rough, they

227

were as highly esteemed by the Indians as the finest frescoes of more civilised people. This tribe is called the Chilluckittequaw, and their language although somewhat different from that of the Echeloots, has many of the same words, and is sufficiently intelligible to the neighbouring Indians. We procured from them a vocabulary, and then after buying five small dogs, some dried berries, and a white bread or cake made of roots, we left them. The wind however rose so high, that we were obliged after going one mile to land on the left side opposite to a rocky island, and pass the day there. We formed our camp in a niche above a point of high rocks, and as it was the only safe harbour we could find, submitted to the inconvenience of lying on the sand, exposed to the wind and rain during all the evening. The high wind, which obliged us to consult the safety of our boats by not venturing further, did not at all prevent the Indians from navigating the river. We had not been long on shore, before a canoe with a man, his wife and two children, came from below through the high waves with a few roots to sell; and soon after we were visited by many Indians from the village above, with whom we smoked and conversed. The canoes used by these people are like those already described, built of white cedar or pine, very light, wide in the middle, and tapering towards the ends, the bow being raised and ornamented with carvings of the heads of animals. As the canoe is the vehicle of transportation, the Indians have acquired great dexterity in the management of it, and guide it safely over the highest waves. They have among their utensils bowls and baskets very neatly made of small bark and grass, in which they boil their provisions. The only game seen to-day were two deer, of which only one was killed, the other was wounded but escaped.

Tuesday 29.—The morning was still cloudy, and the wind from the west, but as it had abated its violence, we set out at daylight. At the distance of four miles we passed a creek on the right, one mile below which is a village of seven houses on the same side. This is the residence of the principal chief of the Chilluckittequaw nation, whom we now found to be the same between whom and our two chiefs we had made a peace at the Echeloot village. He received us very kindly, and set before us pounded fish, filberts, nuts, the berries of the Sacacommis, and white bread made of roots. We gave in return a bracelet of ribbon to each of the women of the house, with which they were very much pleased. The chief had several articles, such as scarlet and blue cloth, a sword, a jacket and hat, which must have been procured from the whites, and on one side of the room were two wide split boards placed together, so as to make space for a rude figure of a man cut and painted on them. On pointing to this and asking them what it meant, he said something, of which all we understood was "good," and then stepped to the image and brought out his bow and quiver, which, with some other warlike instruments, were kept behind it. The chief then directed his wife to hand him his medicine-bag, from which he brought out fourteen fore-fingers, which he told us had once belonged to the same number of his enemies, whom he had killed in fighting with the nations to the southeast, to which place he pointed, alluding no doubt to the Snake Indians, the common enemy of the nations on the Columbia. This bag is about two feet in length, containing roots, pounded dirt, &c. which the Indians only know how to appreciate. It is suspended in the middle of the lodge, and it is supposed to be a species of sacrilege to be touched by any but the owner. It is an object of religious fear, and it is from its sanctity the safest place to deposit their medals and their more valuable articles. The Indians have likewise small bags which they preserve in their great medicine-bag, from whence they are taken and worn around their waists and necks as amulets against any real or imaginary evils. This was the first time we had ever known the Indians to carry from the field any other trophy except the scalp. They were shown with great exultation, and after an harangue which we were left to presume was in praise of his exploits, the fingers were carefully replaced among the valuable contents of the red medicine-bag. This village being part of the same nation with the village we passed above, the language of the two is the same, and their houses of similar form and materials, and calculated to contain about thirty souls. The inhabitants were unusually hospitable and good-humoured, so that we gave to the place the name of the Friendly village. We breakfasted here, and after purchasing twelve dogs, four sacks of fish, and a few dried berries, proceeded on our journey. The hills as we passed are high with steep and rocky sides, and some pine and white oak, and an undergrowth of shrubs scattered over them. Four miles below this village is a small river on the right side; immediately below is a village of Chilluckittequaws, consisting of eleven houses. Here we landed and smoked a pipe with the inhabitants, who were very cheerful and friendly. They as well as the people of the last village inform us, that this river comes a considerable distance from the N. N. E. that it has a

great number of falls, which prevent the salmon
from passing up, and that there are ten nations
residing on it who subsist on berries, or such
game as they can procure with their bows and
arrows. At its mouth the river is sixty yards
wide, and has a deep and very rapid channel.
From the number of falls of which the Indians
spoke, we gave it the name of Cataract river.
We purchased four dogs, and then proceeded.
The country as we advance is more rocky and
broken, and the pine and low white oak on the
hills increase in great quantity. Three miles below Cataract river we passed three large rocks in
the river; that in the middle is large and longer
than the rest, and from the circumstance of its
having several square vaults on it, obtained the
name of Sepulchre island. A short distance below
are two huts of Indians on the right: the river
now widens, and in three miles we came to two
more houses on the right; one mile beyond which
is a rocky island in a bend of the river towards
the left. Within the next six miles we passed fourteen huts of Indians, scattered on the right bank,
and then reached the entrance of a river on the
left, which we called Labieshe's river, after Labieshe one of our party. Just above this river is a
low ground more thickly timbered than usual,
and in front are four huts of Indians on the bank,
which are the first we have seen on that side of
the Columbia. The exception may be occasioned
by this spot's being more than usually protected
from the approach of their enemies, by the creek,
and the thick wood behind.

We again embarked, and at the distance of a
mile passed the mouth of a rapid creek on the
right eighteen yards wide: in this creek the Indians whom we left take their fish, and from the

number of canoes which were in it, we called it Canoe creek. Opposite to this creek is a large sandbar, which continues for four miles along the left side of the river. Just below this a beautiful cascade falls in on the left over a precipice of rock one hundred feet in height. One mile further are four Indian huts in the low ground on the left: and two miles beyond this a point of land on the right, where the mountains become high on both sides, and possess more timber and greater varieties of it than hitherto, and those on the left are covered with snow. One mile from this point we halted for the night at three Indian huts on the right, having made thirty-two miles. On our first arrival they seemed surprised, but not alarmed at our appearance, and we soon became intimate by means of smoking and our favourite entertainment for the Indians, the violin. They gave us fruit, some roots, and root-bread, and we purchased from them three dogs. The houses of these people are similar to those of the Indians above, and their language the same: their dress also, consisting of robes or skins of wolves, deer, elk, and wild-cat, is made nearly after the same model: their hair is worn in plaits down each shoulder, and round their neck is put a strip of some skin with the tail of the animal hanging down over the breast: like the Indians above they are fond of otter skins, and give a great price for them. We here saw the skin of a mountain sheep, which they say live among the rocks in the mountains: the skin was covered with white hair, the wool long, thick, and coarse, with long coarse hair on the top of the neck, and the back resembling somewhat the bristles of a goat. Immediately behind the village is a pond, in which were great numbers of small swan.

Wednesday, 30.—A moderate rain fell during all last night, but the morning was cool, and after taking a scanty breakfast of deer, we proceeded. The river is now about three-quarters of a mile wide, with a current so gentle, that it does not exceed one mile and a half an hour; but its course is obstructed by the projection of large rocks, which seemed to have fallen promiscuously from the mountains into the bed of the river. On the left side four different streams of water empty themselves in cascades from the hills: what is, however, most singular is, that there are stumps of pine trees scattered to some distance in the river, which has the appearance of being dammed below and forced to encroach on the shore: these obstructions continue till at the distance of twelve miles, when we came to the mouth of a river on the right, where we landed: we found it sixty yards wide, and its banks possess two kinds of timber which we had not hitherto seen: one is a very large species of ash; the other resembling in its bark the beech; but the tree itself, as also the leaves, are smaller. We called this stream Crusatte's river, after Crusatte, one of our men: opposite to its mouth the Columbia widens to the distance of a mile, with a large sandbar, and large stones and rocks scattered through the channel. We here saw several of the large buzzards, which are of the size of the largest eagle, with the under part of their wings white: we also shot a deer and three ducks; on part of which we dined, and then continued down the Columbia. Above Crusatte's river the low grounds are about three quarters of a mile wide, rising gradually to the hills, and with a rich soil covered with grass, fern, and other small undergrowth; but below, the country rises with a steep ascent, and soon the mountains approach to the river with steep rugged sides, covered with a very thick growth of pine, cedar, cottonwood, and oak. The river is still strewed with large rocks. Two and a half miles below Crusatte's river is a large creek on the right, with a small island in the mouth. Just below this creek we passed along the right side of three small islands on the right bank of the river, with a larger island on the opposite side, and landed on an island very near the right shore at the head of the great shoot, and opposite two smaller islands at the fall or shoot itself. Just above the island on which we were encamped is a small village of eight large houses in a bend on the right, where the country, from having been very mountainous, becomes low for a short distance. We had made fifteen miles to-day, during all which time we were kept constantly wet with the rain; but as we were able to get on this island some of the ash which we saw for the first time to-day, and which makes a tolerable fire, we were as comfortable as the moistness of the evening would permit. As soon as we landed, captain Lewis went with five men to the village, which is situated near the river, with ponds in the low grounds behind: the greater part of the inhabitants were absent collecting roots down the river: the few, however, who were at home, treated him very kindly, and gave him berries, nuts, and fish; and in the house were a gun and several articles which must have been procured from the whites; but not being able to procure any information, he returned to the island. Captain Clark had in the meantime gone down to examine the shoot, and to discover the best route for a portage. He followed an Indian path, which, at the distance of a mile, led to a village on an elevated situation, the

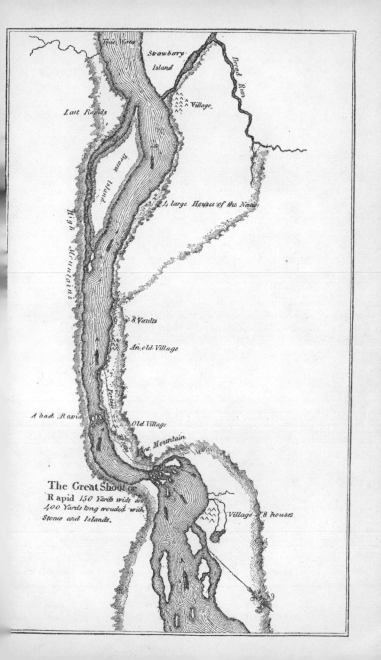

Last Rapids

Strawberry
Island

Village

Broad Run

High Mountains

Brant Island

24 large Houses of the Nation

8 Vaults

An old Village

A bad Rapid

Old Village

low Mountain

The Great Shoot or
Rapid 150 Yards wide and
400 Yards long crouded with
Stones and Islands.

Village 78 houses

houses of which had been large, but built in a different form from any we had yet seen, but which had been lately abandoned, the greater part of the boards being put into a pond near the village: this was most probably for the purpose of drowning the fleas, which were in immense quantities near the houses. After going about three miles the night obliged him to return to camp: he resumed his search in the morning,

Thursday, 31st, through the rain. At the extremity of the basin, in which is situated the island where we are encamped, several rocks and rocky islands are interspersed through the bed of the river. The rocks on each side have fallen down from the mountains; that on the left being high, and on the right the hill itself, which is lower, slipping into the river; so that the current is here compressed within a space of one hundred and fifty yards. Within this narrow limit it runs for the distance of four hundred yards with great rapidity, swelling over the rocks with a fall of about twenty feet: it then widens to two hundred paces, and the current for a short distance becomes gentle; but at the distance of a mile and a half, and opposite to the old village mentioned yesterday, it is obstructed by a very bad rapid, where the waves are unusually high, the river being confined between large rocks, many of which are at the surface of the water. Captain Clark proceeded along the same path he had taken before, which led him through a thick wood and along a hill side, till two and a half miles below the shoots, he struck the river at the place whence the Indians make their portage to the head of the shoot: he here sent Crusatte, the principal waterman, up the stream, to examine if it were practicable to bring the canoes down the water. In the meantime, he, with Joseph Fields, continued his route down the river, along which the rapids seem to stretch as far as he could see. At half a mile below the end of the portage, he came to a house, the only remnant of a town, which, from its appearance, must have been of great antiquity. The house was uninhabited, and being old and decayed, he felt no disposition to encounter the fleas, which abound in every situation of that kind, and therefore did not enter. About half a mile below this house, in a very thick part of the woods, is an ancient burial place: it consists of eight vaults made of pine or cedar boards closely connected, about eight feet square and six in height; the top secured, covered with wide boards sloping a little, so as to convey off the rain: the direction of all of them is east and west, the door being on the eastern side, and partially stopped with wide boards decorated with rude pictures of men and other animals. On entering we found in some of them four dead bodies, carefully wrapped in skins, tied with cords of grass and bark, lying on a mat in a direction east and west: the other vaults contained only bones, which were in some of them piled to the height of four feet: on the tops of the vaults, and on poles attached to them, hung brass kettles and frying-pans with holes in their bottoms, baskets, bowls, sea-shells, skins, pieces of cloth, hair, bags of trinkets and small bones, the offerings of friendship or affection, which have been saved by a pious veneration from the ferocity of war, or the more dangerous temptations of individual gain: the whole of the walls as well as the door were decorated with strange figures cut and painted on them; and besides these were several wooden images of men, some of them so old and decayed as to have almost lost their

236

shape, which were all placed against the sides of the vaults. These images, as well as those in the houses we have lately seen, do not appear to be at all the objects of adoration: in this place they were most probably intended as resemblances of those whose decease they indicate; and when we observe them in houses, they occupy the most conspicuous part; but are treated more like ornaments than objects of worship. Near the vaults which are standing, are the remains of others on the ground completely rotted and covered with moss; and as they are formed of the most durable pine and cedar timber, there is every appearance, that for a very long series of years this retired spot has been the depository for the Indians near this place. After examining this place captain Clark went on, and found the river as before strewed with large rocks, against which the water ran with great rapidity. Just below the vaults the mountain, which is but low on the right side, leaves the river, and is succeeded by an open stony level, which extends down the river, while on the left the mountain is still high and rugged. At two miles distance he came to a village of four houses, which were now vacant and the doors barred up: on looking in he saw the usual quantity of utensils still remaining, from which he concluded that the inhabitants were at no great distance collecting roots or hunting, in order to lay in their supply of food for the winter: he left them and went on three miles to a difficult rocky rapid, which was the last in view. Here, on the right, are the remains of a large and ancient village, which could be plainly traced by the holes for the houses and the deposits for fish: after he had examined these rapids and the neighbouring country he returned to camp by the same route:

the only game he had obtained was a sandhill crane. In the meantime we had been occupied in preparations for making the portage, and in conference with the Indians, who came down from the village to visit us. Towards evening two canoes arrived from the village at the mouth of Cataract river, loaded with fish and bears' grease for the market below: as soon as they landed they unloaded the canoes, turned them upside down on the beach, and encamped under a shelving rock near our camp. We had an opportunity of seeing to-day the hardihood of the Indians of the neighbouring village: one of the men shot a goose, which fell into the river, and was floating rapidly towards the great shoot, when an Indian observing it plunged in after it: the whole mass of the waters of the Columbia, just preparing to descend its narrow channel, carried the animal down with great rapidity: the Indian followed it fearlessly to within one hundred and fifty feet of the rocks, where he would inevitably have been dashed to pieces; but seizing his prey he turned round and swam ashore with great composure. We very willingly relinquished our right to the bird in favour of the Indian who had thus saved it at the imminent hazard of his life: he immediately set to work, and picked off about half the feathers, and then without opening it ran a stick through it and carried it off to roast.

Friday, November 1, 1805.—The morning was cool and the wind high from the northeast. The Indians who arrived last night, took their empty canoes on their shoulders and carried them below the great shoot, where they put them in the water and brought them down the rapid, till at the distance of two and a half miles they stopped to take in their loading, which they had been afraid to trust in the last rapid, and had therefore carried by land from the head of the shoot.

After their example we carried our small canoe, and all the baggage across the slippery rocks, to the foot of the shoot. The four large canoes were next brought down, by slipping them along poles, placed from one rock to another, and in some places by using partially streams which escaped along side of the river. We were not, however, able to bring them across without three of them receiving injuries, which obliged us to stop at the end of the shoot to repair them. At this shoot we saw great numbers of sea-otters; but they are so shy that it is difficult to reach them with the musket: one of them that was wounded to-day sunk and was lost. Having by this portage avoided the rapid and shoot of four hundred yards in length, we re-embarked, passed at a mile and a half the bad rapid opposite to the old village on the right, and making our way through the rocks, saw the house just below the end of the portage; the eight vaults near it; and at the distance of four miles from the head of the shoot, reached a high rock, which forms the upper part of an island near the left shore. Between this island and the right shore we proceeded, leaving at the distance of a mile and a half, the village of four houses on our right, and a mile and a half lower came to the head of a rapid near the village on the right. Here we halted for the night, having made only seven miles from the head of the shoot. During the whole of the passage the river is very much obstructed by rocks. The island, which is about three miles long, reaches to the rapid which its lower extremity contributes to form. The meridian altitude of to-day gave us the latitude of 45° 44′ 3″ north. As we passed the village of four houses, we found that the inhabitants had returned, and stopped to visit them. The houses are similar to those already described, but larger, from thirty-five to fifty feet long, and thirty feet wide, being sunk in the ground about six feet, and raised the same height above. Their beds are raised about four feet and a half above the floor, and the ascent is by a new painted ladder, with which every family is provided, and under them are stored their dried fish, while the space between the part of the bed on which they lie and the wall of the house is occupied by the nuts, roots, berries, and other provisions, which are spread on mats. The fireplace is about eight feet long, and six feet wide, sunk a foot below the floor, secured by a frame, with mats placed around for the family to sit on. In all of the houses are images of men of different shapes, and placed as ornaments in the parts of the house where they are most seen. They gave us nuts, berries, and some dried fish to eat, and we purchased, among other articles, a hat made after their own taste, such as they wear, without a brim. They ask high prices for all that they sell, observing that the whites below, pay dearly for all which they carry there. We cannot learn precisely the nature of the trade carried on by the Indians with the inhabitants below. But as their knowledge of the whites seems to be very imperfect, and the only articles which they carry to market, such as pounded fish, bear-grass and roots, cannot be an object of much foreign traffic, their intercourse appears to be an intermediate trade with the natives near the mouth of the Columbia: from them these people obtain in ex-

change for their fish, roots and bear-grass, blue
and white beads, copper tea-kettles, brass armbands, some scarlet and blue robes, and a few
articles of old European clothing. But their great
object is to obtain beads, an article which holds
the first place in their ideas of relative value, and
to procure which they will sacrifice their last article of clothing or the last mouthful of food. In-
dependently of their fondness for them as an
ornament, these beads are the medium of trade,
by which they obtain from the Indians still higher
up the river, robes, skins, chappelel bread, bear-
grass, &c. Those Indians in turn, employ them to
procure from the Indians in the Rocky mountains,
bear-grass, pachico, roots, robes, &c.

These Indians are rather below the common
size, with high cheek-bones, their noses pierced,
and in full dress, ornamented with a tapering
piece of white shell or wampum about two inches
long. Their eyes are exceedingly sore and weak,
many of them have only a single eye, and some
perfectly blind. Their teeth prematurely decayed,
and in frequent instances, altogether worn away.
Their general health, however, seems to be good,
the only disorder we have remarked, being
tumours in different parts of the body. The
women are small and homely in their appearance,
their legs and thighs much swelled, and their
knees remarkably large; deformities, which are no
doubt owing to the manner in which they set on
their hams. They go nearly naked, having only a
piece of leather tied round the breast, falling
thence, nearly as low as the waist; a small robe
about three feet square, and a piece of leather,
which ill supplies the place of a cover, tied between their legs. Their hair is suffered to hang
loose in every direction; and in their persons, as

well as in their cookery, they are filthy to a most disgusting degree. We here observe that the women universally have their heads flattened, and in many of the villages, we have lately seen the female children undergo the operation.

CHAPTER XX.

Saturday, November 2.—We now examined the rapid below more particularly, and the danger appearing to be too great for the loaded canoes, all those who could not swim were sent with the baggage by land. The canoes then passed safely, and were reloaded; at the foot of the rapid we took a meridian altitude of 59° 45′ 45″. Just as we were setting out seven squaws arrived across the portage loaded with dried fish and bear-grass, neatly packed in bundles, and soon after four Indians came down the rapid in a large canoe. After breakfasting we left our camp at one o'clock, passed the upper point of an island which is separated from the right shore by a narrow chan- nel, through which in high tides the water passes. But at present it contains no running water, and a creek which falls into it from the mountains on the right, is in the same dry condition, though it has the marks of discharging immense torrents at some seasons. The island thus made is three miles in length and about one in width; its situa-

243

tion is high and open, the land rich, and at this
time covered with grass and a great number of
strawberry vines, from which we gave it the name
of Strawberry island. In several places we observed that the Indians had been digging for
roots, and indeed the whole island bears every
appearance of having been at some period in a
state of cultivation. On the left side of the river
the low ground is narrow and open: the rapid
which we have just passed is the last of all the
descents of the Columbia. At this place the first
tide-water commences, and the river in consequence widened immediately below the rapid. As
we descended, we reached at the distance of one
mile from the rapid a creek under a bluff on the
left, at three miles is the lower point of Strawberry island. To this immediately succeed three
small islands covered with wood; in the meadow
to the right, and at some distance from the hills,
stands a high perpendicular rock, about eight hundred feet high, and four hundred yards round the
base; this we called the Beacon rock. Just below
is an Indian village of nine houses, situated between two small creeks.

At this village the river widens to nearly a mile
in extent, the low grounds too become wider, and
they as well as the mountains on each side are
covered with pine, spruce-pine, cottonwood, a
species of ash, and some alder. After being so
long accustomed to the dreary nakedness of the
country above, the change is as grateful to the
eye, as it is useful in supplying us with fuel. Four
miles from the village is a point of land on the
right, where the hills become lower, but are still
thickly timbered. The river is now about two
miles wide, the current smooth and gentle, and
the effect of the tide has been sensible since leaving

the rapid. Six miles lower is a rock rising from the middle of the river to the height of one hundred feet, and about eighty yards at its base. We continued six miles further, and halted for the night under a high projecting rock on the left side of the river opposite the point of a large meadow. The mountains, which from the great shoot to this place are high, rugged, and thickly covered with timber chiefly of the pine species, here leave the river on each side; the river becomes two and a half miles in width, and the low grounds are extensive and well supplied with wood. The Indians whom we left at the portage passed us, on their way down the river, and seven others who were descending in a canoe for the purpose of trading below, encamped with us. We had made from the foot of the great shoot twenty-nine miles to-day. The ebb-tide rose at our camp about nine inches, the flood must rise much higher. We saw great numbers of water-fowl, such as swan, geese, ducks of various kinds, gulls, plover, and the white and grey brant, of which last we killed eighteen.

Sunday 3.—We were detained until ten o'clock by a fog so thick that a man could not be discerned at the distance of fifty steps. As soon as it cleared off we set out in company with our new Indian acquaintances, who came from a village near the great falls. The low grounds along the river are covered so thickly with rushes, vines, and other small growth, that they are almost impassable. At the distance of three miles we reached the mouth of a river on the left, which seemed to lose its waters in a sandbar opposite; the stream itself being only a few inches in depth. But on attempting to wade across, we discovered that the bed was a very bad quicksand, too deep

245

to be passed on foot. We went up a mile and a half to examine this river, and found it to be at this distance a very considerable stream one hundred and twenty yards wide at its narrowest part, with several small islands. Its character resembles very much that of the river Platte. It drives its quicksand over the low grounds with great impetuosity, and such is the quantity of coarse sand which it discharges, that the accumulation has formed a large sandbar or island, three miles long, and a mile and a half wide, which divides the waters of the Quicksand river into two channels. This sand island compresses the Columbia within a space of half a mile, and throws its whole current against the right shore. Opposite to this river, which we call Quicksand river, is a large creek to which we gave the name of Seal river. The first appears to pass through the low country, at the foot of the high range of mountains towards the southeast, while the second as well as all the large creeks on the right side of the Columbia, rise in the same ridge of mountains N. N. E. from this place. The mountain, which we have supposed to be the mount Hood of Vancouver, bears S. 85° E. about forty-seven miles from the mouth of the Quicksand river. After dinner we proceeded, and at the distance of three miles reached the lower mouth of Quicksand river. On the opposite side a large creek falls in near the head of an island, which extends for three miles and a half down the river; it is a mile and a half in width, rocky at the upper end, has some timber round its borders, but in the middle is open and has several ponds. Half a mile lower is another island in the middle of the river, to which from its appearance we gave the name of Diamond island. Here we met fifteen

Indians ascending the river in two canoes, but the only information we could procure from them was, that they had seen three vessels, which we presume to be European, at the mouth of the Columbia. We went along its right side for three miles, and encamped opposite to it, after making to-day thirteen miles. A canoe soon after arrived from the village at the foot of the last rapid, with an Indian and his family, consisting of a wife, three children, and a woman who had been taken prisoner from the Snake Indians, living on a river from the south, which we afterwards found to be the Multnomah. Sacajawea was immediately introduced to her, in hopes that being a Snake Indian also, they might understand each other, but their language was not sufficiently intelligible to permit them to converse together. The Indian had a gun with a brass barrel and cock, which he appeared to value very highly.

Below Quicksand river the country is low, rich and thickly wooded on each side of the river: the islands have less timber, but are furnished with a number of ponds near which are vast quantities of fowls, such as swan, geese, brants, cranes, storks, white gulls, cormorants and plover. The river is wide, and contains a great number of sea otters.

In the evening the hunters brought in game for a sumptuous supper, which we shared with the Indians, both parties of whom spent the night with us.

Monday 4.—The weather was cloudy and cool, and the wind from the west. During the night, the tide rose eighteen inches near our camp. We set out about eight o'clock, and at the distance of three miles came to the lower end of Diamond island. It is six miles long, nearly three in width,

and like the other islands, thinly covered with
timber, and has a number of ponds or small lakes
scattered over its surface. Besides the animals
already mentioned we shot a deer on it this morning. Near the end of Diamond island are two
others, separated by a narrow channel filled at
high tides only, which continue on the right for
the distance of three miles, and like the adjacent
low grounds, are thickly covered with pine. Just
below the last, we landed on the left bank of the
river, at a village of twenty-five houses; all of
these were thatched with straw, and built of
bark, except one which was about fifty feet long,
built of boards in the form of those higher up the
river, from which it differed however, in being
completely above ground, and covered with broad
split boards; this village contains about two hundred men of the Skilloot nation, who seem well
provided with canoes, of which there were at
least fifty-two, and some of them very large,
drawn up in front of the village. On landing we
found the Indian from above, who had left us this
morning, and who now invited us into a lodge
of which he appeared to own a part. Here he
treated us with a root, round in shape, and about
the size of a small Irish potato, which they call
wappatoo, it is the common arrowhead or sagit-
tifolia, so much cultivated by the Chinese, and
when roasted in the embers till it becomes soft,
has an agreeable taste, and is a very good substitute for bread. After purchasing some more of
this root, we resumed our journey, and at seven
miles distance came to the head of a large island
near the left. On the right shore is a fine open
prairie for about a mile, back of which the country rises, and is supplied with timber, such as
white oak, pine of different kinds, wild crab, and

several species of undergrowth, while along the borders of the river, there are only a few cotton-wood and ash trees. In this prairie were also signs of deer and elk. When we landed for dinner, a number of Indians from the last village, came down for the purpose, as we supposed, of paying us a friendly visit, as they had put on their favourite dresses. In addition to their usual covering they had scarlet and blue blankets, sailors' jackets and trowsers, shirts and hats. They had all of them either war axes, spears and bow arrows, or muskets and pistols, with tin powder flasks. We smoked with them and endeavoured to show them every attention, but we soon found them very assuming and disagreeable companions. While we were eating they stole the pipe with which they were smoking, and the great coat of one of the men. We immediately searched them all, and discovered the coat stuffed under the root of a tree near where they were sitting; but the pipe we could not recover. Finding us determined not to suffer any imposition, and discontented with them, they showed their displeasure in the only way which they dared, by returning in an ill humour to their village. We then proceeded and soon met two canoes with twelve men of the same Skilloot nation, who were on their way from below. The larger of the canoes was ornamented with the figure of a bear in the bow, and a man in the stern, both nearly as large as life, both made of painted wood, and very neatly fixed to the boat. In the same canoe were two Indians finely dressed and with round hats. This circumstance induced us to give the name of Image canoe to the large island, the lower end of which we now passed at the distance of nine miles from its head. We had seen two smaller islands to the right, and three more near its lower extremity. The Indians in the canoe here made signs that there was a village behind those islands, and indeed we presumed there was a channel on that side of the river, for one of the canoes passed in that direction between the small islands, but we were anxious to press forward, and therefore did not stop to examine more minutely. The river was now about a mile and a half in width, with a gentle current, the bottoms extensive and low, but not subject to be overflowed. Three miles below the Image canoe island we came to four large houses on the left side, at which place we had a full view of the mountain which we first saw on the 19th of October, from the Muscleshell rapid, and which we now find to be the mount St. Helen of Vancouver. It bears north 25° east, about ninety miles distant; it rises in the form of a sugar-loaf to a very great height, and is covered with snow. A mile lower we passed a single house on the left, and another on the right. The Indians had now learnt so much of us, that their curiosity was without any mixture of fear, and their visits became very frequent and troublesome. We therefore continued on till after night, in hopes of getting rid of them; but after passing a village on each side, which on account of the lateness of the hour we saw indistinctly, we found there was no escaping from their importunities. We therefore landed at the distance of seven miles below Image canoe island, and encamped near a single house on the right, having made during the day twenty-nine miles.

The Skilloots whom we passed to-day, speak a language somewhat different from that of the Echeloots or Chilluckittequaws near the long narrows. Their dress is similar, except that the Skilloots possess more articles procured from the white traders; and there is further difference between them, inasmuch as the Skilloots, both males and females, have the head flattened. Their principal food is fish, and wappatoo roots, and some elk and deer, in killing which with their arrows, they seem very expert, for during the short time we remained at the village three deer were brought in. We also observed there a tame brairo.

As soon as we landed we were visited by two canoes loaded with Indians, from whom we purchased a few roots. The grounds along the river continue low and rich, and among the shrubs which cover them is a large quantity of vines resembling the raspberry. On the right the low grounds are terminated at the distance of five miles by a range of high hills covered with tall timber, and running southeast and northwest. The game as usual very abundant, and among other birds we observe some white geese with a part of their wings black.

Tuesday, 5.—Our choice of a camp had been very unfortunate; for on a sand island opposite to us were immense numbers of geese, swan-ducks, and other wild fowl, who, during the whole night, serenaded us with a confusion of noises which completely prevented our sleeping. During the latter part of the night it rained, and we therefore willingly left our encampment at an early hour. We passed at three miles a small prairie, where the river is only three quarters of a mile in width, and soon after two houses on the left, half a mile distant from each other; from one of which three men came in a canoe merely to look at us, and having done so returned home. At eight miles we came to the lower point of an island, separated from the right side by a narrow channel, on which, a short distance above the end of the island, is situated a large village: it is built more compactly than the generality of the Indian villages, and the front has fourteen houses, which are ranged for a quarter of a mile along the channel. As soon as we were discovered seven canoes came out to see us, and after some traffic, during which they seemed well-disposed and orderly, accompanied us a short distance below. The river here again widens to the space of a mile and a half. As we descended we soon observed, behind a sharp point of rocks, a channel a quarter of a mile wide, which we suppose must be the one taken by the canoes yesterday on leaving Imagecanoe island. A mile below the channel are some low cliffs of rocks, near which is a large island on the right side, and two small islands a little further on. Here we met two canoes ascending the river. At this place the shore on the right becomes bold and rocky, and the bank is bordered by a range of high hills covered with a thick growth of pine: on the other side is an extensive low island, separated from the left side by a narrow channel. Here we stopped to dine, and found the island open, with an abundant growth of grass, and a number of ponds well supplied with fowls; and at the lower extremity are the remains of an old village. We procured a swan, several ducks, and a brant, and saw some deer on the island. Besides this island, the lower extremity of which is seventeen miles from the channel just mentioned, we passed two or three smaller ones in the same distance. Here the hills on the right retire from the river, leaving a high plain, between which, on the left bank, a range of high hills running southeast and covered with pine, forms a bold and rocky shore. At the distance of six miles, however, these hills again return and close the river on both sides. We proceeded on, and at four miles reached a creek on the right, about twenty yards in width, immediately below which is an old village. Three miles further, and at the distance of thirty-two miles from our camp of last night, we halted under a point of highland, with thick pine trees on the left bank of the river. Before landing we met two canoes, the largest of which had at the bow the image of a bear, and that of a man on the stern: there were twenty-six Indians on board, but they all proceeded upwards, and we were left, for the first time since we reached the waters of the Columbia, without any of the natives with us during the night. Besides the game already mentioned, we killed a grouse much larger than the common size, and observed along the shore a number of striped snakes. The river is here deep, and about a mile and a half in width. Here too the ridge of low mountains running northwest and southeast, cross the river, and form the western boundary of the plain through which we have just passed. This great plain or valley begins above the mouth of Quicksand river, and is about sixty miles wide in a straight line, while on the right and left it extends to a great distance: it is a fertile and delightful country, shaded by thick groves of tall timber, watered by small ponds, and running on both sides of the river. The soil is rich, and capable of any species of culture; but in the present condition of the Indians, its chief production is the wappatoo root, which grows spontaneously and exclusively in this region. Sheltered as it is on both sides, the temperature is much milder than that of the surrounding country; for even at this season of the year we observe very little appearance of frost. During its whole extent it is inhabited by numerous tribes of Indians, who either reside in it permanently, or visit its waters in quest of fish and wappatoo roots: we gave it the name of the Columbia valley.

Wednesday, 6.—The morning was cool, wet, and rainy. We proceeded at an early hour between the high hills on both sides of the river, till at the distance of four miles we came to two tents of Indians in a small plain on the left, where the hills on the right recede a few miles from the river, and a long narrow island stretches along the right shore. Behind this island is the mouth of a large river a hundred and fifty yards wide, and called by the Indians, Coweliske. We halted for dinner on the island, but the red wood and green briars are so interwoven with the pine, alder, ash, a species of beech, and other trees, that the woods form a thicket, which our hunters could not penetrate. Below the mouth of the Coweliske a very remarkable knob rises from the water's edge to the height of eighty feet, being two hundred paces round the base; and as it is in a low part of the island, and some distance from the high grounds, the appearance of it is very singular. On setting out after dinner we overtook two canoes going down to trade: one of the Indians, who spoke a few words of English, mentioned, that the principal person who traded with them was a Mr. Haley, and he showed a bow of iron and several other things which he said Mr. Haley had given him. Nine miles below that river is a creek on the same; and between them three smaller islands; one on the left shore, the other about the middle of the river; and a third near the lower end of the long narrow island, and opposite a high cliff of black rocks on the left, sixteen miles from our camp. Here we were overtaken by the Indians from the two tents we passed in the morning, from whom we now purchased wappatoo roots, salmon, trout, and two beaver skins, for which last we gave five small fishhooks. At these cliffs the mountains, which had continued high and rugged on the left, retired from the river, and as the hills on the other side had left the water at the Coweliske, a beautiful extensive plain now presented itself before us: for a few miles we passed along side of an island a mile in width and three miles long, below which is a smaller island, where the high rugged hills, thickly covered with timber, border the right bank of the river, and terminate the low grounds: these were supplied with common rushes, grass, and nettles; in the moister parts with bullrushes and flags, and along the water's edge some willows. Here also were two ancient villages, now abandoned by their inhabitants, of whom no vestige remains, except two small dogs almost starved, and a prodigious quantity of fleas. After crossing the plain and making five miles, we proceeded through the hills for eight miles. The river is about a mile in width, and the hills so steep that we could not for several miles find a place sufficiently level to suffer us to sleep in a level position: at length, by removing the large stones, we cleared a place fit for our purpose above the reach of the tide, and after a journey of twenty-nine miles slept among the smaller stones under a mountain to the right. The weather was rainy during the whole day; we therefore made large fires to dry our bedding and to kill the fleas, who have accumulated upon us at every old village we have passed.

Thursday 7.—The morning was rainy and the

fog so thick that we could not see across the river. We observed however, opposite to our camp, the upper point of an island, between which and the steep hills on the right we proceeded for five miles. Three miles lower is the beginning of an island separated from the right shore by a narrow channel; down this we proceeded under the direction of some Indians whom we had just met going up the river, and who returned in order to show us their village. It consists of four houses only, situated on this channel behind several marshy islands formed by two small creeks. On our arrival they gave us some fish, and we afterwards purchased wappatoo roots, fish, three dogs, and two otter skins, for which we gave fishhooks chiefly, that being an article of which they are very fond.

These people seem to be of a different nation from those we have just passed: they are low in stature, ill shaped, and all have their heads flattened. They call themselves Wahkiacum, and their language differs from that of the tribes above, with whom they trade for wappatoo roots. The houses too are built in a different style, being raised entirely above ground, with the eaves about five feet high, and the door at the corner. Near the end opposite to this door is a single fireplace, round which are the beds, raised four feet from the floor of earth; over the fire are hung the fresh fish, and when dried they are stowed away with the wappatoo roots under the beds. The dress of the men is like that of the people above, but the women are clad in a peculiar manner, the robe not reaching lower than the hip, and the body being covered in cold weather by a sort of corset of fur, curiously plaited, and reaching from the arms to the hip; added to this is a sort of

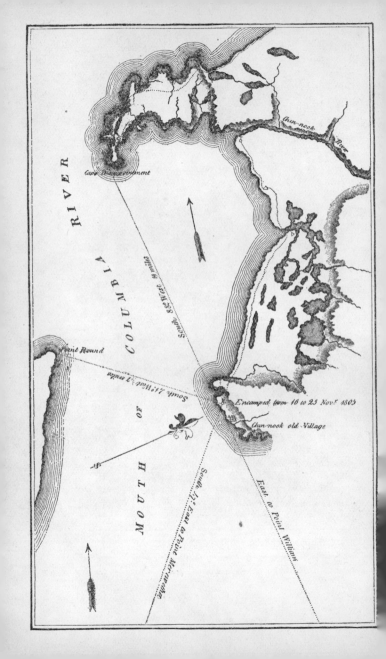

RIVER

COLUMBIA

OF

MOUTH

Cape Disappointment

Point Round

South 86° West 9 miles

South 41° West 4 miles

South 17° East 6 Point Meridth

Chin-nook River

Encamped from 16 to 25 Nov.ʳ 1805

Chin-nook old Village

East to Point William

petticoat, or rather tissue of white cedar bark, bruised or broken into small strands, and woven into a girdle by several cords of the same material. Being tied round the middle, these strands hang down as low as the knee in front, and to midleg behind, and are of sufficient thickness to answer the purpose of concealment whilst the female stands in an erect position, but in any other attitude is but a very ineffectual defence. Sometimes the tissue is strings of silk grass, twisted and knotted at the end.

After remaining with them about an hour, we proceeded down the channel with an Indian dressed in a sailor's jacket for our pilot, and on reaching the main channel were visited by some Indians who have a temporary residence on a marshy island in the middle of the river, where is a great abundance of water fowl. Here the mountainous country again approaches the river on the left, and a higher mountain is distinguished towards the southwest. At a distance of twenty miles from our camp we halted at a village of Wahkiacums, consisting of seven ill-looking houses, built in the same form with those above, and situated at the foot of the high hills on the right, behind two small marshy islands. We merely stopped to purchase some food and two beaver skins, and then proceeded. Opposite to these islands the hills on the left retire, and the river widens into a kind of bay crowded with low islands, subject to be overflowed occasionally by the tide. We had not gone far from this village when the fog cleared off, and we enjoyed the delightful prospect of the ocean; that ocean, the object of all our labours, the reward of all our anxieties. This cheering view exhilarated the spirits of all the party, who were still more delighted on hearing the distant roar of the breakers. We went on with great cheerfulness under the high mountainous country which continued along the right bank; the shore was however so bold and rocky, that we could not, until after going fourteen miles from the last village, find any spot fit for an encampment. At that distance, having made during the day thirty-four miles, we spread our mats on the ground, and passed the night in the rain. Here we were joined by our small canoe, which had been separated from us during the fog this morning. Two Indians from the last village also accompanied us to the camp, but, having detected them in stealing a knife, they were sent off.

Friday 8.—It rained this morning; and having changed the clothing which had been wet during yesterday's rain, we did not set out till nine o'clock. Immediately opposite our camp is a rock at the distance of a mile in the river, about twenty feet in diameter and fifty in height, and towards the southwest some high mountains, one of which is covered with snow at the top. We proceeded past several low islands in the bay or bend of the river to the left, which is here five or six miles wide. We were here overtaken by three Indians in a canoe who had salmon to sell. On the right side we passed an old village, and then, at the distance of three miles, entered an inlet or niche about six miles across, and making a deep bend of nearly five miles into the hills on the right shore, where it receives the waters of several creeks. We coasted along this inlet, which, from its little depth, we called Shallow bay, and at the bottom of it halted to dine near the remains of an old village, from which, however, we kept at a cautious distance, as it was occupied by great numbers of fleas. At this place we observed a

258

number of fowl, among which we killed a goose and two ducks, exactly resembling in appearance and flavour the canvassback duck of the Susquehannah. After dinner the three Indians left us, and we then took advantage of the returning tide, to go on about three miles to a point on the right, eight miles distant from our camp; but here the waves ran so high, and dashed about our canoes so much, that several of the men became seasick. It was therefore judged imprudent to go on in the present state of the weather, and we landed at the point. The situation was extremely uncomfortable; the high hills jutted in so closely that there was not room for us to lie level, nor to secure our baggage free from the tide; and the water of the river is too salt to be used; but the waves increasing every moment so much, that we could not move from the spot with safety: we therefore fixed ourselves on the beach left by the ebb-tide, and having raised the baggage on poles, passed a disagreeable night, the rain during the day having wet us completely, as indeed we have been for some days past.

Saturday 9.—Fortunately for us, the tide did not rise as high as our camp during the night; but being accompanied by high winds from the south, the canoes, which we could not place beyond its reach, were filled with water, and were saved with much difficulty: our position was very uncomfortable, but as it was impossible to move from it, we waited for a change of weather. It rained, however, during the whole day, and at two o'clock in the afternoon, the flood tide set in, accompanied by a high wind from the south, which, about four o'clock, shifted to the southwest, and blew almost a gale directly from the sea. The immense waves now broke over the place where we were encamped, and the large trees, some of them five or six feet thick, which had lodged at the point, were drifted over our camp, and the utmost vigilance of every man could scarcely save our canoes from being crushed to pieces. We remained in the water and drenched with rain during the rest of the day; our only food being some dried fish, and some rain-water which we caught. Yet, though wet and cold, and some of them sick from using the salt-water, the men are cheerful, and full of anxiety to see more of the ocean. The rain continued all night, and,

Sunday 10th, the following morning, the wind, however, lulled, and the waves not being so high, we loaded our canoes and proceeded. The mountains on the right are high, covered with timber, chiefly pine, and descend in a bold and rocky shore to the water. We went through a deep niche and several inlets on the right, while on the opposite side is a large bay, above which the hills are close on the river. At the distance of ten miles the wind rose from the northwest and the waves became so high that we were forced to return for two miles to a place where we could with safety unload. Here we landed at the mouth of a small run, and having placed our baggage on a pile of drifted logs waited until low water. The river then appeared more calm: we therefore started, but after going a mile found the waves too high for our canoes and were obliged to put to shore. We unloaded the canoes, and having placed the baggage on a rock above the reach of the tide, encamped on some drift logs which formed the only place where we could lie, the hills rising steep over our heads to the height of five hundred feet. All our baggage as well as ourselves were thoroughly wet with the rain, which did not cease

260

during the day; it continued violently during the night, in the course of which the tide reached the logs on which we lay, and set them afloat.

Monday, 11.—The wind was still high from the southwest, and drove the waves against the shore with great fury: the rain too fell in torrents, and not only drenched us to the skin, but loosened the stones on the hill sides, which then came rolling down upon us. In this comfortless situation we remained all day wet, cold, with nothing but dried fish to satisfy our hunger; the canoes in one place at the mercy of the waves; the baggage in another, and all the men scattered on floating logs, or sheltering themselves in the crevices of the rocks and hill sides. A hunter was despatched in hopes of finding some fresh meat, but the hills were so steep, and covered with undergrowth and fallen timber, that he could not penetrate them, and he was forced to return. About twelve o'clock we were visited by five Indians in a canoe: they came from above this place on the opposite side of the river, and their language much resembles that of the Wahkiacum: they called themselves *Cathlamahs*. In person they are small, ill made, and badly clothed; though one of them had on a sailor's round jacket and pantaloons, which, as he explained by signs, he had received from the whites below the point: we purchased from them thirteen red char, a fish which we found very excellent. After some time they went on board the boat, and crossed the river, which is here five miles wide, through a very heavy sea.

Tuesday, 12.—About three o'clock a tremendous gale of wind arose, accompanied with lightning, thunder, and hail: at six it became light for a short time, but a violent rain soon began and lasted during the day. During this storm one of our boats, secured by being sunk with great quantities of stone, got loose, but drifting against a rock, was recovered without having received much injury. Our situation became now much more dangerous, for the waves were driven with fury against the rocks and trees, which till now had afforded us refuge: we therefore took advantage of a low tide, and moved about half a mile round a point to a small brook, which we had not observed till now on account of the thick bushes and driftwood which concealed its mouth. Here we were more safe; but still cold and wet, our clothes and bedding rotten as well as wet, our baggage at a distance, and the canoes, our only means of escape from this place, at the mercy of the waves: we were, however, fortunate enough to enjoy good health, and even had the luxury of getting some fresh salmon and three salmon trout in the brook. Three of the men attempted to go round a point in our small Indian canoe, but the high waves rendered her quite unmanageable; these boats requiring the seamanship of the natives themselves to make them live in so rough a sea.

Wednesday, 13.—During the night we had short intervals of fair weather, but it began to rain in the morning, and continued through the day. In order to obtain a view of the country below, captain Clark followed up the course of the brook, and with much fatigue, and after walking three miles, ascended the first spur of the mountains. The whole lower country was covered with almost impenetrable thickets of small pine, with which is mixed a species of plant resembling arrowwood, twelve or fifteen feet high, with a thorny stem, almost interwoven with each other, and scattered among the fern and fallen timber: there is also a red berry, somewhat like the solomon's seal, which is called by the natives, solme, and used as an article of diet. This thick growth rendered travelling almost impossible, and it was rendered more fatiguing by the steepness of the mountain, which was so great as to oblige him to draw himself up by means of the bushes. The timber on the hills is chiefly of a large tall species of pine, many of them eight or ten feet in diameter at the stump, and rising sometimes more than one hundred feet in height. The hail which fell two nights since is still to be seen on the mountains: there was no game, and no traces of any, except some old signs of elk: the cloudy weather prevented his seeing to any distance, and he therefore returned to camp, and sent three men in the Indian canoe to try if they could double the point and find some safer harbour for our canoes. At every flood-tide the seas break in great swells against the rocks, and drifts the trees among our establishment, so as to render it very insecure. We were confined as usual to dried fish, which is our last resource.

Thursday, 14.—It rained without intermission during last night and to-day: the wind too is very high, and one of our canoes much injured by being dashed against rocks. Five Indians from below came to us in a canoe, and three of them having landed, informed us that they had seen the men sent down yesterday. At this moment one of them arrived, and informed us that these Indians had stolen his gig and basket: we therefore ordered the two women who remained in the canoe, to restore them; but this they refused, till we threatened to shoot, when they gave back the articles, and we then ordered them to leave us. They were of the Wahkiacum nation. The man now informed us that they had gone round the

263

point as far as the high sea would suffer them in the canoe, and then landed, and that in the night he had separated from his companions, who had gone further down: that at no great distance from where we are is a beautiful sand beach and a good harbour. Captain Lewis concluded to examine more minutely the lower part of the bay, and taking one of the large canoes was landed at the point, whence he proceeded by land with four men, and the canoe returned nearly filled with water.

Friday, 15.—It continued raining all night, but in the morning the weather became calm and fair: we therefore began to prepare for setting out, but before we were ready a high wind sprang up from the southeast, and obliged us to remain. The sun shone until one o'clock, and we were thus enabled to dry our bedding and examine our baggage. The rain, which has continued for the last ten days without an interval of more than two hours, has completely wet all our merchandise, and spoiled some of our fish, destroyed the robes, and rotted nearly one half of our few remaining articles of clothing, particularly the leather dresses. About three o'clock the wind fell, and we instantly loaded the canoes, and left the miserable spot to which we have been confined the last six days. On turning the point we came to the sand beach, through which runs a small stream from the hills; at the mouth of which is an ancient village of thirty-six houses, which has at present no inhabitants except fleas. Here we met Shannon, who had been sent back to meet us by captain Lewis. The day Shannon left us in the canoe, he and Willard proceeded on till they met a party of twenty Indians, who never having heard of us, did not know where they came from: they however behaved with so much civility, and seemed so anxious that the men should go with them towards the sea, that their suspicions were excited, and they declined going on: the Indians, however, would not leave them, and the men being confirmed in their suspicions, and fearful if they went into the woods to sleep they would be cut to pieces in the night, thought it best to pass the night in the midst of the Indians: they therefore made a fire, and after talking with them to a late hour, laid down with their rifles under their heads. As they awoke this morning they found that the Indians had stolen and concealed their guns: having demanded them in vain, Shannon seized a club, and was about assaulting one of the Indians whom he suspected as a thief, when another Indian began to load a fowling piece with an intention of shooting him. He therefore stopped and explained by signs, that if they did not give up the guns, a large party would come down the river before the sun rose to such a height, and put every one of them to death. Fortunately, captain Lewis and his party appeared at this time, and the terrified Indians immediately brought the guns, and five of them came on with Shannon. To these men we declared, that if ever any of their nation stole any thing from us he should be instantly shot. They reside to the north of this place, and speak a language different from that of the people higher up the river. It was now apparent that the sea was at all times too rough for us to proceed further down the bay by water: we therefore landed, and having chosen the best spot we could select, made our camp of boards from the old village. We were now situated comfortably, and being visited by four Wahkiacums with wappatoo roots, were enabled to make an agreeable addition to our food.

265

Saturday 16.—The morning was clear and beautiful. We therefore, put out all our baggage to dry, and sent several of the party to hunt. Our camp is in full view of the ocean, on the bay laid down by Vancouver, which we distinguish by the name of Haley's bay, from a trader who visits the Indians here, and is a great favourite among them. The meridian altitude of this day gave $46°\ 19'\ 11''\ \frac{7}{10}$ as the latitude of our camp. The wind was strong from the southwest, and the waves very high, yet the Indians were passing up and down the bay in canoes, and several of them encamped near us. We smoked with them, but after our recent experience of their thievish disposition, treated them with caution. Though so much exposed to the bad weather, none of the party have suffered, except one, who has a violent cold, in consequence of sleeping for several nights in wet leather. The hunters brought in two deer, a crane, some geese and ducks, and several brant, three of which were white, except a black part of the wing, and much larger than the grey brant, which is itself a size beyond the duck.

Sunday 17.—A fair cool morning and easterly wind. The tide rises at this place eight feet six inches in height, and rolls over the beach in great waves.

About one o'clock captain Lewis returned, after having coasted down Haley's bay to cape Disappointment, and some distance to the north along the sea coast. He was followed by several Chinnooks, among whom were the principal chief and his family. They made us a present of a boiled root, very much like the common liquorice in taste and size, and called culwhamo: in return we gave double the value of their present, and now learnt the danger of accepting any thing from them, since no return, even if ten times the value of their gift, can satisfy them. We were chiefly occupied in hunting, and were able to procure three deer, four brant and two ducks, and also saw some signs of elk. Captain Clark now prepared for an excursion down the bay, and accordingly started,

Monday 18, at daylight, accompanied by eleven men. He proceeded along the beach one mile to a point of rocks about forty feet high, where the hills retire, leaving a wide beach, and a number of ponds covered with water-fowl, between which and the mountain is a narrow bottom of alder and small balsam trees. Seven miles from the rocks is the entrance of a creek, or rather drain from the ponds and hills, where is a cabin of Chinnooks. The cabin contained some children, and four women, one of whom was in a most miserable state, covered with ulcers, proceeding as we imagine, from the venereal disease, with which several of the Chinnooks we have seen appear to be afflicted. We were taken across in a canoe by two squaws, to each of whom we gave a fish-hook, and then coasting along the bay, passed at two miles the low bluff of a small hill, below which are the ruins of some old huts, and close to it the remains of a whale. The country is low, open and marshy; interspersed with some high pine and a thick undergrowth. Five miles from the creek, we came to a stream forty yards wide at low water, which we called Chinnook river. The hills up this river and towards the bay are not high, but very thickly covered with large pine of several species: in many places pine trees, three or four feet in thickness, are seen growing on the bodies of large trees, which though fallen and covered with moss, were in part sound. Here we dined on some brant and plover, killed as we came along, and after crossing in a boat lying in the sand near some old houses, proceeded along a bluff of yellow clay and soft stone to a little bay or harbour, into which a drain from some ponds empties: at this harbour the land is low, but as we went on it rose to hills of eighty or ninety feet above the water. At the distance of one mile is a second bay, and a mile beyond it, a small rocky island in a deep bend, which seems to afford a very good harbour, and where the natives inform us European vessels anchor for the purpose of trading. We went on round another bay, in which is a second small island of rocks, and crossed a small stream, which rises in a pond near the sea coast, and after running through a low isthmus empties into the bay. This narrow low ground, about two or three hundred yards wide, separates from the main hills a kind of peninsula, the extremity of which is two miles from the anchoring place; and this spot, which was called cape Disappointment, is an elevated, circular knob, rising with a steep ascent one hundred and fifty or one hundred and sixty feet above the water, formed like the whole shore of the bay, as well as of the seacoast, and covered with thick timber on the inner side, but open and grassy in the exposure next the sea. From this cape a high point of land bears south 20° west, about twenty-five miles distant. In the range between these two eminences, is the opposite point of the bay, a very low ground, which has been variously called cape Rond by Lapeyrouse, and point Adams by Vancouver. The water for a great distance off the mouth of the river, appears very shallow, and within the mouth nearest to point Adams, is a large sandbar, almost covered at high tide. We could not ascertain the direction of the deepest channel, for the waves break with tremendous force the whole distance across the bay, but the Indians point nearer to the opposite side as the best passage. After remaining for some time on this elevation, we descended across the low isthmus, and reached the ocean at the foot of a high hill, about a mile in circumference, and projecting into the sea. We crossed this hill, which is open and has a growth of high coarse grass, and encamped on the north side of it, having made nineteen miles. Besides the pounded fish and brant, we had for supper a flounder, which we picked up on the beach.

Tuesday 19.—In the night it began to rain, and continued till eleven o'clock. Two hunters were sent on to kill something for breakfast, and the rest of the party after drying their blankets soon followed. At three miles we overtook the hunters, and breakfasted on a small deer, which they had been fortunate enough to kill. This, like all those we have seen on this coast, are much darker than our common deer. Their bodies too, are deeper, their legs shorter, and their eyes larger. The branches of the horns are similar, but the upper part of the tail is black, from the root to the end, and they do not leap, but jump like a sheep frightened. We then continued over rugged hills and steep hollows, near the sea, on a course about north 20° west, in a direct line from the cape, till at the distance of five miles, we reached a point of high land, below which a sandy beach extends, in a direction north 10° west, to another high point about twenty miles distant. This eminence we distinguished by the name of point Lewis. It is there that the highlands, which at the commencement of the sandy beach, recede towards Chinnook river, again approach the ocean. The intermediate country is low, with many small ponds, crowded with birds, and watered by the Chinnook, on the borders of which resides the nation of the same name. We went four miles along the sandy beach to a small pine tree, on which captain Clark marked his name, with the year and day, and then returned to the foot of the hills, passing on the shore a sturgeon ten feet long, and several joints of the back bone of a whale, both which seem to have been thrown ashore and foundered. After dining on the remains of the small deer, we crossed in a south-eastern direction to the bay, where we arrived at the distance of two miles, then continued along the bay, crossed Chinnook river, and encamped on its upper side, in a sandy bottom.

Wednesday 20.—It rained in the course of the night. A hunter despatched early to kill some food, returned with eight ducks, on which we breakfasted, and then followed the course of the bay to the creek or outlet of the ponds. It was now high tide, the stream three hundred yards wide, and no person in the cabin to take us across. We therefore made a small raft, on which one of the men passed and brought a canoe to carry us over. As we went along the beach we were overtaken by several Indians, who gave us dried sturgeon and wappatoo roots, and soon met several parties of Chinnooks returning from the camp. When we arrived there we found many Chinnooks, and two of them being chiefs, we went through the ceremony of giving to each a medal, and to the most distinguished a flag. Their names were Comcommoly and Chillahlawil. One of the Indians had a robe made of two sea-otter skins, the fur of which was the most beautiful we had ever seen; the owner resisted every tempta-

tion to part with it, but at length could not resist the offer of a belt of blue beads which Chaboneau's wife wore round her waist. During our
absence the camp had been visited by many Indians, and the men who had been employed in
hunting killed several deer, and a variety of wild
fowls.

Thursday 21.—The morning was cloudy, and
from noon till night it rained. The wind too was
high from the southeast, and the sea so rough
that the water reached our camp. Most of the
Chinnooks returned home, but we were visited in
the course of the day by people of different bands
in the neighbourhood, among whom are the
Chiltz, a nation residing on the seacoast near
Point Lewis, and the Clatsops, who live immediately opposite on the south side of the Columbia. A chief from the grand rapid also came to
see us, and we gave him a medal. To each of our
visitors we made a present of a small piece of
ribbon, and purchased some cranberries and some
articles of their manufacture, such as mats, and
household furniture, for all which we paid high
prices. After we had been relieved from these
Indians, we were surprised at a visit of a different
kind; an old woman who is the wife of a Chinnook chief, came with six young women, her
daughters and nieces, and having deliberately encamped near us, proceeded to cultivate an intimacy between our men and her fair wards.

CHAPTER XXI.

Extravagant passion of the natives for blue beads, which constitute amongst them the circulating medium of the country—
The party still in search of a suitable place for winter quarters
—Still suffering from the constant deluges of rain—Are visited
by the Indians, with whom they traffic but little, on account of
the extravagant prices they ask for every article—Return of
captain Lewis, who reports that he has found a suitable place
for winter quarters—The rain still continues—They prepare to
form an encampment on a point of highland on the banks of
the river Nutel—Captain Clark goes with a party to find a place
suitable for the manufacture of salt—He is hospitably entertained by the Clatsops—This tribe addicted to the vice of
gambling—Sickness of some of the party, occasioned by the incessant rains—They form, notwithstanding, a permanent encampment for their winter quarters.

Friday 22.—It rained during the whole night,
and about daylight a tremendous gale of wind
rose from the S. S. E. and continued during the
whole day with great violence. The sea runs so
high that the water comes into our camp, which
the rain prevents us from leaving. We purchased
from the old squaw for armbands and rings, a
few wappatoo roots, on which we subsisted.
They are nearly equal in flavour to the Irish potato, and afford a very good substitute for
bread. The bad weather has driven several Indians to our camp, but they are still under the
terrors of the threat which we made on first seeing them, and now behave with the greatest
decency.

Saturday 23.—The rain continued through the
night, but the morning was calm and cloudy.
The hunters were sent out and killed three deer,
four brant, and three ducks. Towards evening

seven Clatsops came over in a canoe with two skins of the sea-otter. To this article they attach an extravagant value, and their demands for it were so high that we were fearful of reducing our small stock of merchandise, on which we must depend for subsistence as we return, to venture on purchasing. To ascertain however their ideas as to the value of different objects, we offered for one of the skins a watch, a handkerchief, an American dollar, and a bunch of red beads; but neither the curious mechanism of the watch, nor even the red beads could tempt him; he refused the offer, but asked for tiacomoshack or chief beads, the most common sort of coarse blue-coloured beads, the article beyond all price in their estimation. Of these blue beads we have but few, and therefore reserve them for more necessitous circumstances.

Sunday 24.—The morning being fair, we dried our wet articles and sent out the hunters, but they returned with only a single brant. In the evening a chief and several men of the Chinnooks came to see us; we smoked with them, and bought a sea-otter skin for some blue beads. Having now examined the coast, it becomes necessary to decide on the spot for our wintering quarters. The people of the country subsist chiefly on dried fish and roots, but of these there does not seem to be a sufficient quantity for our support, even were we able to purchase, and the extravagant prices as well as our small store of merchandise forbid us to depend on that resource. We must therefore rely for subsistence on our arms, and be guided in the choice of our residence by the abundance of game which any particular spot may offer. The Indians say that the deer is most numerous at some distance above on the river, but that the country on the opposite side of the bay is better supplied with elk, an animal much larger and more easily killed than deer, with a skin better fitted for clothing, and the meat of which is more nutritive during the winter, when they are both poor. The climate too is obviously much milder here than above the first range of mountains, for the Indians are thinly clad, and say they have little snow; indeed since our arrival the weather has been very warm, and sometimes disagreeably so: and dressed as we are altogether in leather, the cold would be very unpleasant if not injurious. The neighbourhood of the sea is moreover recommended by the facility of supplying ourselves with salt, and the hope of meeting some of the trading vessels, who are expected in about three months, and from whom we may procure a fresh supply of trinkets for our route homewards. These considerations induced us to determine on visiting the opposite side of the bay, and if there was an appearance of much game to establish ourselves there during the winter. Next day,

Monday 25, however, the wind was too high to suffer us to cross the river, but as it blew generally from the east southeast, the coast on the north was in some degree sheltered by the highlands. We therefore set out, and keeping near the shore, halted for dinner in the shallow bay, and after dark, reached a spot near a rock, at some distance in the river, and close to our former camp of the 7th inst. On leaving our camp, seven Clatsops accompanied us in a canoe, but after going a few miles crossed the bay through immense high waves, leaving us in admiration, at the dexterity with which they threw aside each wave as it threatened to come over their canoe. The evening was cloudy, and in the morning,

Tuesday 26, it rained. We set out with the

wind from east northeast, and a short distance
above the rock, near our camp, began to cross the
river. We passed between some low, marshy
islands, which we called the Seal islands, and
reached the south side of the Columbia at a bottom three miles below a point, to which we gave
the name of point Samuel. After going along the
shore for five miles, we entered a channel two
hundred yards in width, which separates from the
main land a large, but low island. On this channel, and at the foot of some highlands, is a village
where we landed. It consists of nine large wooden
houses, inhabited by a tribe called Cathlamahs,
who seem to differ neither in dress, language, nor
manners, from the Chinnooks and Wahkiacums:
like whom they live chiefly on fish and wappatoo
roots. We found, however, as we hoped, some elk
meat: after dining on some fresh fish and roots,
which we purchased from them at an immoderate
price, we coasted along a deep bend of the river
towards the south, and at night encamped under
a high hill; all the way from the village the land
is high, and has a thick growth of pine balsam,
and other timber; but as it was still raining very
hard, it was with difficulty we procured wood
enough to make fires. Soon after we landed, three
Indians from the Cathlamah village came down
with wappatoo roots, some of which we purchased with fish-hooks. At daylight the next
morning,

Wednesday 27, eleven more came down with
provisions, skins and mats for sale, but the prices
were too high for our reduced finances, and we
bought nothing. As we were preparing to set out
we missed an axe, which was found under the
robe of one of the Indians, and they were all pro-
hibited in consequence from following us. We

went on in the rain, which had continued through the night, and passing between a number of islands came to a small river, called by the Indians Kekemahke. We afterwards came to a very remarkable knob of land, projecting about a mile and a half towards Shallow bay, and about four miles round, while the neck of land which connects it to the main shore is not more than fifty yards wide. We went round this projection, which we named point William; but the waves then became so high that we could not venture any farther, and we therefore landed on a beautiful shore of pebbles of various colours, and encamped near an old Indian hut on the isthmus. In drawing our canoes in shore, we had the misfortune to make a split two feet long in one of them. This isthmus opposed a formidable barrier to the sea, for we now found that the water below is salt, while that above is fresh and well tasted. It rained hard during the whole day; it continued all night, and in the morning,

Thursday 28, began more violently, attended with a high wind from the southwest. It was now impossible to proceed on so rough a sea. We therefore sent several men to hunt, and the rest of us remained during the day, in a situation the most cheerless and uncomfortable. On this little neck of land we are exposed with a miserable covering, which does not deserve the name of a shelter to the violence of the winds; all our bedding and stores, as well as our bodies are completely wet, our clothes rotting with constant exposure, and no food except the dried fish brought from the falls, to which we are again reduced. The hunters all returned hungry, and drenched with rain, having seen neither deer nor elk, and the swan and brant too shy to be approached. At noon the wind shifted to the north-west, and blew with such tremendous fury that many trees were blown down near us. This gale lasted with short intervals during the whole night; but towards morning,

Friday, 29th, the wind lulled, though the rain continued, and the waves were still high. Captain Lewis took the Indian canoe, which is better calculated for rough weather, and with five men went down to a small bay below us, where we expect to find elk. Three other men set out at the same time to hunt in different directions, and the rest remained round the smoke of our fires drying leather, in order to make some new clothes. The night brought only a continuation of rain and hail, with short intervals of fair weather, till in the morning,

Saturday, 30th, it cleared up about nine o'clock, and the sun shone for several hours. Other hunters were now sent out, and we passed the remainder of the day in drying our merchandise so long exposed. Several of the men complain of disorders in their bowels, which can be ascribed only to their diet of pounded fish mixed with salt-water: and they are therefore directed to use for that purpose, the fresh water above the point. The hunters had seen three elk, but could not obtain any of them: they however brought in three hawks and a few black ducks, of a species common in the United States, living in large flocks, and feeding on grass: they are distinguished by a sharp white beak, toes separated, and by having no craw. Besides these wild fowls, there are in this neighbourhood a large kind of buzzard with white wings, the grey and the bald eagle, the large red-tailed hawk, the blue magpie, and great numbers of ravens and crows. We observe, however, few small birds, the one which has most attracted our attention being a small brown bird, which seems to frequent logs and the roots of trees. Of other animals there is a great abundance. We see great quantities of snakes, lizards, worms, and spiders, as well as small bugs, flies, and insects of different kinds. The vegetable productions are also numerous. The hills along the coast are high and steep, and the general covering is a growth of lofty pines of different species, some of which rise more than two hundred feet, and are ten or twelve feet in diameter near the root. Besides these trees we observe on the point a species of ash, the alder, the laurel, one species of the wild crab, and several kinds of underbrush, among which the rosebushes are conspicuous.

Sunday, December 1, 1805.—Again we had a cloudy day, and the wind so high from the east, that having ventured in a boat with a view to hunt at some distance, we were obliged to return. We resumed our occupation of dressing leather and mending our old clothes, in which we passed the day. The hunters came in with a report of their having seen two herds of elk, but they could kill nothing, and we therefore again fed upon dried fish. At sunset it began to rain violently, and continued all night, and

Monday, 2d, the next day. This disagreeable food, pounded fish, has occasioned so much sickness among the men that it is now absolutely necessary to vary it. Three hunters therefore set out, and three more were sent up the Kekemahke creek in search of fish or birds. Towards evening one of them returned: he had observed great appearances of elk, and even seen two herds of them; but it rained so hard that he could with difficulty get a shot: he had, however, at last killed one, at the distance of six miles from the camp, and a canoe was now sent to bring it. The party from Kekemahke creek were less successful: they had seen no fish, and all the birds, in consequence probably of being much hunted by the Indians, were too shy to be approached.

Tuesday, 3.—The wind was from the east, and the morning fair; but, as if a whole day of fine weather was not permitted, towards night it began to rain. Even this transient glimpse of sunshine revived the spirits of the party, who were still more pleased, when the elk killed yesterday was brought into camp. This was the first elk we had killed on the west side of the Rocky mountains, and condemned as we have been to the dried fish, forms a most nourishing food. After eating the marrow of the shank-bones, the squaw chopped them fine, and by boiling, extracted a pint of grease, superior to the tallow itself of the animal. A canoe of eight Indians, who were carrying down wappatoo roots to trade with the Clatsops, stopped at our camp: we bought a few roots for small fish-hooks, and they then left us: but accustomed as we are to the sight, we could not but view with admiration the wonderful dexterity with which they guide their canoes over the most boisterous seas; for though the waves were so high, that before they had gone half a mile the canoe was several times out of sight, they proceeded with the greatest calmness and security. Two of the hunters who set out yesterday had lost their way, and did not return till this evening: they had seen in their ramble great signs of elk, and had killed six elk, which they had butchered and left at a great distance. A party was sent in the morning,

Wednesday, December 4, to carry the elk to a

279

bay, some distance below, to which place, if the weather permitted, we would all remove our camp this evening; but the rain which had continued during the night lasted all next day, and was accompanied by so high a wind from the southeast and south, that we dared not risk our canoes on the water. It was high water at eleven o'clock, when the spring-tide rose two feet higher than the common flood-tides. We passed the day around our fires, and as we are so situated that the smoke will not immediately leave the camp, we are very much incommoded, and our eyes injured by it. No news has yet been received from captain Lewis, and we begin to have much uneasiness for his safety.

Thursday, December 5.—It rained during the whole night, and this morning the rain and high wind compelled us to remain at our camp. Besides the inconvenience of being thus stopped on our route, we now found that all our stores and bedding are again wet with rain. The high water was at twelve o'clock, and rose two inches beyond that of yesterday. In the afternoon we were rejoiced at the return of captain Lewis, who came in a canoe with three of his men, the other two being left to guard six elk and five deer which they had killed: he had examined the coast, and found a river a short distance below, on which we might encamp during the winter, with a sufficiency of elk for our subsistence within reach. This information was very satisfactory, and we decided on going thither as soon as we could move from the point; but all night and the following day,

Friday 6, it rained, and the wind blew hard from the southwest, so that the sea was still too rough for us to proceed. The high-tide of to-day rose thirteen inches higher than it did yesterday, and obliged us to move our camp to a high situation. Here we remained waiting for better weather, till about dark the wind shifted to the north, and the sky was clear. We had now some prospect of being able to leave our situation, and indeed although some rain fell in the course of the night, the next morning,

Saturday 7, was fair; we therefore loaded our canoes, and proceeded. But the tide was against us, and the waves very high, so that we were obliged to proceed slowly and cautiously. We at length turned a point, and found ourselves in a deep bay; here we landed for breakfast, and were joined by the party sent out three days ago to look for the six elk. In seeking for the elk they had missed their way for a day and a half, and when they reached the place, found the elk so much spoiled that they brought the skins only of four of them. After breakfast we coasted round the bay, which is about four miles across, and receives, besides several small creeks, two rivers called by the Indians, the one Killowanakcl, the other Netul. We called it Meriwether's bay, from the christian name of captain Lewis, who was no doubt the first white man who surveyed it. As we went along the wind was high from the northeast, and in the middle of the day it rained for two hours, and then cleared off. On reaching the south side of the bay, we ascended the Netul for three miles to the first point of highland on its western bank, and formed our camp in a thick grove of lofty pines, about two hundred yards from the water, and thirty feet above the level of the high tides.

Sunday 8.—This seemed the most cligible spot for our winter establishment. In order therefore

to find a place for making salt, and to examine
the country further, captain Clark set out with
five men, and pursuing a course south, 60° west,
over a dividing ridge, through thick pine timber,
much of which had fallen, passed the heads of
two small brooks. In the neighbourhood of these
the land was swampy and overflowed, and we
waded knee-deep till we came to an open ridgy
prairie, covered with the plant known on our
frontier by the name of sacacommis. Here is a
creek about sixty yards wide, and running towards point Adams; they passed it on a small
raft. At this place they discovered a large herd of
elk, and after pursuing them for three miles over
bad swamps and small ponds, we killed one of
them. The agility with which the elk crossed the
swamps and bogs, seems almost incredible; as we
followed their track, the ground for a whole acre
would shake at our tread, and sometimes we sunk
to our hips without finding any bottom. Over
the surface of these bogs is a species of moss,
among which are great numbers of cranberries,
and occasionally there rise from the swamp steep
and small knobs of earth, thickly covered with
pine and laurel. On one of these we halted at
night, but it was scarcely large enough to suffer
us to lie clear of the water, and had very little
dry wood. We succeeded however in collecting
enough to make a fire, and having stretched the
elk skin to keep off the rain, which still continued,
slept till morning,

Monday 9, when we rose, perfectly wet with
rain during the night. Three men were then sent
in pursuit of the elk, while with the other three,
captain Clark proceeded westward towards the
sea. He passed over three swamps, and then arrived at a creek, which was too deep to ford, and

there was no wood to make a raft. He therefore proceeded down it for a short distance, till he found that he was between the forks of a creek. One branch of which he had passed yesterday, turns round towards the southwest to meet another of equal size from the south, and together they form a small river, about seventy yards wide. He returned to the place where he had left the raft, and having crossed proceeded down about a mile, when he met three Indians. They were loaded with fresh salmon which they had taken with a gig, and were now returning to their village on the seacoast, where they invited him to accompany them. He agreed, and they brought out a canoe hid along the banks of the creek. In this they passed over the branch which he had just crossed on a raft, and then carried the canoe a quarter of a mile to the other fork, which they crossed and continued down to the mouth of the river. At this place it makes a great bend, where the river is seventy yards wide; just above, or to the south of which is the village. We crossed over, and found that it consisted of three houses, inhabited by twelve families of Clatsops. They were on the south exposure of a hill, and sunk about four feet deep into the ground; the walls, roof, and gable-ends being formed of split pine boards; the descent through a small door down a ladder. There are two fires in the middle of the room, and the beds disposed round the walls two or three feet from the fall, so as to leave room under them for their bags, baskets and household articles. The floor itself is covered with mats. Captain Clark was received with much attention. As soon as he entered, clean mats were spread, and fish, berries and roots set before him on small neat platters of rushes. After he had eaten, the men of the other houses came and smoked with him. They all appeared much neater in their persons and diet than Indians generally are, and frequently wash their hands and faces, a ceremony by no means frequent elsewhere. While he was conversing with them, a flock of brant lighted on the water, and he with a small rifle shot one of them at a great distance. They immediately jumped in, and brought it on shore, very much astonished at the shot, which contributed to make them increase their attention. Towards evening it began to rain and blow very violently from the southwest; and captain Clark therefore, determined to remain during the night. When they thought his appetite had returned, an old woman presented him in a bowl, made of light coloured horn, a kind of syrup, pleasant to the taste, and made from a species of berry common in this country, about the size of a cherry, and called by the Indians shelwel: of these berries a bread is also prepared, which being boiled with roots forms a soup, which was served in neat wooden trenchers: this, with some cockles, was his repast. The men of the village now collected, and began to gamble. The most common game, was one in which one of the company was banker, and played against all the rest. He had a piece of bone, about the size of a large bean, and having agreed with any individual as to the value of the stake, would pass the bone from one hand to the other, with great dexterity, singing at the same time, to divert the attention of his adversary; and then holding it in his hands, his antagonist was challenged to guess in which of them the bone was, and lost or won as he pointed to the right or wrong hand. To this game of hazard they abandoned themselves with great ardour; sometimes every thing they possess is sacrificed to it, and this evening several of the Indians lost all the beads which they had with them. This lasted for three hours, when captain Clark appearing disposed to sleep, the man who had been most attentive, and whose name was Cuskalah, spread two new mats near the fire, and ordering his wife to retire to her own bed, the rest of the company dispersed at the same time. Captain Clark then lay down, but the violence with which the fleas attacked him, did not leave his rest unbroken, and he rose,

Tuesday 10, early. The morning was cloudy, with some rain: he walked out on the seashore, and observed the Indians walking up and down the creek and examining the shore: he was at a loss to understand their object, till one of them came to him and explained that they were in search of fish which had been thrown on shore and left by the tide, adding in English, "sturgeon is very good." There is indeed, every reason to suppose, that these Clatsops depend for their subsistence during the winter, chiefly on the fish thus casually thrown on the coast. After amusing himself for some time on the beach, he returned towards the village, and shot on his way two brant. As he came near the village, one of the Indians asked him to shoot a duck about thirty steps distant: he did so, and having accidentally shot off its head, the bird was brought to the village by the Indians, all of whom came round in astonishment: they examined the duck, the musket, and the very small bullet, which were a hundred to the pound, and then exclaimed, Clouch musquet, wake, commatax musquet: a good musket, do not understand this kind of musket. They now placed before him their best roots, fish, and syrup, after which he attempted to purchase a sea-otter skin with some red beads which he happened to have about him; but they declined trading, as they valued none except blue or white beads: he therefore bought nothing but a little berry bread and a few roots in exchange for fish-hooks, and then set out to return by the same route on which he came. He was accompanied by Cuskalah and his brother as far as the third creek, and then proceeded to the camp through a heavy rain. The whole party had been occupied during his absence in cutting down trees to make huts, and in hunting.

Wednesday, 11.—The rain continued last night and the whole of this day. We were, however, all employed in putting up our winter cabins, which we are anxious to finish, as several of the men are beginning to suffer from the excessive dampness: four of them have very violent colds, one has a dysentery, a third has tumours on his legs, and two have been injured by dislocation and straining of their limbs.

Thursday, 12.—We continued to work in the rain at our houses. In the evening there arrived two canoes of Clatsops, among whom was a principal chief, called Comowol. We gave him a medal, and treated his companions with great attention; after which we began to bargain for a small sea-otter skin, some wappatoo roots, and another species of root called shanataque. We readily perceived that they were close dealers, stickled much for trifles, and never closed the bargain until they thought they had the advantage. The wappatoo is dear, as they themselves are obliged to give a high price for it to the Indians above. Blue beads are the articles most in request, the white occupy the next place in their estimation; but they do not value much those of any other colour. We succeeded at last in purchasing their whole cargo for a few fish-hooks and a small sack of Indian tobacco, which we had received from the Shoshonees. The next morning,

Friday, 13th, we treated them to a breakfast on elk meat, of which they seemed very fond, and having purchased from them two skins of the lucervia, and two robes made of the skin of an animal about the size of a cat, they left us. Two hunters returned with the pleasing intelligence of their having killed eighteen elk about six miles off. Our huts begin to rise, for though it rains all day we continue our labours, and are rejoiced to find that the beautiful balsam pine splits into excellent boards, more than two feet in width. In the evening three Indians came in a canoe with provisions and skins for sale, and spent the night with us.

Saturday, 14.—Again it rained all day, but by working constantly we finished the walls of our huts, and nearly completed a house for our provisions. The constant rains have completely spoiled our last supply of elk; but notwithstanding that scarcely a man has been dry for a great number of days, the sick are recovering. Four men were despatched to guard the elk which were killed yesterday, till a larger party joined them. Accordingly,

Sunday 15, captain Clark with sixteen men set out in three canoes, and having rowed for three miles up the river turned up a large creek from the right, and after going three miles further landed about the height of the tide water. The men were then despatched in small parties to bring in the elk, each man returning with a quarter of the animal. In bringing the third and last load, nearly half the men missed their way, and did not return till after night; five of them indeed were not able to find their way at all. It had been cloudy all day, and in the night began to rain, and as we had no cover were obliged to sit up the greater part of the night, for as soon as we lay down the rain would come under us, and compel us to rise. It was indeed a most uncomfortable situation, but the five men who joined us in the morning,

Monday 16, had been more unlucky, for in addition to the rain which had poured down upon them all night, they had no fire, and drenched and cold as they were when they reached us, exhibited a most distressing sight. They had left their loads where they slept, and some men were sent after them, while others were despatched after two more elk in another bend of the creek, who after taking these last on board, proceeded to our camp. It rained and hailed during the day, and a high wind from the southeast not only threw down trees as we passed along, but made the river so rough that we proceeded with great risk. We now had the meat house covered, and all our game carefully hung up in small pieces.

Tuesday 17.—It rained all night, and this morning there was a high wind, and hail as well as rain fell; and on the top of a mountain about ten miles to the southeast of us we observed some snow. The greater part of our stores is wet, and our leathern tent is so rotten that the slightest touch makes a rent in it, and it will now scarcely shelter a spot large enough for our beds. We were all busy in finishing the inside of the huts. The after part of the day was cool and fair. But this respite was of very short duration, for all night it continued raining and snowing alternately, and in the morning,

Wednesday 18, we had snow and hail till twelve o'clock, after which it changed to rain. The air now became cool and disagreeable, the wind high and unsettled, so that being thinly dressed in leather, we were able to do very little on the houses.

Thursday 19.—The rain continued all night with short intervals, but the morning was fair and the wind from the southwest. Situated as we are, our only occupation is to work as diligently as we can on our houses, and to watch the changes of the weather, on which so much of our comfort depends. We availed ourselves of this glimpse of sunshine, to send across Meriwether's bay for the boards of an old Indian house; but before the party returned with them, the weather clouded, and we again had hail and rain during the rest of the day. Our only visitors were two Indians who spent a short time with us.

Friday 20.—A succession of rain and hail during the night. At ten o'clock it cleared off for a short time, but the rain soon recommenced; we now covered in four of our huts; three Indians came in a canoe with mats, roots, and the berries of the sacacommis. These people proceed with a dexterity and finesse in their bargains, which, if they have not learnt from their foreign visitors, it may show how nearly allied is the cunning of savages to the little arts of traffic. They begin by asking double or treble the value of what they have to sell, and lower their demand in proportion to the greater or less degree of ardour or knowledge of the purchaser, who with all his management is not able to procure the article for less than its real value, which the Indians perfectly understand. Our chief medium of trade consists of blue and white beads, files with which they sharpen their tools, fish-hooks, and tobacco: but of all these articles blue beads and tobacco are the most esteemed.

Saturday 21.—As usual it rained all night and continued without intermission during the day. One of our Indian visitors was detected in stealing a horn spoon, and turned out of the camp. We find that the plant called sacacommis forms an agreeable mixture with tobacco, and we therefore despatched two men to the open lands near the ocean, in order to collect some of it, while the rest continued their work.

Sunday 22.—There was no interval in the rain last night and to-day; so that we cannot go on rapidly with our buildings. Some of the men are indeed quite sick, others have received bruises, and several complain of biles. We discover too, that part of our elk meat is spoiling in consequence of the warmth of the weather, though we have kept a constant smoke under it.

Monday 23.—It continued raining the whole day, with no variation except occasional thunder and hail. Two canoes of Clatsops came to us with various articles for sale; we bought three mats and bags neatly made of flags and rushes, and also the skin of a panther seven feet long, including the tail. For all these we gave six small fish-hooks, a worn-out file, and some pounded fish which had become so soft and mouldy by exposure, that we could not use it: it is, however, highly prized by the Indians of this neighbourhood. Although a very portable and convenient food, the mode of curing seems known, or at least practised only by the Indians near the great falls, and coming from such a distance, has an additional value in the eyes of these people, who are anxious to possess some food less precarious than

290

their ordinary subsistence. Among these Clatsops was a second chief to whom we gave a medal, and sent some pounded fish to Cuscalah, who could not come to see us, on account of sickness. The next day,

Tuesday 24, however, he came in a canoe with his young brother and two squaws. Having treated captain Clark so kindly at his village we were pleased to see him, and he gave us two mats and a parcel of roots. These we accepted, as it would have been offensive to decline the offer but afterwards two files were demanded in return for the presents, and not being able to spare those articles, we restored the mats and roots. Cuscalah was a little displeased: in the evening however he offered each of us one of the squaws, and even this being declined, Cuscalah as well as the whole party of Indians were highly offended: the females particularly seemed to be much incensed at our indifference about their favours. The whole stock of meat being now completely spoiled, our pounded fish became again our chief dependence. It had rained constantly all day, but we still continued working and at last moved into our huts.

Wednesday 25.—We were awaked at daylight by a discharge of firearms, which was followed by a song from the men, as a compliment to us on the return of Christmas, which we have always been accustomed to observe as a day of rejoicing. After breakfast we divided our remaining stock of tobacco, which amounted to twelve carrots, into two parts; one of which we distributed among such of the party as made use of it, making a present of a handkerchief to the others. The remainder of the day was passed in good spirits, though there was nothing in our situation to excite much gaiety. The rain confined us to the house, and our only luxuries in honour of the season, were some poor elk, so much spoiled that we eat it through mere necessity, a few roots, and some spoiled pounded fish. The next day,

Thursday 26, brought a continuation of rain, accompanied with thunder, and a high wind from the southeast. We were therefore still obliged to remain in our huts, and endeavoured to dry our wet articles before the fire. The fleas which annoyed us near the portage of the great falls, have taken such possession of our clothes, that we are obliged to have a regular search every day through our blankets as a necessary preliminary to sleeping at night. These animals indeed are so numerous, that they are almost a calamity to the Indians of this country. When they have once obtained the mastery of any house it is impossible to expel them, and the Indians have frequently different houses, to which they resort occasionally when the fleas have rendered their permanent residence intolerable; yet in spite of these precautions, every Indian is constantly attended by multitudes of them, and no one comes into our houses without leaving behind him swarms of these tormenting insects.

Friday 27.—The rain did not cease last night, nor the greater part of the day. In the evening we were visited by Comowool, the chief, and four men of the Clatsop nation, who brought a very timely supply of roots and berries. Among these was one called culhomo, resembling liquorice in size and taste, and which they roast like a potato; there was also the shanataque, a root of which they are very fond. It is of a black colour, sweet to the taste, and is prepared for eating in a kiln, as the Indians up the Columbia dry the pasheco. These as well as the shellwell berries, they value highly, but were perfectly satisfied with the return we made them, consisting of a small piece of sheepskin, to wear round the chief's head, a pair of earbobs for his son, a small piece of brass, and a little ribbon. In addition to our old enemies the fleas, we observed two mosquitoes, or insects so completely resembling them, that we can perceive no difference in their shape and appearance.

Saturday, 28.—Again it rained during the greater part of last night, and continued all day. Five men were sent out to hunt, and five others despatched to the seaside, each with a large kettle, in order to begin the manufacture of salt. The route to the seacoast is about seven miles in length, in a direction nearly west. Five miles of the distance is through thick wood varied with hills, ravines and swamps, though the land in general possesses a rich black mould. The remaining two miles is formed of open waving prairies of sand, with ridges running parallel to the river, and covered with green grass. The rest of the men were employed in making pickets and gates for our new fort. Although we had no sun, the weather was very warm.

Sunday, 29.—It rained the whole night, but ceased this morning, and but little rain fell in the course of the day; still the weather was cloudy and the wind high from the southeast. The Clatsop chief and his party left us, after begging for a great number of articles, which, as we could not spare them, we refused except a razor. We were employed all day in picketting the fort: in the evening a young Wahkaicum chief, with four men and two women, arrived with some dressed elk skin and wappatoo for sale. We purchased about a bushel and a half of those roots for some red beads, and small pieces of brass wire and old check. The chief too made us a present of half a bushel more, for which we gave him a medal, and a piece of ribbon, to tie round his hat. These roots are extremely grateful, since our meat has become spoiled, and we were desirous of purchasing the remainder; but the chief would not dispose of any more, as he was on his way to trade with the Clátsops. They remained with us however till the next day,

Monday, 30, when they were joined by four more of their countrymen, from the Wahkiacum village. These last began by offering us some roots; but as we had now learned that they always expect three or four times as much in return, as the real value of the articles, and are even dissatisfied with that, we declined such dangerous presents. Towards evening the hunters brought in four elk, and after a long course of abstinence and miserable diet, we had a most sumptuous supper of elk's tongues and marrow. Besides this agreeable repast, the state of the weather had been quite exhilarating. It had rained during the night, but in the morning, though the high wind continued, we enjoyed the fairest and most pleasant weather since our arrival; the sun having shone at intervals, and there being only three showers in the course of the day. By sunset we had completed the fortification, and now announced to the Indians that every day at that hour the gates would be closed, and they must leave the fort and not enter it till sunrise. The Wahkiacums, who had remained with us, and who are very forward in their deportment, complied very reluctantly with this order; but being excluded from our houses, formed a camp near us.

Tuesday, 31.—As if it were impossible to have

twenty-four hours of pleasant weather, the sky last evening clouded, and the rain began and continued through the day. In the morning there came down two canoes, one from the Wahkiacum village, the other contained three men and a squaw of the Skilloot nation. They brought wappatoo, and shanataque roots, dried fish, mats made of flags and rushes, dressed elk skins and tobacco; for which, particularly the skins, they asked a very extravagant price. We purchased some wappatoo, and a little tobacco, very much like that we had seen among the Shoshonees, put up in small neat bags made of rushes. These we obtained in exchange for a few articles, among which fish-hooks are the most esteemed. One of the Skilloots brought a gun which wanted some repair, and having put it in order, we received from him a present of about a peck of wappatoo; we then gave him a piece of sheep skin and blue cloth, to cover the lock, and he very thankfully offered a further present of roots. There is, in fact, an obvious superiority in these Skilloots over the Wahkiacums, who are intrusive, thievish, and impertinent. Our new regulations, however, and the appearance of the sentinel, have improved the behaviour of all our Indian visitors. They left the fort before sunset, even without being ordered.

Besides the fleas, we observe a number of insects in motion to-day. Snakes are yet to be seen; snails too, without covers, are common. On the rivers, and along the shores of Meriwether's bay, are many kinds of large water fowls, but at this period they are excessively wild. The early part of the night was fair.

Wednesday, January 1, 1806.—We were awaked at an early hour, by a discharge of a volley of small arms, to salute the new year. This is the only mode of doing honour to the day which our situation permits, for though we have reason to be gayer than we were at Christmas, our only dainties are the boiled elk and wappatoo, enlivened by draughts of pure water. We were visited by a few Clatsops, who came by water, bringing roots and berries for sale. Among this nation we have observed a man about twenty-five years old, of a much lighter complexion than the Indians generally: his face was even freckled, and his hair long, and of a colour inclining to red. He was in habits and manners perfectly Indian; but, though he did not speak a word of English, he seemed to understand more than the others of his party; and, as we could obtain no account of his origin, we concluded that one of his parents, at least, must have been completely white.

These Indians stayed with us during the night, and left the fort next morning,

Thursday 2, having disposed of their cargo for fishing-hooks and other trifling articles. The hunters brought in two elk, and we obtained from the traps another. This animal, as well as the beaver and the raccoon, are in plenty near the seacoast, and along the small creeks and rivers as high as the grand rapids, and in this country possess an extremely good fur.

The birds which most strike our attention are the large as well as the small or whistling swan, the sandhill crane, the large and small geese, cormorants, brown and white brant, duck and mallard, the canvass and several other species of ducks. There is also a small crow, the blue crested corvus, and the smaller corvus with a white breast, the little brown wren, a large brown sparrow, the bald eagle, and the beautiful buzzard of the Columbia. All these wild fowl continue with us, though they are not in such numbers as on our first arrival in this neighbourhood.

Friday 4.—At eleven o'clock we were visited by our neighbour the Fia, or chief Comowool, who is also called Coone, and six Clatsops. Besides roots, and berries, they brought for sale three dogs and some fresh blubber. Having been so long accustomed to live on the flesh of dogs, the greater part of us have acquired a fondness for it, and our original aversion for it is overcome, by reflecting that while we subsisted on that food we were fatter, stronger, and in general enjoyed better health than at any period since leaving the buffalo country eastward of the mountains. The blubber, which is esteemed by the Indians an excellent food, has been obtained, they tell us, from their neighbours the Killamucks, a nation who live on the seacoast to the southeast, and near one of whose villages a whale had recently been thrown and foundered. Three of the hunters who had been despatched on the 28th, returned about dark; they had been fifteen miles up the river to the east of us, which falls into Meriwether's bay, and had hunted a considerable distance to the east; but they had not been able to kill more than a single deer, and a few fowls, scarcely sufficient for their subsistence; an incident which teaches us the necessity of keeping out several parties of hunters, in order to procure a supply against any exigency.

Saturday 4.—Comowool left us this morning with his party, highly pleased with a present of an old pair of satin breeches. The hunters were all sent in different directions, and we are now becoming more anxious for their success since our store of wappatoo is all exhausted.

Sunday 5.—Two of the five men who had been

despatched to make salt returned. They had carefully examined the coast, but it was not till the fifth day after their departure that they discovered a convenient situation for their manufacture. At length they formed an establishment about fifteen miles southwest of the fort, near some scattered houses of the Clatsop and Killamuck nation, where they erected a comfortable camp, and had killed a stock of provisions. The Indians had treated them very kindly, and made them a present of the blubber of the whale, some of which the men brought home. It was white and not unlike the fat of pork, though of a coarser and more spongy texture, and on being cooked was found to be tender and palatable, and in flavour resembling the beaver. The men also brought with them a gallon of the salt, which was white, fine, and very good, but not so strong as the rock salt common to the western parts of the United States. It proves to be a most agreeable addition to our food, and as the saltmakers can manufacture three or four quarts a day, we have a prospect of a very plentiful supply. The appearance of the whale seemed to be a matter of importance to all the neighbouring Indians, and as we might be able to procure some of it for ourselves, or at least purchase blubber from the Indians, a small parcel of merchandise was prepared, and a party of the men held in readiness to set out in the morning. As soon as this resolution was known, Chaboneau and his wife requested that they might be permitted to accompany us. The poor woman stated very earnestly that she had travelled a great way with us to see the great water, yet she had never been down to the coast, and now that this monstrous fish was also to be seen, it seemed hard that she should not be permitted to see neither the ocean nor the whale. So reasonable a request could not be denied; they were therefore suffered to accompany captain Clark, who,

Monday 6, after an early breakfast set out with twelve men in two canoes. He proceeded down the Netul into Meriwether bay, intending to go to the Clatsop town, and there procure a guide through the creeks, which there was reason to believe communicated not only with the bay, but with a small river running towards the sea, near where our saltmakers were encamped. Before however he could reach the Clatsop village, the high wind from the northwest compelled him to put into a small creek. He therefore resolved to attempt the passage without a guide, and proceeded up the creek three miles, to some high open land where he found a road. He therefore left the canoes, and followed the path over three deep marshes to a pond about a mile long, and two hundred yards wide. He kept on the left of this pond, and at length came to the creek which he had crossed on a raft, when he had visited Cuscalah's village on the ninth of December. He proceeded down it, till he found a small canoe, fit to hold three persons, in which the whole party crossed the creek. Here they saw a herd of elk, and the men were divided into small parties, and hunted them till after dark, when they met again at the forks of the river. Three of the elk were wounded, but night prevented their taking more than one, which was brought to the camp, and cooked with some sticks of pine which had drifted down the creeks. The weather was beautiful, the sky clear, the moon shone brightly, a circumstance the more agreeable as this is the first fair evening we have enjoyed for two months.

CHAPTER XXII.

A party, headed by captain Clark, go in quest of a whale driven on the shore of the Pacific to obtain some of the oil—They pass Clatsop river, which is described—The perilous nature of this jaunt, and the grandeur of the scenery described—Indian mode of extracting whale oil—The life of one of captain Clark's party preserved by the kindness of an Indian woman—A short account of the Chinnooks, of the Clatsops, Killamucks, the Lucktons, and an enumeration of several other tribes—The manner of sepulchre among the Chinnooks, Clatsops, &c.—Description of their weapons of war and hunting—Their mode of building houses—Their manufactures, and cookery—Their mode of making canoes—Their great dexterity in managing that vehicle.

Tuesday, 7.—There was a frost this morning. We rose early, and taking eight pounds of flesh, which were all the remains of the elk, proceeded up the south fork of the creek. At the distance of two miles we found a pine tree, which had been felled by one of our saltmakers, and on which we crossed the deepest part of the creek, and waded through the rest. We then went over an open ridgy prairie, three quarters of a mile, to the seabeach; after following which for three miles, we came to the mouth of a beautiful river, with a bold, rapid current, eighty-five yards wide, and three feet deep, in its shallowest crossings. On its northeast side are the remains of an old village of Clatsops, inhabited by only a single family, who appeared miserably poor and dirty. We gave a man two fish-hooks, to ferry the party over the river, which, from the tribe on its banks, we called Clatsop river. The creek which we had passed on a tree, approaches this river within about an hundred yards, and by means of a portage, supplies a

communication with the villages near Point
Adams. After going on for two miles, we found
the saltmakers encamped near four houses of Clatsops and Killamucks, who, though poor, dirty,
and covered with fleas, seemed kind and well disposed. We persuaded a young Indian, by a present of a file, and a promise of some other articles,
to guide us to the spot where the whale lay. He
led us for two and a half miles over the round
slippery stones at the foot of a high hill projecting
into the sea, and then suddenly stopping, and
uttering the word peshack or bad, explained by
signs that we could no longer follow the coast,
but must cross the mountain. This promised to
be a most laborious undertaking, for the side is
nearly perpendicular, and the top lost in clouds.
He, however, followed an Indian path which
wound along as much as possible, but still the
ascent was so steep, that at one place we drew
ourselves for about an hundred feet by means of
bushes and roots. At length, after two hours'
labour, we reached the top of the mountain, where
we looked down with astonishment on the prodigious height of ten or twelve hundred feet, which
we had ascended. Immediately below us, in the
face of this precipice, is a stratum of white earth,
used, as our guide informed us, as a paint by the
neighbouring Indians. It obviously contains
argile, and resembles the earth of which the
French porcelain is made, though whether it
contains silex or magnesia, or in what propor-
tions, we could not observe. We were here met
by fourteen Indians, loaded with oil and blubber,
the spoils of the whale, which they were carrying
in very heavy burdens, over this rough mountain.
On leaving them, we proceeded over a bad road
till night, when we encamped on a small run. we

were all much fatigued, but the weather was pleasant, and, for the first time since our arrival here, an entire day has passed without rain. In the morning,

Wednesday, 8, we set out early and proceeded to the top of the mountain, the highest point of which is an open spot facing the ocean. It is situated about thirty miles southeast of cape Disappointment, and projects nearly two and a half miles into the sea. Here one of the most delightful views in nature presents itself. Immediately in front is the ocean, which breaks with fury on the coast, from the rocks of cape Disappointment as far as the eye can discern to the northwest, and against the highlands and irregular piles of rock which diversify the shore to the southeast. To this boisterous scene, the Columbia, with its tributary waters, widening into bays as it approaches the ocean, and studded on both sides with the Chinnook and Clatsop villages, forms a charming contrast; while immediately beneath our feet, are stretched the rich prairies, enlivened by three beautiful streams, which conduct the eye to small lakes at the foot of the hills. We stopped to enjoy the romantic view from this place, which we distinguished by the name of Clark's Point of View, and then followed our guide down the mountain. The descent was steep and dangerous: in many places the hill sides, which are formed principally of yellow clay, has been washed by the late rains, and is now slipping into the sea, in large masses of fifty and an hundred acres. In other parts, the path crosses the rugged perpendicular rocks which overhang the sea, into which a false step would have precipitated us. The mountains are covered with a very thick growth of timber, chiefly pine and fir; some of which, near

302

Clark's Point of View, perfectly sound and solid, rise to the height of two hundred and ten feet, and are from eight to twelve in diameter. Intermixed is the white cedar, or arbor vitae, and a small quantity of black alder, two or three feet thick, and sixty or seventy in height. At length we reached a single house, the remains of an old Killamuck village, situated among some rocks, in a bay immediately on the coast. We then continued for two miles along the sand beach; and after crossing a creek, eighty yards in width, near which are five cabins, reached the place where the waves had thrown the whale on shore. The animal had been placed between two Killamuck villages, and such had been their industry, that there now remained nothing more than the skeleton, which we found to be one hundred and five feet in length. Captain Clark then returned to the village of five huts, on the creek, to which he gave the name of Ecola, or Whale creek. The natives were all busied in boiling the blubber, in a large square trough of wood, by means of heated stones, and preserving the oil, thus extracted, in bladders and the entrails of the whale. The refuse of the blubber, which still contained a portion of oil, are hung up in large flitches, and when wanted for use, are warmed on a wooden spit before the fire, and eaten either alone, or dipped in oil, or with roots of the rush and shanataque. These Killamucks, though they had great quantities, parted with it reluctantly, and at such high prices, that our whole stock of merchandise was exhausted in the purchase of about three hundred pounds of blubber, and a few gallons of oil. With these we set out to return; and having crossed Ecola creek, encamped on its bank, where there was abundance of fine timber. We were soon joined by the men of the village, with whom we smoked, and who gave us all the information they possessed, relative to their country. These Killamucks are part of a much larger nation of the same name, and they now reside chiefly in four villages, each at the entrance of a creek, all of which fall into a bay on the southwest coast; that at which we now are, being the most northern, and at the distance of about forty-five miles southeast of Point Adams. The rest of the nation are scattered along the coast, and on the banks of a river, which, as we found it in their delineations, we called Killamuck's river, emptying itself in the same direction. During the salmon season they catch great quantities of that fish, in the small creeks, and when they fail, their chief resource was the sturgeon and other fish stranded along the coast. The elk were very numerous in the mountains, but they could not procure many of them with their arrows; and their principal communication with strangers, was by means of the Killamuck river, up which they passed to the Shocatilcum (or Columbia) to trade for wappatoo roots. In their dress, appearance, and indeed every circumstance of life, they differ very little from the Chinnooks, Clatsops, and other nations in the neighbourhood. The chief variation we have observed is in the manner of burying the dead; the bodies being secured in an oblong box of plank, which is placed in an open canoe, lying on the ground, with a paddle, and other small articles of the deceased by his side.

Whilst smoking with the Indians, captain Clark was surprised about ten o'clock by a loud shrill outcry from the opposite village; on hearing which, all the Indians immediately started up to cross the creek, and the guide informed him that some one had been killed. On examination, one of the men was discovered to be absent, and a guard despatched, who met him crossing the creek in great haste. An Indian belonging to another band, and who happened to be with the Killamucks that evening, had treated him with much kindness, and walked arm in arm with him to a tent where our man found a Chinnook squaw, who was an old acquaintance. From the conversation and manner of the stranger, this woman discovered that his object was to murder the white man, for the sake of the few articles on his person, and when he rose, and pressed our man to go to another tent where they would find something better to eat, she held M'Neal by the blanket; not knowing her object, he freed himself from her, and was going on with his pretended friend, when she ran out and gave the shriek which brought the men of the village over, and the stranger ran off before M'Neal knew what had occasioned the alarm.

Thursday, 9.—The morning was fine, the wind from the northeast; and having divided our stock of the blubber, we began at sunrise to retread our steps, in order to reach fort Clatsop, at the distance of thirty-five miles. We met several parties of Indians on their way to trade for blubber and oil with the Killamucks; (our route lay across the same mountains which we had already passed) we also overtook a party returning from the village, and could not but regard with astonishment the heavy loads which the women carry over these fatiguing and dangerous paths. As one of the women was descending a steep part of the mountain, her load slipped from her back, and she stood holding it by a strap with one hand, and with the other supporting herself by a bush: captain Clark being near her, undertook to replace the load, and found it almost as much as he could lift, and above one hundred pounds in weight. Loaded as they were, they kept pace with us, till we reached the saltmakers' tents, where we passed the night, while they continued their route.

Friday, 10.—We proceeded across Clatsop river, to the place where we had left our canoes; and as the tide was coming in, immediately embarked for the fort, at which place we arrived about ten o'clock at night. During their absence, the men had been occupied in hunting and dressing skins, but in this they were not very successful, as the deer have become scarce, and are, indeed, seen chiefly near the prairies and open grounds, along the coast. This morning, however, there came to the fort twelve Indians, in a large canoe. They are of the Cathlamah nation, our nearest neighbours above, on the south side of the river. The tia, or chief, whose name was Shahawacap, having been absent on a hunting excursion, as we passed his village, had never yet seen us, and we therefore showed him the honours of our country, as well as our reduced finances would permit. We invested him with a small medal, and received a present of Indian tobacco and a basket of wappatoo in return, for which we gave him a small piece of our tobacco, and thread for a fishing net. They had brought dried salmon, wappatoo, dogs, and mats made of rushes and flags: but we bought only some dogs and wappatoo. These Cathlamahs speak the same language as the Chinnooks and Clatsops, whom they also resemble in dress and manners.

Saturday, 11.—A party was sent out to bring in some elk killed yesterday, and several were despatched after our Indian canoe, which drifted away last night; but, though the whole neighbourhood was diligently searched, we were unable to find it. This is a serious loss, as she is much superior to our own canoes, and so light that four men can carry her readily without fatigue, though she will carry from ten to twelve hundred pounds, besides a crew of four. In the evening the Cathlamahs left us, on their way to barter their wappatoo with the Clatsops, for some blubber and oil, which these last have procured from the Killamucks, in exchange for beads and other articles.

Sunday, 12.—Our meat is now becoming scarce; we, therefore, determined to jerk it, and issue it in small quantities, instead of dividing it among the four messes, and leaving to each the care of its own provisions; a plan by which much is lost, in consequence of the improvidence of the men. Two hunters had been despatched in the morning, and one of them, Drewyer, had before evening, killed seven elk. We should scarcely be able to subsist, were it not for the exertions of this most excellent hunter. The game is scarce, and nothing is now to be seen, except elk, which to almost all the men, are very difficult to be procured: but Drewyer, who is the offspring of a Canadian Frenchman, and an Indian woman, has passed his life in the woods, and unites, in a wonderful degree, the dexterous aim of the frontier huntsman, with the intuitive sagacity of the Indian, in pursuing the faintest tracks through the forest. All our men, however, have indeed, become so expert with the rifle, that we are never under apprehensions as to food, since, whenever there is game of any kind, we are almost certain of procuring it.

Monday, 13.—Captain Lewis took all the men who could be spared, and brought in the seven elk, which they had found untouched by the

wolves, of which there are a few in the neighbourhood. The last of the candles which we brought
with us being exhausted, we now began to make
others of elk tallow. From all that we have seen
and learnt of the Chinnooks, we have been induced
to estimate the nation at about twenty-eight
houses, and four hundred souls. They reside
chiefly along the banks of a river, to which we
gave the same name; and which, running parallel
to the seacoast, waters a low country with many
stagnant ponds, and then empties itself into
Haley's bay. The wild fowl of these ponds, and
the elk and deer of the neighbourhood, furnish
them with occasional luxuries; but their chief subsistence is derived from the salmon and other fish,
which are caught in the small streams, by means
of nets and gigs, or thrown on shore by the violence of the tide. To these are added some roots,
such as the wild liquorice, which is the most common, the shanataque, and the wappatoo, brought
down the river by the traders.

The men are low in stature, rather ugly, and ill
made; their legs being small and crooked, their
feet large, and their heads, like those of the
women, flattened in a most disgusting manner.
These deformities are in part concealed by robes
made of sea-otter, deer, elk, beaver, or fox skins.
They also employ in their dress, robes of the skin
of a cat peculiar to this country, and of another
animal of the same size, which is light and durable, and sold at a high price by the Indians, who
bring it from above. In addition to these are
worn blankets, wrappers of red, blue, or spotted
cloth, and some old sailors' clothes, which were
very highly prized. The greater part of the men
have guns, powder, and ball.

The women have, in general, handsome faces,

but are low and disproportioned, with small feet and large legs and thighs, occasioned, probably, by strands of beads, or various strings, drawn so tight above the ankles, as to prevent the circulation of the blood. Their dress, like that of the Wahkiacums, consists of a short robe, and a tissue of cedar bark. Their hair hangs loosely down the shoulders and back; and their ears, neck, and wrists are ornamented with blue beads. Another decoration which is very highly prized, consists of figures made by puncturing the arms or legs; and on the arm of one of the squaws, we observed the name of J. Bowman, executed in the same way. In language, habits, and in almost every other particular, they resemble the Clatsops, Cathlamahs, and indeed all the people near the mouth of the Columbia. They, however, seem to be inferior to their neighbours in honesty as well as spirit. No ill treatment or indignity, on our part, seems to excite any feeling, except fear; nor, although better provided than their neighbours with arms, have they enterprise enough to use them advantageously against the animals of the forest, nor offensively against their neighbours; who owe their safety more to the timidity than the forbearance of the Chinnooks. We had heard instances of pilfering whilst we were amongst them, and therefore had a general order, excluding them from our encampment; so that whenever an Indian wished to visit us, he began by calling out "No Chinnook." It may be probable that this first impression left a prejudice against them, since when we were among the Clatsops, and other tribes at the mouth of the Columbia, the Indians had less opportunity of stealing, if they were so disposed.

Tuesday, 14, we were employed in jerking the meat of the elk, and searching for one of the

309

canoes which had been carried off by the tide last night. Having found it, we now had three of them drawn up out of reach of the water, and the other secured by a strong cord, so as to be ready for any emergency.

After many inquiries and much observation, we are at length enabled to obtain a connected view of the nations, who reside along the coast, on both sides of the Columbia.

To the south, our personal observation has not extended beyond the Killamucks; but we obtained from those who were acquainted with the sea-coast, a list of the Indian tribes, in the order in which they succeed each other, to a considerable distance. The first nation to the south are the Clatsops, who reside on the southern side of the bay, and along the seacoast, on both sides of Point Adams. They are represented as the remains of a much larger nation; but about four years ago, a disorder, to which till then they were strangers, but which seems, from their description, to have been the small-pox, destroyed four chiefs, and several hundreds of the nation. These are deposited in canoes, a few miles below us on the bay, and the survivors do not number more than fourteen houses, and about two hundred souls. Next to them along the southeast coast, is a much larger nation, the Killamucks, who number fifty houses, and a thousand souls. Their first establishment are the four huts at the mouth of Ecola creek, thirty-five miles from Point Adams; and two miles below are a few more huts; but the principal town is situated twenty miles lower, at the entrance of a creek, called Nielee, into the bay, which we designate by the name of Killamucks bay. Into the same bay empties a second creek, five miles further, where is a Killamuck village, called Kilherhurst; at two miles a third creek, and a town called Kilherner; and at the same distance a town called *Chishuck*, at the mouth of Killamuck river. Towerquotton and *Chucktin*, are the names of two other towns, situated on creeks which empty into the bottom of the bay, the last of which is seventy miles from Point Adams. The Killamuck river is about one hundred yards wide, and very rapid; but having no perpendicular fall, is the great avenue for trade. There are two small villages of Killamucks settled above its mouth, and the whole trading part of the tribe ascend it, till by a short portage, they carry their canoes over to the Columbian valley, and descend the Multnomah to Wappatoo island. Here they purchase roots, which they carry down the Chockalilum or Columbia; and, after trafficking with the tribes on its banks for the various articles which they require, either return up the Columbia, or cross over through the country of the Clatsops. This trade, however, is obviously little more than a loose and irregular barter, on a very small scale; for the materials for commerce are so extremely scanty and precarious, that the stranding of a whale was an important commercial incident, which interested all the adjoining country. The Killamucks have little peculiar, either in character or manners, and resemble, in almost every particular, the Clatsops and Chinnooks.

Adjoining the Killamucks, and in a direction S. S. E. are the Lucktons, a small tribe inhabiting the seacoast. They speak the same language as the Killamucks, but do not belong to the same nation. The same observation applies to the Kahunkle nation, their immediate neighbours, who are supposed to consist of about four hundred souls.

The Lickawis, a still more numerous nation, who have a large town of eight hundred souls.

The Youkone nation, who live in very large houses, and number seven hundred souls.

The Necketo nation, of the same number of persons.

The Ulseah nation, a small town of one hundred and fifty souls.

The Youitts, a tribe who live in a small town, containing not more than one hundred and fifty souls.

·The Shiastuckle nation, who have a large town of nine hundred souls.

The Killawats nation of five hundred souls collected into one large town.

With this last nation ends the language of the Killamucks: and the coast, which then turns towards the southwest, is occupied by nations whose languages vary from that of the Killamucks, and from each other. Of these, the first in order are,

The Cookoooose, a large nation of one thousand five hundred souls, inhabiting the shore of the Pacific and the neighbouring mountains. We have seen several of this nation who were taken prisoners by the Clatsops and Killamucks. Their complexion was much fairer than that of the Indians near the mouth of the Columbia, and their heads were not flattened. Next to these are,

The Shalalahs, of whom we know nothing, except their numbers, which are computed at twelve hundred souls. Then follow,

The Luckasos, of about the same number, and

The Hannakalals, whom we estimate at six hundred souls.

This is the extent of the Indian information, and judging, as we can do, with considerable accuracy from the number of sleeps, or days journey, the distance which these tribes occupy along the coast, may be estimated at three hundred and sixty miles.

On the north of the Columbia, we have already seen the Chinnooks, of four hundred souls, along the shores of Haley's bay, and the low grounds on Chinnook river. Their nearest neighbours to the northeast are

The Killaxthokle, a small nation on the coast, of not more than eight houses, and a hundred souls. To these succeed

The Chilts, who reside above Point Lewis, and who are estimated at seven hundred souls, and thirty-eight houses. Of this nation, we saw, transiently, a few among the Chinnooks, from whom they did not appear to differ. Beyond the Chilts we have seen none of the northwest Indians, and all that we learnt, consisted of an enumeration of their names and numbers. The nations next to the Chilts, are

The Clamoitomish, of twelve houses, and two hundred and sixty souls.

The Potoashees, of ten houses, and two hundred souls.

The Pailsk, of ten houses, and two hundred souls.

The Quinults, of sixty houses, and one thousand souls.

The Chillates, of eight houses, and one hundred and fifty souls.

The Calasthorte, of ten houses, and two hundred souls.

The Quinnechant, consisting of two thousand souls.

A particular detail of the characters, manners, and habits of the tribes, must be left to some future adventurers, who may have more leisure and a better opportunity than we had to accomplish this object. Those who first visit the ground, can only be expected to furnish sketches rude and imperfect.

Wednesday, 15.—Two hunting parties intended setting out this morning, but they were prevented by incessant rain, which confined us all to the fort.

The Chinnooks, Clatsops, and most of the adjoining nations dispose of the dead in canoes. For this purpose a scaffold is erected, by fixing perpendicularly in the ground four long pieces of split timber. These are placed two by two just wide enough apart to admit the canoe, and sufficiently long to support its two extremities. The boards are connected by a bar of wood run through them at the height of six feet, on which is placed a small canoe containing the body of the deceased, carefully wrapped in a robe of dressed skins, with a paddle, and some articles belonging to the deceased, by his side. Over this canoe is placed one of a larger size, reversed, with its gunwale resting on the crossbars, so as to cover the body completely. One or more large mats of rushes or flags are then rolled round the canoes, and the whole secured by cords usually made of the bark of the white cedar. On these crossbars are hung different articles of clothing, or culinary utensils. The method practised by the Killamucks differs somewhat from this; the body being deposited in an oblong box, of plank, which, with the paddle, and other articles, is placed in a canoe, resting on the ground. With the religious opinions of these people we are but little acquainted, since we understand their language too imperfectly to converse on a subject so abstract; but it is obvious, from the different deposits which they place by their dead, that they believe in a future state of existence.*

Thursday, 16.—To-day we finished curing our meat, and having now a plentiful supply of elk, and salt, and our houses dry and comfortable, we wait patiently for the moment of resuming our journey.

The implements used in hunting, by the Clatsops, Chinnooks, and other neighbouring nations, are the gun, bow and arrow, deadfall, pits, snares, and spears or gigs. The guns are generally old American or British muskets repaired for this trade; and although there are some good pieces among them, they are constantly out of order, as the Indians have not been sufficiently accustomed to arms to understand the management of them. The powder is kept in small japanned tin flasks, in which the traders sell it; and when the ball or shot fails, they make use of gravel or pieces of metal from their pots, without being sensible of the injury done to their guns. These arms are reserved for hunting elk, and the few deer and bears in this neighbourhood; but as they have no rifles, they are not very successful hunters. The most common weapon is the bow and arrow, with which every man is provided, even though he carries a gun, and which is used in every kind of hunting. The bow is extremely neat, and being very thin and flat, possesses great elasticity. It is made of the heart of the white cedar, about two feet and a half in length, two inches wide at the

---

* This fact is much too equivocal to warrant an inference so important. These deposits might have been intended for nothing more than the testimonials of surviving affection. Amongst those savages, where the language was better understood, it does not appear, that the Indians intended any thing more by such sacrifices than to testify their reverence for the dead.—EDITOR.

centre, whence it tapers to the width of half an inch at the extremities; and the back is covered with the sinews of elk, fastened on by means of a glue made from the sturgeon. The string is formed of the same sinews. The arrow generally consists of two parts; the first is about twenty inches long, and formed of light white pine, with the feather at one end, and at the other a circular hole, which receives the second part, formed of some harder wood, and about five inches long, and secured in its place by means of sinews. The barb is either stone, or else of iron or copper, in which latter place, the angle is more obtuse than any we have seen. If, as sometimes happens, the arrow is formed of a single piece, the whole is of a more durable wood, but the form just described is preferred; because, as much of the game consists of wild fowl, on the ponds, it is desirable that they should be constructed so as to float, if they fall into the water. These arrows are kept in a quiver of elk or young bear skin, opening not at the ends, as the common quivers, but at the sides; which, for those who hunt in canoes, is much more convenient. These weapons are not, however, very powerful, for many of the elk we kill have been wounded with them; and, although the barb with the small end of the arrows remain, yet the flesh closes, and the animal suffers no permanent injury. The deadfalls and snares are used in taking the wolf, the raccoon, and the fox, of which there are, however, but few in this country. The spear or gig employed in pursuit of the sea-otter, (which they call spuck) the common otter, and beaver, consists of two points of barbs, and is like those already described, as common among the Indians on the upper part of the Columbia. The pits are chiefly for the elk, and are therefore usually large and deep cubes of twelve or fourteen feet in depth, and are made by the side of some fallen tree lying across the path frequented by the elk: They are covered with slender boughs and moss, and the elk either sinks into it as he approaches the tree, or in leaping over the tree, falls into the pit on the other side.

Friday 17.—Comowool and seven other Clatsops spent the day with us. He made us a present of some roots and berries, and in return we gave him an awl and some thread, which he wanted for the purpose of making a net. We were not able to purchase any more of their provisions, the prices being too high for our exhausted stock of merchandise. One of the Indians was dressed in three very elegant skins of the sea-otter: for these we were very desirous of trafficking; but he refused every exchange except that of blue beads, of which he asked six fathom for each skin, and as we had only four fathom left, he would not accept for the remaining two, either a knife, or any quantity of beads of another sort.

In fishing, the Clatsops, Chinnooks and other nations near this place employ the common straight net, the scooping or dipping net with a long handle, the gig, and the hook and line. The first is of different lengths and depths, and used in taking salmon, char, and trout, in the deep inlets among the marshy grounds, and the mouths of deep creeks. The scooping net is used for small fish in the spring and summer season; and in both kinds the net is formed of silk grass, or the bark of white cedar. The gig is used at all seasons, and for all kinds of fish they can procure with it; so too is the hook and line, of which the line is made of the same material as the net, and the hook generally brought by the traders; though before the whites came, they made hooks out of two small pieces of bone, resembling the European hook, but with a much more acute angle, where the two pieces were joined.

Saturday 18.—We were all occupied in dressing skins, and preparing clothes for our journey homewards. The houses in this neighbourhood are all large wooden buildings, varying in length from twenty to sixty feet, and from fourteen to twenty in width. They are constructed in the following manner. Two posts of split timber or more, agreeably to the number of partitions, are sunk in the ground, above which they rise to the height of fourteen or eighteen feet. They are hollowed at the top, so as to receive the ends of a round beam or pole, stretching from one to the other, and forming the upper point of the roof for the whole extent of the building. On each side of this range is placed another, which forms the eaves of the house, and is about five feet high; but as the building is often sunk to the depth of four or five feet, the eaves come very near the surface of the earth. Smaller pieces of timber are now extended by pairs, in the form of rafters, from the lower to the upper beam, where they are attached at both ends with cords of cedar bark. On these rafters two or three ranges of small poles are placed horizontally, and secured in the same way with strings of cedar bark. The sides are now made with a range of wide boards, sunk a small distance into the ground, with the upper ends projecting above the poles at the eaves, to which they are secured by a beam passing outside, parallel with the eave-poles, and tied by cords of cedar bark passing through holes made in the boards at certain distances. The gable ends and partitions are formed in the same way, being fastened by beams on the outside, parallel to the rafters. The roof is then covered with a double range of thin boards, except an aperture of two or three feet in the centre, for the smoke to pass through. The entrance is by a small hole, cut out of the boards, and just large enough to admit the body. The very largest houses only are divided by partitions, for though three or four families reside in the same room, there is quite space enough for all of them. In the centre of each room is a space six or eight feet square, sunk to the depth of twelve inches below the rest of the floor, and enclosed by four pieces of square timber. Here they make the fire, for which purpose pine bark is generally preferred. Around this fireplace, mats are spread, and serve as seats during the day, and very frequently as beds at night; there is however a more permanent bed made, by fixing, in two or sometimes three sides of the room, posts reaching from the roof down to the ground, and at the distance of four feet from the wall. From these posts to the wall itself, one or two ranges of boards are placed so as to form shelves, on which they either sleep, or where they stow away their various articles of merchandise. The uncured fish is hung in the smoke of their fires, as is also the flesh of the elk, when they are fortunate enough to procure any, which is but rarely.

Sunday 20.—This morning we sent out two parties of hunters in different directions. Soon after we were visited by two Clatsop men and a woman, who brought several articles to trade: we purchased a small quantity of train oil for a pair of brass armbands, and succeeded in obtaining a sea-otter skin, for which we gave our only remaining four fathoms of blue beads, the same quantity of white ones, and a knife: we gave a fish-hook also in exchange for one of their hats. These are made of cedar bark and bear-grass, interwoven together in the form of an European hat, with a small brim of about two inches, and a high crown, widening upwards. They are light, ornamented with various colours and figures, and being nearly water-proof, are much more durable than either chip or straw hats. These hats form a small article of traffic with the whites, and the manufacture is one of the best exertions of Indian industry. They are, however, very dexterous in making a variety of domestic utensils, among which are bowls, spoons, skewers, spits, and baskets. The bowl or trough is of different shapes, sometimes round, semicircular, in the form of a canoe, or cubic, and generally dug out of a single piece of wood, the larger vessels having holes in the sides by way of handle, and all executed with great neatness. In these vessels they boil their food, by throwing hot stones into the water, and extract oil from different animals in the same way. Spoons are not very abundant, nor is there any thing remarkable in their shape, except that they are large and the bowl broad. Meat is roasted on one end of a sharp skewer, placed erect before the fire, with the other fixed in the ground. The spit for fish is split at the top into two parts, between which the fish is placed, cut open, with its sides extended by means of small splinters. The usual plate is a small mat of rushes or flags, on which every thing is served. The instrument with which they dig up roots, is a strong stick, about three feet and a half long, sharpened and a little curved at the lower end, while the upper is inserted into a handle, standing transversely, and made of part of an elk or buck's horn. But the most curious workmanship is that of the basket. It is formed of cedar bark and bear-grass, so closely interwoven, that it is water tight, without the aid of either gum or resin. The form is generally conic, or rather the segment of a cone, of which the smaller end is the bottom of the basket; and being made of all sizes, from that of the smallest cup to the capacity of five or six gallons, answer the double purpose of a covering for the head or to contain water. Some of them are highly ornamented with strands of bear-grass, woven into figures of various colours, which require great labour; yet they are made very expeditiously and sold for a trifle. It is for the construction of these baskets, that the bear-grass forms an article of considerable traffic. It grows only near the snowy region of the high mountains, and the blade, which is two feet long and about three-eighths of an inch wide, is smooth, strong and pliant; the young blades particularly, from their not being exposed to the sun and air, have an appearance of great neatness, and are generally preferred. Other bags and baskets, not water-proof, are made of cedar bark, silk-grass, rushes, flags, and common coarse sedge, for the use of families. In the manufactures, as well as in the ordinary work of the house, the instrument most in use is a knife, or rather a dagger. The handle of it is small, and has a strong loop of twine for the thumb, to prevent its being wrested from the hand. On each side is a blade, double-edged and pointed; the longer from nine to ten inches, the shorter from four to five. This knife is carried about habitually in the hand, sometimes exposed, but mostly when in company with strangers, put under the robe.

Monday, 20.—We were visited by three Clatsops, who came merely for the purpose of smoking and conversing with us. We have now only three days' provision, yet so accustomed have the men become to live sparingly, and fast occasionally, that such a circumstance excites no concern, as we all calculate on our dexterity as hunters. The industry of the Indians is not confined to household utensils: the great proof of their skill is the construction of their canoes. In a country, indeed, where so much of the intercourse between different tribes is carried on by water, the ingenuity of the people would naturally direct itself to the improvement of canoes, which would gradually become, from a mere safe conveyance, to an elegant ornament. We have accordingly seen, on the Columbia, canoes of many forms, beginning with the simple boats near the mountains, to those more highly decorated, because more useful nearer the mouth of the Columbia. Below the grand cataract there are four forms of canoes: the first and smallest is about fifteen feet long, and calculated for one or two persons: it is, indeed, by no means remarkable in its structure, and is chiefly employed by the Cathlamahs and Wahkiacums among the marshy islands. The second is from twenty to thirty-five feet long, about two and a half or three feet in the beam, and two feet in the hold. It is chiefly remarkable in having the bowsprit, which rises to some height above the bow, formed by tapering gradually from the sides into a sharp point. Canoes of this shape are common to all the nations below the grand rapids.

But the canoes most used by the Columbia Indians, from the Chilluckittequaws inclusive, to the ocean, are about thirty or thirty-five feet long. The bow, which looks more like the stern of our boats, is higher than the other end, and is ornamented with a sort of comb, an inch in thickness, cut out of the same log which forms the canoe, and extending nine or eleven inches from the bowsprit to the bottom of the boat. The stern is nearly rounded off, and gradually ascends to a point. This canoe is very light and convenient; for though it will contain ten or twelve persons, it may be carried with great ease by four.

The fourth and largest species of canoe we did not meet till we reached tide-water, near the grand rapids below, in which place they are found among all the nations, especially the Killamucks, and others residing on the seacoast. They are upwards of fifty feet long, and will carry from eight to ten thousand pounds weight, or from twenty to thirty persons. Like all the canoes we have mentioned, they are cut out of a single trunk of a tree, which is generally white cedar, though the fir is sometimes used. The sides are secured by cross-bars, or round sticks, two or three inches in thickness, which are inserted through holes made just below the gunwale, and made fast with cords. The upper edge of the gunwale itself is about five-eighths of an inch thick, and four or five in breadth, and folds outwards, so as to form a kind of rim, which prevents the water from beating into the boat. The bow and stern are about the same height, and each provided with a comb, reaching to the bottom of the boat. At each end, also, are pedestals, formed of the same solid piece, on which are placed strange grotesque figures of men or animals, rising sometimes to the height of five feet, and composed of small pieces of wood, firmly united, with great ingenuity, by inlaying and mortising, without a spike of any kind. The paddle is usually from four feet and a half to five feet in length; the handle being thick for one third of its length, when it widens, and is hollowed and thinned on each side of the centre, which forms a sort of rib. When they embark, one Indian sits in the stern, and steers with a paddle, the others kneel in pairs in the bottom of the canoe, and sitting on their heels, paddle over the gunwale next to them. In this way they ride with perfect safety the highest waves, and venture without the least concern in seas, where other boats or seamen could not live an instant. They sit quietly and paddle, with no other movement; except, when any large wave throws the boat on her side, and, to the eye of a spectator, she seems lost: the man to windward then steadies her by throwing his body towards the upper side, and sinking his paddle deep into the wave, appears to catch the water and force it under the boat, which the same stroke pushes on with great velocity. In the management of these canoes the women are equally expert with the men; for in the smaller boats, which contain four oarsmen, the helm is generally given to the female. As soon as they land, the canoe is generally hauled on shore, unless she be very heavily laden; but at night the load is universally discharged, and the canoe brought on shore.

Our admiration of their skill in these curious constructions was increased by observing the very inadequate implements with which they are made. These Indians possess very few axes, and the only tool employed in their building, from felling of the tree to the delicate workmanship of the images, is a chisel made of an old file, about an inch or an inch and a half in width. Even of this too, they have not yet learnt the management, for the chisel is sometimes fixed in a large block of wood, and being held in the right hand, the block is pushed with the left without the aid of a mallet. But under all these disadvantages, these canoes, which one would suppose to be the work of years, are made in a few weeks. A canoe, however, is very highly prized: in traffic, it is an article of the greatest value, except a wife, which is of equal consideration; so that a lover generally gives a canoe to the father in exchange for his daughter.

CHAPTER XXIII.

An account of the Clatsops, Killamucks, Chinnooks and Cathlamahs—Their uniform custom of flattening the forehead—The dress of these savages, and their ornaments, described—The licensed prostitution of the women, married and unmarried, of which a ludicrous instance is given—The character of their diseases—The common opinion, that the treatment of women is the standard by which the virtues of an Indian may be known, combatted, and disproved by examples—The respect entertained by these Indians for old age, compared with the different conduct of those nations who subsist by the chase—Their mode of government—Their ignorance of ardent spirits, and their fondness for gambling—Their dexterity in traffic—In what articles their traffic consists—Their extraordinary attachment to blue beads, which forms their circulating medium.

Tuesday, 21.—Two of the hunters came back with three elk, which form a timely addition to our stock of provisions. The Indian visitors left us at twelve o'clock.

The Killamucks, Clatsops, Chinnooks, and Cathlamahs, the four neighbouring nations with whom we have had most intercourse, preserve a general resemblance in person, dress, and manners. They are commonly of a diminutive stature, badly shaped, and their appearance by no means prepossessing. They have broad thick flat feet, thick ankles, and crooked legs: the last of which deformities is to be ascribed, in part, to the universal practice of squatting, or sitting on the calves of their legs and heels, and also to the tight bandages of beads and strings worn round the ankles, by the women, which prevent the circulation of the blood, and render the legs, of the females, particularly, ill shaped and swollen. The complexion is the usual copper coloured brown of the North American tribes, though the complexion is rather lighter than that of the Indians of the Missouri, and the frontier of the United States: the mouth is wide and the lips thick; the nose of a moderate size, fleshy, wide at the extremities, with large nostrils, and generally low between the eyes, though there are rare instances of high aquiline noses; the eyes are generally black, though we occasionally see them of a dark yellowish brown, with a black pupil. But the most distinguishing part of their physiognomy, is the peculiar flatness and width of their forehead, a peculiarity which they owe to one of these customs by which nature is sacrificed to fantastic ideas of beauty. The custom, indeed, of flattening the head by artificial pressure during infancy, prevails among all the nations we have seen west of the Rocky mountains. To the east of that barrier, the fashion is so perfectly unknown, that there the western Indians, with the exception of the Alliatan or Snake nation, are designated by the common name of Flatheads. The singular usage, which nature could scarcely seem to suggest to remote nations, might perhaps incline us to believe in the common and not very ancient origin of all the western nations. Such an opinion might well accommodate itself with the fact, that while on the lower parts of the Columbia, both sexes are universally flatheads, the custom diminishes in receding eastward, from the common centre of the infection, till among the remoter tribes near the mountains, nature recovers her rights, and the wasted folly is confined to a few females. Such opinions, however, are corrected or weakened by considering that the flattening of the head is not, in fact, peculiar to that part of the continent, since it was among the first objects which struck the attention of Columbus.

But wherever it may have begun, the practice is now universal among these nations. Soon after the birth of her child, the mother, anxious to procure for her infant the recommendation of a broad forehead, places it in the compressing machine, where it is kept for ten or twelve months; though the females remain longer than the boys. The operation is so gradual, that it is not attended with pain; but the impression is deep and permanent. The heads of the children, when they are released from the bandage, are not more than two inches thick about the upper edge of the forehead, and still thinner above: nor with all its efforts can nature ever restore its shape; the heads of grown persons being often in a straight line from the nose to the top of the forehead.

The hair of both sexes is parted at the top of the head, and thence falls loosely behind the ears, over the back and shoulders. They use combs, of which they are very fond, and indeed, contrive without the aid of them, to keep their hair in very good order. The dress of the man consists in a small robe, reaching to the middle of the thigh, tied by a string across the breast, with its corners hanging loosely over their arms. These robes are, in general, composed of the skins of a small animal, which we have supposed to be the brown mungo. They have besides, those of the tiger, cat, deer, panther, bear, and elk, which last is principally used in war parties. Sometimes they have a blanket woven with the fingers, from the wool of their native sheep; occasionally a mat is thrown over them to keep off rain; but except this robe, they have no other article of clothing during winter or summer, so that every part of the body, but the back and shoulders, is exposed to view. They are very fond of the dress of the whites, whom they call pashisheooks or cloth-men; and whenever they can procure any clothes, wear them in our manner: the only article, indeed, which we have not seen among them is the shoe.

The robe of the women is like that worn by the men, except that it does not reach below the waist. Those most esteemed are made of strips of sea-otter skin, which being twisted are inter-woven with silk-grass, or the bark of the white cedar, in such a manner that the fur appears equally on both sides, so as to form a soft and warm covering. The skin of the raccoon or beaver are also employed in the same way, though on other occasions these skins are simply dressed in the hair, and worn without further preparation. The garment which covers the body from the waist as low as the knee before and the thigh behind, is the tissue already described, and is made either of the bruised bark of white cedar, the twisted cords of silk-grass, or of flags and rushes. Neither leggings nor moccasins are ever used, the mildness of the climate not requiring them as a security from the weather, and their being so much in the water rendering them an incum-brance. The only covering for the head is a hat made of bear-grass, and the bark of cedar, inter-woven in a conic form, with a knob of the same shape at the top. It has no brim, but is held on the head by a string passing under the chin, and tied to a small rim inside of the hat. The colours are generally black and white only, and these are made into squares, triangles, and sometimes rude figures of canoes and seamen harpooning whales. This is all the usual dress of females; but if the weather be unusually severe, they add a vest formed of skins like the robe, tied behind, without any shoulder-straps to keep it up. As this vest covers the body from the armpits to the waist, it conceals the breasts, but on all other occasions they are suffered to remain loose and exposed, and present, in old women especially, a most disgusting appearance.

Sometimes, though not often, they mark their skins by puncturing and introducing some coloured matter: this ornament is chiefly confined to the women, who imprint on their legs and arms, circular or parallel dots. On the arm of one of the squaws we read the name of J. Bowman, apparently a trader who visits the mouth of the Columbia. The favourite decoration however of both sexes, are the common coarse blue or white beads, which are folded very tightly round their wrists and ankles, to the width of three or four inches, and worn in large loose rolls round the neck, or in the shape of earrings, or hanging from the nose, which last mode is peculiar to the men. There is also a species of wampum very much in use, which seems to be worn in its natural form without any preparation. Its shape is a cone somewhat curved, about the size of a raven's quill at the base, and tapering to a point, its whole length being from one to two and a half inches, and white, smooth, hard and thin. A small thread is passed through it, and the wampum is either suspended from the nose, or passed through the cartilage horizontally, and forms a ring, from which other ornaments hang. This wampum is employed in the same way as the beads, but is the favourite decoration for the noses of the men. The men also use collars made of bears' claws, the women and children those of elks' tusks, and both sexes are adorned with bracelets of copper, iron, or brass, in various forms.

Yet all these decorations are unavailing to conceal the deformities of nature and the extravagance of fashion; nor have we seen any more disgusting object than a Chinnook or Clatsop beauty in full attire. Their broad flat foreheads, their falling breasts, their ill shaped limbs, the awkwardness of their positions, and the filth which intrudes through their finery; all these render a Chinnook or Clatsop beauty in full attire, one of the most disgusting objects in nature. Fortunately this circumstance conspired with the low diet and laborious exercise of our men, to protect them from the persevering gallantry of the fair sex, whose kindness always exceeded the ordinary courtesies of hospitality. Among these people, as indeed among all Indians, the prostitution of unmarried women is so far from being considered criminal or improper, that the females themselves solicit the favours of the other sex, with the entire approbation of their friends and connections. The person is in fact often the only property of a young female, and is therefore the medium of trade, the return for presents, and the reward for services. In most cases, however, the female is so much at the disposal of her husband or parent, that she is farmed out for hire. The Chinnook woman, who brought her six female relations to our camp, had regular prices, proportioned to the beauty of each female; and among all the tribes, a man will lend his wife or daughter for a fishhook or a strand of beads. To decline an offer of this sort is indeed to disparage the charms of the lady, and therefore gives such offence, that although we had occasionally to treat the Indians with rigour, nothing seemed to irritate both sexes more than our refusal to accept the favours of the females. On one occasion we were amused by a Clatsop, who having been cured of some disorder by our medical skill, brought his sister as a reward for our kindness. The young lady was quite anxious to join in this expression of her brother's gratitude, and mortified that we did not avail ourselves of it, she could not be prevailed on to leave the fort, but remained with Chaboneau's wife, in the next room to ours, for two or three days, declining all the solicitations of the men, till finding, at last, that we did not relent, she went away, regretting that her brother's obligations were unpaid.

The little intercourse which the men have had with these women is, however, sufficient to apprise us of the prevalence of the venereal disease, with which one or two of the party had been so much afflicted, as to render a salivation necessary. The infection in these cases was communicated by the Chinnook women. The others do not appear to be afflicted with it to any extent: indeed, notwithstanding this disorder is certainly known to the Indians on the Columbia, yet the number of infected persons is very inconsiderable. The existence of such a disorder is very easily detected, particularly in the men, in their open style of dress; yet in the whole route down the Columbia, we have not seen more than two or three cases of gonorrhoea, and about double that number of lues venerea. There does not seem to be any simples which are used as specifics in this disorder, nor is any complete cure ever effected. When once a patient is seized, the disorder ends with his life only; though from the simplicity of their diet, and the use of certain vegetables, they support it for many years with but little inconvenience, and even enjoy tolerable health; yet their life is always abridged by decrepitude or premature old age. The Indians, who are mostly successful in treating this disorder, are the Chippeways. Their specifics are the root of the lobelia, and that of a species of sumac, common to the United States, the neighbourhood of the Rocky mountains, and to the countries westward, and which is readily distinguished by being the smallest of its kind, and by its winged rib, or common footstalk, supporting leaves oppositely pinnate. Decoctions of the roots are used very freely, without any limitation, and are said to soften the violence of the lues, and even to be sovereign in the cure of the gonorrhoea.

The Clatsops and other nations at the mouth of the Columbia, have visited us with great freedom, and we have endeavoured to cultivate their intimacy, as well for the purpose of acquiring information, as to leave behind us impressions favourable to our country. In their intercourse with us they are very loquacious and inquisitive. Having acquired much of their language, we are enabled with the assistance of gestures, to hold conversations with great ease. We find them inquisitive and loquacious, with understandings by no means deficient in acuteness, and with very retentive memories; and though fond of feasts, and generally cheerful, they are never gay. Every thing they see excites their attention and inquiries, but having been accustomed to see the whites, nothing appeared to give them more astonishment than the air-gun. To all our inquiries they answer with great intelligence, and the conversation rarely slackens, since there is a constant discussion of the events, and trade, and politics, in the little but active circle of Killamucks, Clatsops, Cathlamahs, Wahkiacums, and Chinnooks. Among themselves, the conversation generally turns on the subjects of trade, or smoking, or eating, or connection with females, before whom this last is spoken of with a familiarity which would be in the highest degree indecent, if custom had not rendered it inoffensive.

The treatment of women is often considered as the standard by which the moral qualities of savages are to be estimated. Our own observation, however, induced us to think that the importance of the female in savage life, has no necessary relation to the virtues of the men, but is regulated wholly by their capacity to be useful. The Indians whose treatment of the females is mildest, and who pay most deference to their opinions, are by no means the most distinguished for their virtues; nor is this deference attended by any increase of attachment, since they are equally willing with the most brutal husband, to prostitute their wives to strangers. On the other hand, the tribes among whom the women are very much debased, possess the loftiest sense of honour, the greatest liberality, and all the good qualities of which their situation demands the exercise. Where the women can aid in procuring subsistence for the tribe, they are treated with more equality, and their importance is proportioned to the share which they take in that labour; while in countries where subsistence is chiefly procured by the exertions of the men, the women are considered and treated as burdens. Thus, among the Clatsops and Chinnooks, who live upon fish and roots, which the women are equally expert with the men in procuring, the former have a rank and influence very rarely found among Indians. The females are permitted to speak freely before the men, to whom indeed they sometimes address themselves in a tone of authority. On many subjects their judgments and opinions are respected, and in matters of trade, their advice is generally asked and pursued. The labours of the family too, are shared almost equally. The men collect wood and make fires, assist in cleansing the fish, make the houses, canoes, and wooden utensils; and whenever strangers are to be entertained, or a great feast prepared, the meats are cooked and served up by the men. The peculiar province of the female is to collect roots, and to manufacture the various articles which are formed of rushes, flags, cedar-bark, and bear-grass; but the management of the canoes, and many of the occupations, which elsewhere devolves wholly on the female, are here common to both sexes.

The observation with regard to the importance of females, applies with equal force to the treatment of old men. Among tribes who subsist by hunting, the labours of the chase, and the wandering existence to which that occupation condemns them, necessarily throws the burden of procuring provisions on the active young men. As soon, therefore, as a man is unable to pursue the chase, he begins to withdraw something from the precarious supplies of the tribe. Still, however, his counsels may compensate his want of activity; but in the next stage of infirmity, when he can no longer travel from camp to camp, as the tribe roams about for subsistence, he is then found to be a heavy burden. In this situation they are abandoned among the Sioux, Assiniboins, and the hunting tribes on the Missouri. As they are setting out for some new excursion, where the old man is unable to follow, his children, or nearest relations, place before him a piece of meat and some water, and telling him that he has lived long enough, that it is now time for him to go home to his relations, who could take better care of him than his friends on earth, leave him, without remorse, to perish, when his little supply is exhausted. The same custom is said to prevail among the Minnetarees, Ahnahawas, and Ricaras, when they are attended by old men on their hunting excursions. Yet, in their villages, we saw no want of kindness to old men. On the contrary, probably because in villages, the means of more abundant subsistence renders such cruelty unnecessary, the old people appeared to be treated with attention, and some of their feasts, particularly the buffalo dances, were intended chiefly as a contribution for the old and infirm.

The dispositions of these people seem mild and inoffensive, and they have uniformly behaved to us with great friendship. They are addicted to begging and pilfering small articles, when it can be done without danger of detection, but do not rob wantonly, nor to any large amount; and some of them having purloined some of our meat, which the hunters had been obliged to leave in the woods, they voluntarily brought some dogs a few days after, by way of compensation. Our force and great superiority in the use of firearms, enable us always to command, and such is the friendly deportment of these people, that the men have been accustomed to treat them with the greatest confidence. It is therefore with difficulty that we can impress on our men a conviction of the necessity of being always on our guard, since we are perfectly acquainted with the treacherous character of Indians in general. We are always prepared for an attack, and uniformly exclude all large parties of Indians from the fort. Their large houses usually contain several families, consisting of the parents, their sons and daughters-in-law, and grandchildren, among whom the provisions are common, and whose harmony is scarcely ever interrupted by disputes. Although polygamy is permitted by their customs, very few have more than a single wife, and she is brought immediately after the marriage into the husband's family, where she resides until increasing numbers oblige them to seek another house. In this state the old man is not considered as the head of the family, since the active duties, as well as the responsibility, fall on some of the younger members. As these families gradually expand into bands or tribes or nations, the paternal authority is represented by the chief of each association. This chieftain however is not hereditary; his ability to render service to his neighbours, and the popularity which follows it, is at once the foundation and the measure of his authority, the exercise of which does not extend beyond a reprimand for some improper action.

The harmony of their private life is indeed secured by their ignorance of spirituous liquors, the earliest and most dreadful present which civilisation has given to the other natives of the continent. Although they have had so much intercourse with whites, they do not appear to possess any knowledge of those dangerous luxuries; at least they have never inquired after them; which they probably would have done if once they had been introduced among them. Indeed we have not observed any liquor of an intoxicating quality used among these or any Indians west of the Rocky mountains, the universal beverage being pure water. They however sometimes almost intoxicate themselves by smoking tobacco of which they are excessively fond, and the pleasures of which they prolong as much as possible, by retaining vast quantities at a time, till after circulating through the lungs and stomach it issues in volumes from the mouth and nostrils. But the natural vice of all these people is an attachment for games of hazard which they pursue with a strange and ruinous avidity. The games are of two kinds. In the first, one of the company assumes the office of banker, and plays against the rest. He takes a small stone, about the size of a bean, which he shifts from one hand to the other with great dexterity, repeating at the same time a song adapted to the game, and which serves to divert the attention of the company, till having agreed on the stake, he holds out his hands, and the antagonist wins or loses as he succeeds or fails at guessing in which hand the stone is. After the banker has lost his money, or whenever he is tired, the stone is transferred to another, who in turn challenges the rest of the company. The other game is something like the play of ninepins; two pins are placed on the floor, about the distance of a foot from each other, and a small hole made behind them. The players then go about ten feet from the hole, into which they try to roll a small piece resembling the men used at draughts; if they succeed in putting it into the hole, they win the stake; if the piece rolls between the pins, but does not go into the hole, nothing is won or lost; but the wager is wholly lost if the chequer rolls outside of the pins. Entire days are wasted at these games, which are often continued through the night round the blaze of their fires, till the last article of clothing or even the last blue bead is won from the desperate adventurer.

In traffic they are keen, acute and intelligent,

and they employ in all their bargains a dexterity and finesse, which, if it be not learnt from their foreign visitors, may show how nearly the cunning of savages is allied to the little arts of more civilised trade. They begin by asking double or treble the value of their merchandise, and lower the demand in proportion to the ardour or experience in trade of the purchaser; and if he expresses any anxiety, the smallest article, perhaps a handful of roots, will furnish a whole morning's negotiation. Being naturally suspicious, they of course conceive that you are pursuing the same system. They, therefore, invariably refuse the first offer, however high, fearful that they or we have mistaken the value of the merchandise, and therefore cautiously wait to draw us on to larger offers. In this way, after rejecting the most extravagant prices, which we have offered merely for experiment, they have afterwards importuned us for a tenth part of what they had before refused. In this respect, they differ from almost all Indians, who will generally exchange in a thoughtless moment the most valuable article they possess, for any bauble which happens to please their fancy.

These habits of cunning, or prudence, have been formed or increased by their being engaged in a large part of the commerce of the Columbia; of that trade, however, the great emporium is the falls, where all the neighbouring nations assemble. The inhabitants of the Columbian plains, after having passed the winter near the mountains, come down as soon as the snow has left the valleys, and are occupied in collecting and drying roots, till about the month of May. They then crowd to the river, and fixing themselves on its north side, to avoid the incursions of the Snake

Indians, continue fishing, till about the first of September, when the salmon are no longer fit for use. They then bury their fish and return to the plains, where they remain gathering quamash, till the snow obliges them to desist. They come back to the Columbia, and taking their store of fish, retire to the foot of the mountains, and along the creeks, which supply timber for houses, and pass the winter in hunting deer or elk, which, with the aid of their fish, enables them to subsist till in the spring they resume the circle of their employments. During their residence on the river, from May to September, or rather before they begin the regular fishery, they go down to the falls, carrying with them skins, mats, silk grass, rushes, and chappelell bread. They are here overtaken by the Chopunnish, and other tribes of the Rocky mountains, who descend the Kooskooskee and Lewis's river for the purpose of selling bear-grass, horses, quamash, and a few skins which they have obtained by hunting, or in exchange for horses, with the Tushepaws.

At the falls, they find the Chilluckittequaws, Eneeshurs, Echeloots, and Skilloots, which last serve as intermediate traders or carriers between the inhabitants above and below the falls. These tribes prepare pounded fish for the market, and the nations below bring wappatoo roots, the fish of the seacoast, berries, and a variety of trinkets and small articles which they have procured from the whites.

The trade then begins. The Chopunnish, and Indians of the Rocky mountains, exchange the articles which they have brought for wappatoo, pounded fish, and beads. The Indians of the plains being their own fishermen, take only wappatoo, horses, beads, and other articles, procured from Europeans. The Indians, however, from Lewis's river to the falls, consume as food or fuel all the fish which they take; so that the whole stock for exportation is prepared by the nations between the Towahnahiooks and the falls, and amounts, as nearly as we could estimate, to about thirty thousand weight, chiefly salmon, above the quantity which they use themselves, or barter with the more eastern Indians. This is now carried down the river by the Indians at the falls, and is consumed among the nations at the mouth of the Columbia, who in return give the fish of the seacoast, and the articles which they obtain from the whites. The neighbouring people catch large quantities of salmon and dry them, but they do not understand or practise the art of drying and pounding it in the manner used at the falls, and being very fond of it, are forced to purchase it at high prices. This article, indeed, and the wappatoo, form the principal subjects of trade with the people of our immediate vicinity. The traffic is wholly carried on by water; there are even no roads or paths through the country, except across the portages which connect the creeks.

But the circumstance which forms the soul of this trade, is the visit of the whites. They arrive generally about the month of April, and either remain until October, or return at that time; during which time, having no establishment on shore, they anchor on the north side of the bay, at the place already described, which is a spacious and commodious harbour, perfectly secure from all except the south and southeast winds; and as they leave it before winter, they do not suffer from these winds, which, during that season, are the most usual and the most violent. This situation is recommended by its neighbourhood to fresh water and wood, as well as to excellent timber for repairs. Here they are immediately visited by the tribes along the seacoast, by the Cathlamahs, and lastly by the Skilloots, that numerous and active people, who skirt the river between the marshy islands and the grand rapids, as well as the Coweliskee, and who carry down the fish prepared by their immediate neighbours the Chilluckittequaws, Eneeshurs, and Echeeloots, residing from the grand rapids to the falls, as well as all the articles which they have procured in barter at the market in May. The accumulated trade of the Columbia now consists of dressed and undressed skins of elk, sea-otter, the common otter, beaver, common fox, spuck, and tiger cat. The articles of less importance, are a small quantity of dried or pounded salmon, the biscuits made of the chapelell roots, and some of the manufactures of the neighbourhood. In return they receive guns (which are principally old British or American muskets) powder, ball and shot, copper and brass kettles, brass tea-kettles, and coffee-pots, blankets, from two to three points, coarse scarlet and blue cloth, plates and strips of sheet copper and brass, large brass wire, knives, tobacco, fish-hooks, buttons, and a considerable quantity of sailors' hats, trousers, coats and shirts. But as we have had occasion to remark more than once, the object of foreign trade which is the most desired, are the common cheap, blue or white beads, of about fifty or seventy to the pennyweight, which are strung on strands a fathom in length, and sold by the yard, or the length of both arms: of these blue beads, which are called tia commashuck, or chief beads, hold the first rank in their ideas of relative value: the most inferior kind, are esteemed beyond the finest

342

wampum, and are temptations which can always seduce them to part with their most valuable effects. Indeed, if the example of civilised life did not completely vindicate their choice, we might wonder at their infatuated attachment to a bauble in itself so worthless. Yet these beads are, perhaps, quite as reasonable objects of research as the precious metals, since they are at once beautiful ornaments for the person, and the great circulating medium of trade with all the nations on the Columbia.

These strangers who visit the Columbia for the purpose of trade or hunting, must be either English or Americans. The Indians inform us that they speak the same language as we do, and indeed the few words which the Indians have learnt from the sailors, such as musket, powder, shot, knife, file, heave the lead, damned rascal, and other phrases of that description, evidently show that the visitors speak the English language. But as the greater part of them annually arrive in April, and either remain till autumn, or revisit them at that time, which we could not clearly understand, the trade cannot be direct from either England or the United States, since the ships could not return thither during the remainder of the year. When the Indians are asked where these traders go on leaving the Columbia, they always point to the southwest, whence we presume that they do not belong to any establishment at Nootka Sound. They do, however, mention a trader by the name of Moore, who sometimes touches at this place, and the last time he came, he had on board three cows; and when he left them, continued along the northwest coast, which renders it probable, that there may be a settlement of whites in that direction. The names and description of all these persons who visit them in the spring and autumn are remembered with great accuracy, and we took down, exactly as they were pronounced, the following list: The favourite trader is

Mr. Haley, who visits them in a vessel with three masts, and continues some time. The others are

Youens, who comes also in a three masted vessel, and is a trader.

Tallamon, in a three masted vessel, but he is not a trader.

Callalamet in a ship of the same size, he is a trader, and they say has a wooden leg.

Swipton	three masted vessel,	trader.
Moore	four do.	do.
Mackey	three do.	do.
Washington	three do.	do.
Mesship	three do.	do.
Davidson	three do.	does not trade, but hunts elk.
Jackson	three do.	trader.
Bolch	three do.	do.

Skelley, also a trader, in a vessel with three masts, but he has been gone for some years. He had only one eye.

It might be difficult to adjust the balance of the advantages or the dangers of this trade to the nations of the Columbia, against the sale of their furs, and the acquisition of a few bad guns and household utensils.

The nations near the mouth of the Columbia enjoy great tranquillity; none of the tribes being engaged in war. Not long since, however, there was a war on the coast to the southwest, in which the Killamucks took several prisoners. These, as far as we could perceive, were treated very well, and though nominally slaves, yet were adopted into the families of their masters, and the young ones placed on the same footing with the children of the purchaser.

The month of February and the greater part of March were passed in the same manner. Every day, parties as large as we could spare them from our other occupations were sent out to hunt, and we were thus enabled to command some days' provision in advance. It consisted chiefly of deer and elk; the first is very lean, and the flesh by no means as good as that of the elk, which, though poor, is getting better: it is indeed our chief dependence. At this time of the year it is in much better order in the prairies near the point, where they feed on grass and rushes, considerable quantities of which are yet green, than in the woody country up the Netul. There, they subsist on huckleberry bushes and fern, but chiefly on evergreen, called shallun, resembling the laurel, which abounds through all the timbered lands, particularly along the broken sides of hills. Toward the latter end of the month, however, they left the prairies near Point Adams, and retired back to the hills; but fortunately, at the same time the sturgeon and anchovies began to appear, and afforded us a delightful variety of food. In the mean time, the party on the seacoast supplied us with salt: but though the kettles were kept boiling all day and night, the salt was made but slowly; nor was it till the middle of this month that we succeeded in procuring twenty gallons, of which twelve were put in kegs for our journey as far as the deposits on the Missouri.

The neighbouring tribes continued to visit us, for the purpose of trading, or merely to smoke with us. But on the 21st, a Chinnook chief, whom we had never seen, came over with twenty-five of his men. His name was Tahcum, a man of about fifty years of age, with a larger figure and a better carriage than most of his nation. We received him with the usual ceremonies, gave the party something to eat, smoked most copiously with them all, and presented the chief with a small medal. They were all satisfied with their treatment; and though we were willing to show the chief every civility, could not dispense with our rule of not suffering so many strangers to sleep in the fort. They, therefore, left us at sunset. On the twenty-fourth, Comowool, who is by far the most friendly and decent savage we have seen in this neighbourhood, came with a large party of Clatsops, bringing among other articles, sturgeon and a small fish, which has just begun, within a day or two past, to make their appearance in the Columbia.

From this time, as the elk became scarce and lean, we made use of these fish whenever we could catch them, or purchase them from the Indians. But as we were too poor to indulge very largely in these luxuries, the diet was by no means pleasant, and to the sick, especially, was unwholesome. On the 15th of March we were visited by Delashilwilt, the Chinnook chief, and his wife, accompanied by the same six damsels, who in the autumn had encamped near us, on the other side of the bay, and whose favours had been so troublesome to several of the men. They formed a camp close to the fort, and began to renew their addresses very assiduously, but we warned the men of the dangers of intercourse with this frail society, and they cautiously abstained from connection with them.

During the greater part of this month, five or

six of the men were sick; indeed, we have not had so many complaining since we left Wood river; the general complaint is a bad cold and fever, something in the nature of an influenza, which, joined with a few cases of venereal, and accidental injuries, complete our invalid corps. These disorders may chiefly be imputed to the nature of the climate.

CHAPTER XXIV.

A general description of the beasts, birds and plants, &c. found
by the party in this expedition.

The vegetable productions of the country, which
furnish a large proportion of the food of the Indians, are the roots of a species of thistle, the
fern, the rush, the liquorice, and a small cylindric
root, resembling in flavour and consistency the
sweet potato.

1st. The thistle, called by the natives shana-
tanque, is a plant which grows in a deep, rich,
dry loam, with a considerable mixture of sand.
The stem is simple, ascending, cylindric, and his-
pid, and rising to the height of three or four feet.
The cauline life, which, as well as the stem of the
last season is dead, is simple, crenate, and oblong;
rather more obtuse at its apex than at its insertion, which is decurrent, and its position declining; whilst the margin is armed with prickles, and
its disc is hairy. The flower too is dry and mutilated; but the pericarp seems much like that of the
common thistle. The root-leaves, which still possess their verdure, and are about half grown, are
of a pale green colour. The root, however, is the
only part used. It is from nine to fifteen inches
long, about the size of a man's thumb, perpendicular, fusiform, and with from two to four
radicles. The rind is of a brown colour, and
somewhat rough. When first taken from the
earth, it is white, and nearly as crisp as a carrot,
and in this state is sometimes eaten without any
preparation. But after it is prepared by the same
process used for the pasheco quamash, which is

the most usual and the best method, it becomes black, and much improved in flavour. Its taste is exactly that of sugar, and it is indeed the sweetest vegetable employed by the Indians. After being baked in the kiln, it is either eaten simply or with train oil; sometimes pounded fine and mixed with cold water, until it is reduced to the consistence of sagamity, or Indian mush, which last method is the most agreeable to our palates.

2. Three species of fern grow in this neighbourhood, but the root of only one is eaten. It is very abundant in those parts of the open lands and prairies which have a deep, loose, rich, black loam, without any sand. There, it attains the height of four or five feet, and is a beautiful plant with a fine green colour in summer. The stem, which is smooth, cylindric, and slightly grooved on one side, rises erectly about half its height, when it divides into two branches, or rather long footstalks, which put forth in pairs from one side only, and near the edges of the groove, declining backwards from the grooved side. These footstalks are themselves grooved and cylindric, and as they gradually taper toward the extremities, put forth others of a smaller size, which are alternate, and have forty or fifty alternate, pinnate, horizontal, and sessile leaves: the leaves are multi partite for half the length of their footstalk, when they assume the tongue-like form altogether; being, moreover, revolute, with the upper disc smooth, and the lower resembling cotton: the top is annual, and therefore dead at present, but it produces no flower or fruit: the root itself is perennial and grows horizontally; sometimes a little diverging, or obliquely descending, and frequently dividing itself as it proceeds, and shooting up a number of stems. It lies about four inches

under the surface of the earth, in a cylindrical form, with few or no radicles, and varies from the size of a goose quill to that of a man's finger. The bark is black, thin, brittle, and rather rough, and easily separates in flakes from the part which is eaten: the centre is divided into two parts by a strong, flat, and white ligament, like a piece of thin tape; on each side of which is a white substance, resembling, after the root is roasted, both in appearance and flavour, the dough of wheat. It has, however, a pungency which is disagreeable, but the natives eat it voraciously, and it seems to be very nutritious.

3. The rush is most commonly used by the Killamucks, and other Indians on the seacoast, along the sands of which it grows in greatest abundance. From each root a single stem rises erectly to the height of three or four feet, somewhat thicker than a large quill, hollow and jointed; about twenty or thirty long, lineal, stellate, or radiate and horizontal leaves surround the stem at each joint, about half an inch above which, its stem is sheathed like the sand rush. When green, it resembles that plant also in appearance, as well as in having a rough stem. It is not branching; nor does it bear, as far as we can discover, either flower or seed. At the bottom of this stem, which is annual, is a small, strong radicle, about an inch long, descending perpendicularly to the root, while just above the junction of the radicle with the stem, the latter is surrounded in the form of a wheel, with six or nine small radicles, descending obliquely: the root attached to this radicle is a perennial solid bulb, about an inch long, and of the thickness of a man's thumb, of an ovate form, depressed on one or two of its sides, and covered with a thin, smooth, black rind: the pulp is

350

white, brittle, and easily masticated. It is commonly roasted, though sometimes eaten raw; but in both states is rather an insipid root.

4. The liquorice of this country does not differ from that common to the United States. It here delights in a deep, loose, sandy soil, and grows very large, and abundantly. It is prepared by roasting in the embers, and pounding it slightly with a small stick, in order to separate the strong ligament in the centre of the root, which is then thrown away, and the rest chewed and swallowed. In this way it has an agreeable flavour, not unlike that of the sweet potato. The root of the cattail, or cooper's flag, is eaten by the Indians. There is also, a species of small, dry, tuberous root, two inches in length, and about the thickness of the finger. They are eaten raw, are crisp, milky, and of an agreeable flavour.

5. Beside the small cylindric root mentioned above, is another of the same form and appearance, which is usually boiled and eaten with train oil. Its taste, however, is disagreeably bitter. But the most valuable of all the Indian roots, is

6. The wappatoo, or the bulb of the common sagittafolia, or common arrowhead. It does not grow in this neighbourhood, but is in great abundance in the marshy grounds of that beautiful valley, which extends from near Quicksand river for seventy miles westward, and is a principal article of trade between the inhabitants of that valley and those of the seacoast.

The shrub rises to the height of four or five feet; the stem simple and much branched. The bark is of a reddish dark brown; the main stem somewhat rough, while that of the bough is smooth; the leaf is about one-tenth of an inch long, obtuse at the apex, and acute and angular at the inser-

351

tion of the pedicle. The leaf is three fourths of an inch in length, and three eighths in width, smooth, and of a paler green than evergreens generally are. The fruit is a small deep purple berry, and of a pleasant flavour; the natives eat the berry when ripe, but seldom collect such quantities as to dry for winter use.

The native fruits and berries in use among the Indians, are what they call the shallun; the solme; the cranberry; a berry like the black haw; the scarlet berry, of the plant called sacacommis; a purple berry, like the huckleberry.

1. The shallun is an evergreen plant, abounding in this neighbourhood, and its leaves are the favourite food of the elk. It is a thick growth, cylindrically rising to the height of three, and sometimes five feet, and varying from the size of a goose quill, to that of a man's thumb. The stem is simple, branching, reclining, and partially fluxuose, with a bark which, on the elder part, is of a reddish brown colour, while the younger branches are red where exposed to the sun, and green elsewhere. The leaf is three fourths of an inch in length, and two and a half in breadth; of an oval form; the upper disc of a glossy deep green, the under of a pale green; the fruit is a deep purple berry, about the size of a common black cherry, oval, and rather bluntly pointed; the pericarp is divided into five acute angular points, and envelops a soft pulp, containing a great number of small brown seeds.

2. The solme is a small, pale, red berry, the production of a plant, resembling in size and shape that which produces the fruit, called in the United States, Solomon's seal-berry. The berry is attached to the stem in the same manner. It is of a globular form; containing a soft pulp, which

352

envelops four seeds about the size of the seed of the common small grape. It grows amongst the woodland moss, and is, to all appearance, an annual plant.

3. The cranberry is of the low and viny kind, and grows in the marshes or bogs of this neighbourhood: it is precisely the same as the cranberry of the United States.

4. The fruit, which, though rather larger, resembles the black haw, is a light brown berry, the fruit of a tree about the size, shape, and appearance in every respect, of that of the United States, called the wild crab-apple. The leaf is also precisely the same, as also the bark in texture and colour. The berries grow in clumps at the end of the small branches; each berry supported by a separate stem, and as many as from three to eighteen or twenty in a clump: the berry is ovate, with one of its extremities attached to a peduncle, where it is to a small degree concave, the wood of which is excessively hard. The natives make their wedges of this wood, in splitting their boards, their firewood, and in hollowing out their canoes; the wedge when driven into solid dry pine, receives not the slightest injury. Our party made use of it likewise for wedges and axe-handles. The fruit is exceedingly acid, and resembles the flavour of the wild crab. The pericarp of the berry contains a soft pulpy substance, divided into four cells, each containing a single seed; the outer coat of the pericarp, is a thin smooth though firm and tough pellicle.

The plant called sacacommis by the Canadian traders derives its name from this circumstance: that the clerks of the trading companies are generally very fond of smoking its leaves, which they carry about with them in a small bag. It grows generally in an open piny woodland country, or on its borders. We found this berry in the prairies bordering on the Rocky mountains, or in the more open woodlands. It is indiscriminately the growth of a very rich or a very poor soil, and is found in the same abundance in both. The natives on the western side of the Rocky mountains are very fond of this berry, although to us it was a very tasteless and insipid fruit: the shrub is an evergreen, and retains its verdure in the same perfection the whole season round. However inclement the climate, the root puts forth a great number of stems which separate near the surface of the ground, each stem from the size of a small quill to that of a man's finger: these are much branched, the branches forming an acute angle with the stem, and all more properly procumbent than creeping: although it sometimes puts forth radicles from the stems and branches, which strike obliquely into the ground: these radicles are by no means general or equable in their distances from each other, nor do they appear calculated to furnish nutriment to the plant: the bark is formed of several layers of a smooth, thin, brittle and reddish substance easily separated from the stem: the leaves with respect to their position are scattered, yet closely arranged, and particularly near the extremities of the twigs: the leaf is about three-fourths of an inch in length; oval, pointed and obtuse; of a deep green, slightly grooved; and the footstalk is of proportionable length: the berry is attached in an irregular manner to the small boughs among the leaves, and always supported by separate, small and short peduncles: the insertion produces a slight concavity in the berry, while its opposite side is slightly convex. The outer coat of the pericarp is a thin, firm, tough pellicle: the inner coat consists of a dry, mealy powder, of a yellowish white colour, enveloping from four to six large, light, brown seeds: the colour of the fruit is a fine scarlet: the natives eat these berries without any preparation: the fruit ripens in September, and remains on the bushes all winter unaffected by the frost: they are sometimes gathered and hung in the lodges in bags, where they are dried without further trouble.

6. The deep purple berry, like the huckleberry, terminates bluntly, and has a cap or cover at the end: the berries are attached separately to the sides of the boughs by a short stem, hanging underneath and they often grow very near each other, on the same bough: the berry separates very easily from the stem; the leaves adhere closely: the shrub rises to the height of six or eight feet, and sometimes grows on high lands, but more frequently on low marshy grounds: the shrub is an evergreen, and about ten inches in circumference, divides into many irregular branches, and seldom more than one stem springs from one root, although they associate very thickly: the bark is somewhat rough and of a reddish brown colour: the wood is very hard: the leaves are alternate and attached by a short footstalk to the horizontal sides of the boughs: the form is a long oval, rather more acute towards the apex than at the point of insertion: its margin slightly serrate, its sides collapsing, thick, firm, smooth and glossy: the under surface is of a pale or whitish green, and the upper of a fine deep green. This beautiful shrub retains its verdure throughout the year, and is more peculiarly beautiful in winter. The natives sometimes eat the berries without preparation: sometimes they dry them in the sun, and at others in their sweating

kilns: they very frequently pound them, and bake them in large loaves, weighing from ten to fifteen pounds: the bread keeps very well for one season, and retains its juices better by this mode of preparation than any other: this bread when broken is stirred in cold water, until it acquires the consistency of soup, and then eaten.

The trees of a larger growth are very abundant; the whole neighbourhood of the coast is supplied with great quantities of excellent timber. The predominating growth is the fir, of which we have seen several species. There is one singular circumstance attending all the pine of this country, which is, that when consumed it yields not the slightest particle of ashes. The first species grows to an immense size, and is very commonly twenty-seven feet in circumference six feet above the earth's surface: they rise to the height of two hundred and thirty feet, and one hundred and twenty of that height without a limb. We have often found them thirty-six feet in circumference. One of our party measured one, and found it to be forty-two feet in circumference, at a point beyond the reach of an ordinary man. This trunk for the distance of two hundred feet was destitute of limbs: this tree was perfectly sound, and at a moderate calculation, its size may be estimated at three hundred feet. The timber is throughout, and rives better than any other species; the bark scales off in flakes irregularly round, and of a reddish brown colour, particularly the younger growth: the trunk is simple, branching, and not very proliferous. The leaf is acerose, one tenth of an inch in width, and three fourths in length, firm, stiff, and acuminate. It is triangular, a little declining, thickly scattered on all sides of the bough, and springs from small triangular pedestals of soft, spongy, elastic bark at the junction of the boughs. The bud scales continue to encircle their respective twigs for several years. Captain Lewis has counted as many as the growth of four years beyond their scales; it yields but little resin, and we have never been able to discover the cone, although we have killed several.

The second is a much more common species, and constitutes at least one half of the timber in this neighbourhood. It seems to resemble the spruce, rising from one hundred and sixty to one hundred and eighty feet, and is from four to six in diameter, straight, round, and regularly tapering. The bark is thin, of a dark colour, much divided in small longitudinal interstices: the bark of the boughs and young trees is somewhat smooth, but not equal to the balsam fir: the wood is white, very soft, but difficult to rive: the trunk is a simple, branching, and diffuse stem, not so proliferous as the pines and firs usually are. It puts forth buds from the sides of the small boughs, as well as from their extremities: the stem terminates like the cedar, in a slender pointed top: the leaves are petiolate, the footstalks short, acerose, rather more than half a line in width, and very unequal in length; the greatest length seldom exceeds one inch, while other leaves intermixed on every part of the bough, do not exceed a quarter of an inch. The leaf has a small longitudinal channel on the upper disc, which is of a deep and glossy green, while the under disc is of a whitish green only: it yields but little resin. What is remarkable, the cane is not longer than the end of a man's thumb, it is soft, flexible, of an ovate form, and produced at the ends of the small twigs.

The third species resembles in all points, the Canadian balsam fir. It grows from two and a half to four feet in diameter, and rises to the height of eighty or an hundred feet. The stem is simple, branching, and proliferous: its leaves are sessile, acerose, one eighth of an inch in length, and one sixteenth in width, thickly scattered on the twigs, and adhere to the three under sides only; gibbous, a little declining, obtusely pointed, soft, and flexible. The upper disc is longitudinally marked with a slight channel, of a deep glossy-green; the under of a pale green and not glossy. This tree affords in considerable quantities, a fine deep aromatic balsam, resembling the balsam of Canada in taste and appearance. The small pistils filled, rise like a blister on the trunk and the branches. The bark that envelops these pistils, is soft and easily punctured: the general appearance of the bark is dark and smooth; but not so remarkable for that quality as the white pine of our country. The wood is white and soft.

The fourth species in size resembles the second. The stem is simple, branching, ascending, and proliferous; the bark is of a reddish dark brown, and thicker than that of the third species, divided by small longitudinal interstices, not so much magnified as in the second species. The relative position of the leaves resemble those of the balsam fir, excepting that they are only two thirds the width, and little more than half the length, and that the upper disc is not so green and glossy. The wood yields no balsam, and but little resin. The wood is white and tough although rather porous.

The fifth species in size resembles the second, and has a trunk simple, branching, and proliferous. The bark is of a thin dark brown, divided longitudinally by interstices, and scaling off in thin rolling flakes. It yields but little balsam: two-thirds of the diameter of the trunk in the centre, presents a reddish white; the remainder is white, porous, and tough: the twigs are much longer and more slender than in either of the other species; the leaves are acerose, one-twentieth of an inch in width, and one inch in length; sextile, inserted on all sides of the bough, straight, and obliquely pointing towards the extremities. The upper disc has a small longitudinal channel, and is of a deep green, and not so glossy as the balsam fir. The under disc is of a pale green.

We have seen a species of this fir on low marshy grounds, resembling in all points the foregoing, except that it branches more diffusively. This tree is generally thirty feet in height, and two in diameter. The diffusion of its branches may result from its open situation, as it seldom grows in the neighbourhood of another tree. The cone is two and a half inches in length, and three and three-quarters in its greatest circumference. It tapers regularly to a point, and is formed of the imbricated scales, of a bluntly rounded form. A thin leaf is inserted in the pith of the cone, which overlays the centre of, and extends half an inch beyond the point of each scale.

The sixth species does not differ from what is usually denominated the white pine in Virginia. The unusual length of the cone seems to constitute the only difference. It is sometimes sixteen or eighteen inches in length, and is about four in circumference. It grows on the north side of the Columbia, near the ocean.

The seventh, and last species grows in low grounds, and in places frequently overflown by the tide, seldom rising higher than thirty-five feet, and not more than from two and a half to four in diameter: the stem is simple, branching and proliferous: the bark resembles that of the first species, but more rugged: the leaves are acerose, two-tenths of an inch in width, three-fourths in length, firm, stiff, and a little acuminated: they end in short pointed tendrils, gibbous, and thickly scattered on all sides of the branch, though they adhere to the three under sides only: those inserted on the under side incline sidewise, with upward points, presenting the leaf in the shape of a scythe: the others are pointing upwards, sextile and like those of the first species, grow from the small triangular pedestals, of a bark, spongy, soft and elastic. The under disc is of a deep glossy green, the other of a pale whitish green: the boughs retain the leaves of a six years' growth: the bud scales resemble those of the first species: the cone is of an ovate figure, three and a half inches in length, and three in circumference, thickest in the middle, and tapering and terminating in two obtuse points: it is composed of small, flexible scales, imbricated, and of a reddish brown colour. Each of these scales covers two small seeds, and is itself covered in the centre by a small, thin, inferior scale, acutely pointed: these scales proceed from the sides of the bough, as well as from its extremities. It was nowhere seen above the Wappatoo. The stem of the black alder arrives to a great size. It is simple, branching, and diffuse: the bark is smooth, of a light colour, with white spreading spots, resembling those of the beech: the leaf, fructification, &c. resemble precisely those of the common alder of our country: the shrubs grow separately from different roots, and not in clusters, like those of the United States. The black alder does not cast its leaf until the first of December. It is sometimes found growing to the height of sixty or seventy feet, and is from two to four in diameter.

3. There is a tree common to the Columbia river, below the entrance of Cataract river, when divested of its foliage, much resembling the ash. The trunk is simple, branching, and diffuse: the leaf is petiolate, plain, divided by four deep lines, and resembling those of the palm, and considerably lobate: the lobes terminate in from three to five angular points, and their margins are indented with irregular and somewhat circular incissures: the petiolate is cylindrical, smooth, and seven inches long; the leaf itself eight inches in length, and twelve in breadth: this tree is frequently three feet in diameter, and rises from forty to fifty feet: the fruit is a winged seed, somewhat resembling that of the maple.

In the same part of the country there is also another growth, resembling the white maple, though much smaller, and is seldom to be seen of more than six or seven inches in diameter. These trees grow in clusters, from fifteen to twenty feet in height, from the same bed of roots, spreading, and leaning outwards: the twigs are long and slender, the stem simple and branching, the bark, in colour, resembling the white maple, the leaf is petiolate, plain, scattered, nearly circular, with acute, angular incissures round the margin, of an inch in length, and from six to eight in number: the acute angular points so formed, are crenate, three inches in length and four in width; the petiole is cylindric, smooth, and an inch and a quarter in length, and the fruit is not known.

The undergrowth consists of honeysuckles, alder, seven bark or nine bark, huckleberry, a shrub like the quillwood, a plant like the mountain-holly, a green briar, the fern.

1. The honeysuckle common to the United States we found in this neighbourhood. We first

discovered the honeysuckle on the waters of the Kooskooskee, near the Chopunnish nation, and again below the grand rapids.

2. The alder which is also common to our country, was found in great abundance in the woodlands, on this side of the Rocky mountains. It differs in the colour of its berry: this being of a pale sky blue, while that of the United States is of a deep purple.

3. The seven bark, or, as it is usually denominated, the nine bark of the United States, is also common to this country.

4. The huckleberry. There is a species of huckleberry, common to the highlands, from the commencement of the Columbian valley to the seacoast, rising to the height of six or eight feet, branching and diffuse: the trunk is cylindrical, of a dark brown colour; the collateral branches are green, smooth, and square, and put forth a number of alternate branches of the same colour, and from the two horizontal sides only. The fruit is a small deep purple berry, held in much esteem by the natives: the leaf is of a pale green, and small, three-fourths of an inch in length, and three-eighths in width, oval, terminating more acutely at the apex than at the insertion of the footstalk: the base is nearly entire, and but slightly serrate: the footstalks are short; their relative position is alternate, two-ranked, and proceeding from the horizontal sides of the boughs only.

5. There are two species of shrubs, first seen at the grand rapids of the Columbia, and which have since been seen elsewhere; they grow in rich dry grounds, usually in the neighbourhood of some water course: the roots are creeping and cylindrical: the stem of the first species is from a foot to eighteen inches in height, and about as large as

an ordinary goose quill: it is simple, unbranched,
and erect: its leaves are cauline, compound and
spreading: the leaflets are jointed, and oppositely
pinnate, three pair, and terminating in one sextile,
widest at the base, and tapering to an acuminate
point: it is an inch and a quarter in its greatest
width, and three inches and a quarter in length:
each point of the margin is armed with a subulate
thorn, and from thirteen to seventeen in number:
are veined, glossy, carinated and wrinkled: their
points obliquely tending towards the extremity of
the common footstalk: the stem of the second
species is procumbent, about the size of that of the
first species, jointed and unbranched: its leaves are
cauline, compound, and oppositely pinnate: the
rib is from fourteen to sixteen inches in length,
cylindric and smooth: the leaflets are two inches
and a half long, and one inch wide, and of the
greatest width half an inch from the base: this
they regularly surround, and from the same point
tapering to an acute apex: this is usually terminated with a small subulate thorn: they are
jointed and oppositely pinnate, consisting of six
pair, and terminating in one: sessile, serrate, and
ending in a small subulate spire, from twenty-five
to twenty-seven in number: they are smooth,
plain, and of a deep green, and all obliquely tending towards the extremity of the footstalk: they
retain their green all winter. The large leafed
thorn, has a leaf about two inches and a half
long, which is petiolate, and conjugate: the leaflets are petiolate, acutely pointed, having their
margins cut with unequal and irregular incisures:
the shrub, which we had once mistaken for the
large leafed thorn, resembled the stem of that
shrub, excepting the thorn: it bears a large three
headed leaf: the briar is of the class polyandria,

and order poligymnia: the flowers are single: the peduncle long and cylindrical: the calyx is a perianth, of one leaf, five cleft, and acutely pointed: the perianth is proper, erect, inferior in both petals, and germen: the corolla consists of five acute, pale scarlet petals, inserted in the receptacle with a short and narrow cleft: the corolla is smooth, moderately long, situated at the base of the germen, permanent, and in shape resembling a cup: the stamens and filaments are subulate, inserted into the receptacle, unequal and bent inwards, concealing the pystilium: the anther is two lobed and influted, situated on the top of the filament of the pystilium: the germ is conical, imbricated, superior, sessile and short: the styles are short, compared with the stamen, capillary smooth and obtuse: they are distributed over the surface of the germ, and deciduous without any perceptible stamen.

7. The green briar grows most abundantly in rich dry lands, in the vicinity of a water course, and is found in small quantities in piny lands at a distance from the water. In the former situation the stem is frequently of the size of a man's finger, and rises perpendicularly four or five feet: it then descends in an arch, becomes procumbent, or rests on some neighbouring plants: it is simple, unbranched, and cylindric: in the latter situation it grows much smaller, and usually procumbent: the stem is armed with sharped and forked briars: the leaf is petiolate, ternate and resembles in shape and appearance that of the purple raspberry, so common to the Atlantic states: the fruit is a berry resembling the blackberry in all points, and is eaten when ripe by the natives, which they hold in much esteem, although it is not dried for winter consumption. This shrub was first dis-

covered at the entrance of Quicksand river: it grows so abundantly in the fertile valley of Columbia, and the islands, that the country is almost impenetrable: it retains its verdure late in summer.

8. Besides the fern already described, as furnishing a nutritious root, there are two other plants of the same species, which may be divided into the large and the small: the large fern rises three or four feet: the stem is a common footstalk, proceeding immediately from the radix, somewhat flat, about the size of a man's arm, and covered with innumerable black coarse capillary radicles, issuing from every part of its surface: one of these roots will send forth from twenty to forty of these common footstalks, bending outwards from the common centre: the ribs are cylindric and marked longitudinally their whole length, with a groove on the upper side: on either side of this groove, and a little below its edge the leaflets are inserted: these are shortly petiolate for about two thirds the length of the middle rib, commencing from the bottom, and from thence to the extremity sessile: the rib is terminated by a single undivided lanceolate leaflet: these are from two to four inches in length, and have a small acute angular projection, and obliquely cut at the base: the upper surface is smooth, and of a deep green: the under surface of a pale green and covered with a brown protuberance of a woolly appearance, particularly near the central fibre: the leaflets are alternately pinnate, and in number, from one hundred and ten to one hundred and forty: they are shortest at the two extremities of the common footstalk, largest in the centre, gradually lengthening, and diminishing as they succeed each other. The small fern rises likewise with a common footstalk from the radix,

from four to eight in number: from four to eight inches long: the central rib is marked with a slight longitudinal groove throughout its whole length: the leaflets are oppositely pinnate, about one third of the length of the common footstalk, from the bottom, and thence alternately pinnate: the footstalk terminates in a simple undivided lanceolate leaflet: these are oblong, obtuse, convex, absolutely entire, and the upper disc is marked with a slight longitudinal groove: near the upper extremity these leaflets are decursively pinnate, as are all those of the large fern. Both of these species preserve green during the winter.

The quadrupeds of this country from the Rocky mountains to the Pacific ocean, may be conveniently divided into the domestic and the wild animals. The first embraces the horse and dog only.

The horse is confined principally to the nations inhabiting the great plains of Columbia, extending from latitude forty to fifty north, and occupying the tract of territory lying between the Rocky mountains, and a range of mountains which pass the Columbia river about the great falls from longitude sixteen to one hundred and twenty-one west. The Shoshonees, the Chopunnish, Sokulks, Escheloots, Eneshures, and Chilluckittequaws, all enjoy the benefit of that docile, noble, and generous animal; and all of them, except the three last, possess immense numbers.

They appear to be of an excellent race, lofty, elegantly formed, active and durable: many of them appear like fine English coursers; some of them are pied with large spots of white irregularly scattered, and intermixed with a dark brown bay: the greater part, however, are of an uniform colour, marked with stars and white feet, and resemble in fleetness and bottom, as well as in

366

form and colour, the best blooded horses of Virginia. The natives suffer them to run at large in the plains, the grass of which affords them their only winter subsistence; their masters taking no trouble to lay in a winter's store for them: notwithstanding, they will, unless much exercised, fatten on the dry grass afforded by the plains during the winter. The plains are rarely if ever moistened by rain, and the grass is consequently short and thin. The natives, excepting those of the Rocky mountains, appear to take no pains in selecting their male horses for breed; and indeed, those of that class appear much the most indifferent. Whether the horse was originally a native of this country or not, the soil and climate appear to be perfectly well adapted to the nature of this animal. Horses are said to be found wild in many parts of this extensive country. The several tribes of Shoshonees who reside towards Mexico, on the waters of the Mutlomah river, and particularly one of them, called Shaboboah, have also a great number of mules, which the Indians prize more highly than horses. An elegant horse may be purchased of the natives for a few beads or other paltry trinkets, which in the United States, would not cost more than one or two dollars. The abundance and cheapness of horses, will be extremely advantageous to those who may hereafter attempt the fur trade to the East Indies, by the way of Columbia river, and the Pacific ocean.

2. The dog is unusually small, about the size of an ordinary cur: he is usually parti-coloured, amongst which, the black, white, brown, and brindle are the colours most predominant: the head is long, the nose pointed, the eyes small, the ears erect and pointed, like those of the wolf: the hair is short and smooth, excepting on the tail,

where it is long and straight, like that of the ordinary cur-dog. The natives never eat the flesh of this animal, and he appears to be in no other way serviceable to them than in hunting the elk.

The second division comprehends the brown, white, or grisly bear, the black bear; the deer, common red deer, the black-tailed fallow deer, the mule deer, the elk, the wolves, the large brown wolf, the small wolf of the plains, the large wolf of the plains, the tiger-cat, the foxes, the common red fox, the silver fox, the fisher or black fox, the large red fox of the plains, the kit-fox, or small fox of the plains, the antelope, the sheep, beaver, common otter, sea-otter, mink, seal, raccoon, squirrels, large grey squirrel, small grey squirrel, small brown squirrel, ground squirrel, braro, rat, mouse, mole, panther, hare, rabbit, polecat or skunk.

First, the brown, white or grisly bear, which seem to be of the same family, with an accidental variation of colour only, inhabit the timbered parts of the Rocky mountains. There are rarely found on the westerly side, and are more commonly below the Rocky mountains, in the plains, or on their borders, amidst copses of brush and underwood, and near the water courses. We are unable to learn that they inhabit at all in the woody country, bordering on the coast, as far in the interior as the range of mountains which pass the Columbia, between the great falls and the rapids of that river.

2. The black bear differs in no respect from those common to the United States. They chiefly inhabit timbered parts of the Rocky mountains, and likewise the borders of the great plains of the Columbia. They are sometimes found in the tract which lies between those plains and the Pacific

ocean. One of our hunters saw one of this species, which was the only one we have discovered since our residence in fort Clatsop.

3. The deer are of three kinds: the common red deer, the black-tailed fallow deer, and the mule deer.

1. The common red deer inhabit the Rocky mountains, in the neighbourhood of the Chopunnish, and about the Columbia, and down the river as low as where the tide water commences. They do not appear to differ essentially from those of the United States, being the same in shape, size, and appearance. The tail is however different, which is of an unusual length, far exceeding that of the common deer. Captain Lewis measured one, and found it to be seventeen inches long.

2. The black-tailed fallow deer are peculiar to this coast, and are a distinct species, partaking equally of the qualities of the mule and the common deer. Their ears are longer, and their winter coat darker than those of the common deer. The receptacle of the eye more conspicuous, their legs shorter, their bodies thicker and larger. The tail is of the same length with that of the common deer, the hair on the under side white, and on its sides and top of a deep jetty black: the hams resemble in form and colour those of the mule, which it likewise resembles in its gait. The black-tailed deer never runs at full speed, but bounds with every foot from the ground, at the same time, like the mule deer. He sometimes inhabits the woodlands, but more often the prairies and open grounds. It may be generally said, that he is of a size larger than the common deer, and less than the mule deer. The flesh is seldom fat, and in flavour is far inferior to any other of the species.

3. The mule deer inhabit both the seacoast and

the plains of the Missouri, and likewise the borders of the Kooskooskee river, in the neighbourhood of the Rocky mountains. It is not known whether they exist in the interior of the great plains of the Columbia, or on the lower borders, near the mountains which pass the river above the great falls. The properties of this animal have already been noticed.

4. The elk is of the same species with that which inhabits much the greatest part of North America. They are common to every part of this country, as well the timbered lands as the plains, but are much more abundant in the former than in the latter. In the month of March we discovered several which had not cast their horns, and others where the new horns had grown to the length of six inches. The latter were in much the best order, and from hence we draw the inference that the leanest elk retain their horns the longest.

5. The wolf is either the large brown wolf, or the wolf of the plains, of which last there are two kinds, the large and the small. The large brown wolf inhabits the woody countries on the borders of the Pacific, and the mountains which pass the Columbia river, between the great falls and rapids, and resembles in all points those of the United States.

The large and small wolves of the plains, principally inhabit the open country and the woodlands on their borders. They resemble, both in appearance and habit, those of the Missouri plains. They are by no means abundant in the plains of the Columbia, as they meet there but very little game for their subsistence.

6. The tiger-cat inhabits the borders of the plains, and the woody country in the neighbourhood of the Pacific. This animal is of a size

larger than the wild cat of our country, and much the same in form, agility, and ferocity. The colour of the back, neck, and sides is of a reddish brown, irregularly variegated with small spots of dark brown: the tail is about two inches long, and nearly white, except the extremity, which is black. It terminates abruptly, as if it had been amputated: the belly is white, and beautifully variegated with small black spots: the legs are of the same colour with the sides, and the back is marked transversely with black stripes: the ears are black on the outer side, covered with fine, short hair, except at the upper point, which is furnished with a pencil of hair, fine, straight, and black, three-fourths of an inch in length. The hair of this animal is long and fine, far exceeding that of the wild cat of the United States, but inferior in that quality to that of the bear of the north-west. The skin of this animal is in great demand amongst the natives, for of this they form their robes, and it requires four to make up the complement.

7. Of the foxes we have seen several species.

The large red fox of the plains, and the kit-fox or small red fox of the plains, are the same which are found on the banks of the Missouri. They are found almost exclusively in the open plains, or on the tops of brush within the level country: the common red fox of the United States, inhabits the country bordering the coast, nor does this animal appear to have undergone any alteration.

The black fox, or as it is termed in the neighbourhood of Detroit, the fisher, is found in the woody country bordering on the coast. How it should have acquired this appellation it is difficult to imagine, as it certainly does not prey upon fish. These animals are extremely strong and active, and admirably expert in climbing: this they perform with the greatest ease, and bound from tree to tree in pursuit of the squirrel or raccoon, their most usual food. Their colour is of a jetty black, excepting a small white spot upon the breast: the body is long, the legs short, and resembling those of the ordinary turnspit dog. The tail is remarkably long, and not differing in other particulars from that of the ordinary fox.

The silver fox is an animal very rare, even in the country he inhabits. We have seen nothing but the skins of this animal, and those in the possession of the natives of the woody country below the Columbia falls, which makes us conjecture it to be an inhabitant of that country exclusively. From the skin it appeared to be of the size of the large red fox of the plains, resembling that animal in form, and particularly in the dimensions of the tail. The legs captain Lewis conjectured to be somewhat larger. It has a long deep lead coloured fur, for foil, intermixed with long hairs, either of a black or white colour at the lower part, and invariably white at the top, forming a most beautiful silver grey. Captain Lewis thought this the most beautiful of the whole species, excepting one which he discovered on the Missouri near the natural walls.

8. The antelope inhabits the great plains of the Columbia, and resembles those found on the banks of the Missouri, and indeed in every part of the untimbered country, but they are by no means so abundant on this as on the other side of the Rocky mountains. The natives in this place make themselves robes of their skins, and preserve the hair entire. In the summer and autumn, when the salmon begin to decline, the majority of the natives leave the sides of the river, and reside in

the open plains, to hunt the antelope, which they pursue on horseback, and shoot with their arrows.

9. The sheep is found in many places, but mostly in the timbered parts of the Rocky mountains. They live in greater numbers on the chain of mountains forming the commencement of the woody country on the coast, and passing the Columbia between the falls and rapids. We have only seen the skins of these animals, which the natives dress with the wool, and the blankets which they manufacture from the wool. The animal from this evidence appears to be of the size of our common sheep, of a white colour: the wool is fine on many parts of the body, but in length not equal to that of our domestic sheep. On the back, and particularly on the top of the head, this is intermixed with a considerable proportion of long straight hairs. From the Indian account these animals have erect pointed horns: one of our engagees informed us that he had seen them in the black hills, and that the horns were lunated like those of our domestic sheep. We have nevertheless too many proofs to admit a doubt of their existing, and in considerable numbers on the mountains near the coast.

10. The beaver of this country is large and fat: the flesh is very palatable, and at our table was a real luxury. On the 7th of January, 1806, our hunter found a beaver in his traps, of which he made a bait for taking others: this bait will entice the beaver to the trap, as far as he can smell it, and this may be fairly stated to be at the distance of a mile, as their sense of smelling is very acute. To prepare beaver bait, the castor or bark stone is first gently pressed from the bladder like bag which contains it, into a vial of four ounces,

with a large mouth: five or six of these stones are thus taken, to which must be added a nutmeg, a dozen or fifteen cloves, and thirty grains of cinnamon, finely pulverized and stirred together, and as much ardent spirits added to the composition as will reduce the whole to the consistency of mustard. All this must be carefully corked, as it soon loses its efficacy if exposed to open air. The scent becomes much stronger in four or five days after preparation, and, provided proper precaution is exercised, will preserve its efficacy for months. Any strong aromatic spices will answer; their sole virtue being to give variety and pungency to the scent of the bark stone. The male beaver has six stones, two of which contain a substance much like finely pulverized bark, of a pale yellow colour, and in smell resembling tanners' ooze; these are called bark stones or castors. Two others, which like the bark stone resemble small bladders, contain pure strong oil, of a strong rank smell, and are called the oil stone, and the other two are the testicles. The bark stones are two inches in length: the others are somewhat smaller, of an oval form, and lie in a bunch together, between the skin and the root of the tail, with which they are closely connected, and seem to communicate. The female brings forth once in a year only, and has sometimes two and sometimes four at a birth, which usually happens in the latter end of May and the beginning of June: at this time she is said to drive the male from the lodge, who would otherwise destroy the young. They propagate like the fowl, by the gut, and the male has no other sexual distinction that we could discover.

11. The common otter has already been described, and this species does not differ from those inhabiting the other parts of America.

12. The sea-otter resides only on the seacoast, or in the neighbourhood of the salt water. When fully grown, he arrives to the size of a large mastiff dog. The ears and eyes, particularly the former, which are not an inch in length, are thick, pointed, fleshy, and covered with short hair: the tail is ten inches long, thick at the point of insertion and partially covered with a deep fur on the upper side: the legs are very short, and the feet, which have five toes each, are broad, large, and webbed: the legs are covered with fur, and the feet with short hair: the body of this animal is long, and of the same thickness throughout: from the extremity of the tail to the nose they measure five feet. The colour is a uniform dark brown, and, when in good order and season, perfectly black. This animal is unrivalled for the beauty, richness, and softness of his fur: the inner part of the fur, when opened, is lighter than the surface in its natural position: there are some black and shining hairs intermixed with the fur, which are rather longer, and add much to its beauty: the fur about the ears, nose and eyes, in some of this species, presents a lighter colour, sometimes a brown: their young are often seen of a cream-coloured white about the nose, eyes and forehead, and which are always much lighter than their other parts: their fur is however much inferior to that of the full grown otter.

13. The mink inhabits the woody country bordering on the coast, and does not differ in any point from those of the United States.

14. The seal are found on this coast in great numbers, and as far up the Columbia river as the Great Falls, and none have been discovered beyond them. The skins of such as captain Lewis examined, were covered with a short, coarse, stiff,

and glossy hair, of a reddish brown colour. This
animal, when in the water, appeared of a black
colour, and sometimes spotted with white. We
believe that there are several species of this animal
to be found in this country, but we could not procure a sufficient number to make the examination:
the skins were precisely of the same kind as our
countrymen employ in the manufacture of trunks.

15. The raccoon inhabits woody countries bordering on the coast, in considerable numbers, and
are caught by the natives with snares or pitfalls:
they hold their skins in but little or no estimation, and very seldom make them into robes.

16. The squirrels we have seen, are,

The large grey squirrel. This animal appears to
be an inhabitant of a narrow tract of country,
well covered with whiteoak timber, and situated
on the upper side of the mountains just below
Columbia falls. This animal we have only found
in those tracts which have been covered with
timber; for in countries where pine is most abundant, he does not appear: he is much superior in
size to the common grey squirrel, and resembles in
form, colour and size, the fox squirrel of the Atlantic states: the tail exceeds the whole length of
the body and the head: the eyes are dark, the
whiskers long and black: the back, sides of the
head and tail, and outward part of the legs, are
all of a blue-coloured grey: the breast, belly, and
inner part of the body, are all of a pure white:
the hair is short, like that of the fox squirrel,
though much finer, and intermixed with a portion
of fur. The natives hold the skin of this animal
in high estimation, which they use in forming
their robes. He subsists on the acorn and filberts,
which last grows in great abundance in the oak
country.

The small grey squirrel is common to every part of the Rocky mountains where timber abounds. He differs from the dark brown squirrel in colour only. The back, sides, neck, head, tail and outer side of the legs, are of a brownish lead-coloured grey: the tail is slightly touched with a dark reddish colour, near the extremity of some of the hairs: the throat, breast, belly, and inner parts of the legs, are of the colour of a tanner's ooze, and have a narrow strip of black, commencing behind each shoulder, and entering longitudinally about three inches, between the colours of the sides and belly. Their habits are precisely those of the dark brown squirrel, and like them they are extremely nimble and active.

There is also a species of squirrel, evidently distinct, which we have denominated the burrowing squirrel. He inhabits these plains, and somewhat resembles those found on the Missouri: he measures one foot and five inches in length, of which the tail comprises two and a half inches only: the neck and legs are short; the ears are likewise short, obtusely pointed, and lie close to the head, and the aperture larger than will generally be found among burrowing animals. The eyes are of a moderate size, the pupil black, and the iris of a dark sooty brown: the whiskers are full, long, and black: the teeth, and, indeed, the whole contour, resemble those of the squirrel: each foot has five toes; the two inner ones of the fore feet are remarkably short, and are equipped with blunt nails: the remaining toes on the front feet are long, black, slightly curved, and sharply pointed: the hair of the tail is thickly inserted on the sides only, which gives it a flat appearance, and a long oval form: the tips of the hair forming the outer edges of the tail are white, the other extremity of a fox red: the under part of the tail resembles an iron grey; the upper is of a reddish brown: the lower part of the jaws, the under part of the neck, legs and feet, from the body and belly downwards, are of a light brick red: the nose and eyes are of a darker shade, of the same colour: the upper part of the head, neck and body, are of a curious brown grey, with a slight tinge of brick red: the longer hairs of these parts are of a reddish white colour, at their extremities, and falling together, give this animal a speckled appearance. These animals form in large companies, like those on the Missouri, occupying with their burrows sometimes two hundred acres of land: the burrows are separate, and each possesses, perhaps, ten or twelve of these inhabitants. There is a little mound in front of the hole, formed of the earth thrown out of the burrow, and frequently there are three or four distinct holes, forming one burrow, with these entrances around the base of these little mounds. These mounds, sometimes about two feet in height and four in diameter, are occupied as watch-towers by the inhabitants of these little communities. The squirrels, one or more, are irregularly distributed on the tract they thus occupy, at the distance of ten, twenty, or sometimes from thirty to forty yards. When any one approaches, they make a shrill whistling sound, somewhat resembling tweet, tweet, tweet, the signal for their party to take the alarm, and to retire into their entrenchments. They feed on the roots of grass, &c.

The small brown squirrel is a beautiful little animal, about the size and form of the red squirrel of the eastern Atlantic states and western lakes. The tail is as long as the body and neck, and formed like that of the red squirrel: the eyes are

378

black, the whiskers long and black but not abundant: the back, sides, head, neck, and outer part of the legs are of a reddish brown: the throat, breast, belly, and inner part of the legs are of a pale red: the tail is a mixture of black and fox-coloured red, in which the black predominates in the middle, and the other on the edges and extremity: the hair of the body is about half an inch long, and so fine and soft it has the appearance of fur: the hair of the tail is coarser and double in length. This animal subsists chiefly on the seeds of various species of pine and is always found in the pine country.

The ground squirrel is found in every part of this country, as well in the prairies as in the woodlands, and is one of the few animals which we have seen in every part of our journey, and differs in no respect from those of the United States.

There is still another species, denominated by captain Lewis, the barking squirrel, found in the plains of the Missouri. This animal commonly weighs three pounds: the colour is a uniform bright brick red and grey, and the former predominates: the under side of the neck and belly are lighter than the other parts of the body: the legs are short, and the breast and shoulders wide; the head is stout and muscular, and terminates more bluntly, wider, and flatter than that of the common squirrel: the ears are short, and have the appearance of amputation: the jaw is furnished with a pouch to contain his food, but not so large as that of the common squirrel: the nose is armed with whiskers on each side, and a few long hairs are inserted on each jaw, and directly over the eyes: the eye is small and black: each foot has five toes, and the two outer ones are much shorter than those in the centre. The two inner toes of the fore-feet are long, sharp, and well adapted to digging and scratching. From the extremity of the nose to the end of the tail this animal measures one foot and five inches, of which the tail occupies four inches. Notwithstanding the clumsiness of his form, he is remarkably active, and he burrows in the ground with great rapidity. These animals burrow and reside in their little subterraneous villages like the burrowing squirrel. To these apartments, although six or eight usually associate together, there is but one entrance. They are of great depth, and captain Lewis once pursued one to the depth of ten feet, and did not reach the end of the burrow. They occupy, in this manner, several hundred acres of ground, and when at rest their position is generally erect on their hinder feet and rump: they sit with much confidence, and bark at the intruder as he approaches, with a fretful and harmless intrepidity. The note resembles that of the little toy-dog: the yelps are in quick and angry succession, attended by rapid and convulsive motions, as if they were determined to sally forth in defence of their freehold. They feed on the grass of their village, the limits of which they never venture to exceed. As soon as the frost commences, they shut themselves up in their caverns, and continue until the spring opens. The flesh of this animal is not unpleasant to the taste.

17. Sewellel is a name given by the natives to a small animal found in the timbered country on this coast. It is more abundant in the neighbourhood of the great falls and rapids of the Columbia than on the coast which we inhabit.

The natives make great use of the skins of this animal in forming their robes, which they dress

with the fur on, and attach them together with
sinews of the elk or deer: the skin, when dressed,
is from fourteen to eighteen inches long, and from
seven to nine in width: the tail is always separated from the skin by the natives when making
their robes. This animal mounts a tree and burrows in the ground precisely like a squirrel: the
ears are short, thin, and pointed, and covered
with a fine short hair, of a uniform reddish
brown: the bottom or the base of the long hairs,
which exceed the fur but little in length, as well as
the fur itself, are of a dark colour next to the
skin for two-thirds of the length of this animal:
the fur and hair are very fine, short, thickly set,
and silky: the ends of the fur and tip of the hair
are of a reddish brown, and that colour predominates in the usual appearance of the animal.
Captain Lewis offered considerable rewards to the
Indians, but was never able to procure one of
these animals alive.

18. The braro, so called from the French engagees, appears to be an animal of the civet species,
and much resembles the common badger. These
animals inhabit the open plains of the Columbia,
sometimes those of the Missouri, and are sometimes found in the woods: they burrow in hard
grounds with surprising ease and dexterity, and
will cover themselves in a very few moments: they
have five long fixed nails on each foot; those on
the fore feet are much the longest, and one of
those on each hind foot is double, like that of
the beaver: they weigh from fourteen to eighteen
pounds: the body is long in proportion to its
thickness: the fore legs are remarkably large,
muscular, and are formed like those of the turnspit dog, and, as well as the hind legs, are short:
these animals are broad across the shoulders and

breast: the neck is short, the mouth wide, and furnished with sharp, straight teeth, both above and below, with four sharp, straight, pointed tusks, two in the upper, and two in the lower jaw: the eyes are black and small; whiskers are placed in four points on each side near the nose, and on the jaws near the opening of the mouth: the ears are short, wide, and oppressed, as if a part had been amputated: the tail is four inches in length, the hair of which is longest at the point of the junction with the body, and growing shorter until it ends in an acute point: the hairs of the body are much shorter on the sides and rump than those on any other part, which gives the body an apparent flatness, particularly when the animal rests upon his belly: the hair is upwards of three inches in length, especially on the rump, where it extends so far towards the point of the tail, it conceals the shape of that part, and gives to the whole of the hinder parts of the body the appearance of a right angled triangle, of which the point of the tail forms an acute angle: the small quantity of coarse fur intermixed with the hair is of a reddish pale yellow.

19. The rat which inhabits the Rocky mountains, like those on the borders of the Missouri, in the neighbourhood of the mountains, have the distinguishing traits of possessing a tail covered with hair like the other parts of the body. These animals are probably of the same species with those of the Atlantic states, which have not this characteristic distinction: the ordinary house rat we found on the banks of the Missouri, as far up as the woody country extends, and the rat, such as has been described, captain Lewis found in the state of Georgia, and also in Madison's cave in Virginia.

20. The mouse which inhabits this country are precisely the same with those which inhabit the United States.

21. The mole. This animal differs in no respect from the species so common in the United States.

22. The panther is found indifferently, either in the great plains of the Columbia, the western side of the Rocky mountains, or on the coast of the Pacific. He is the same animal so well known on the Atlantic coast, and most commonly found on the frontiers, or unsettled parts of our country. He is very seldom found, and when found, so wary, it is difficult to reach him with a musket.

23. The hare on this side of the Rocky mountains inhabits the great plains of the Columbia. On the eastward of those mountains they inhabit the plains of the Missouri. They weigh from seven to eleven pounds: the eye is large and prominent, the pupil of a deep sea-green, occupying one-third of the diameter of the eye; the iris is of a bright yellowish and silver colour; the ears are placed far back, and very near each other, which the animal can, with surprising ease and quickness, dilate, and throw forward, or contract, and hold upon his back at pleasure: the head, neck, back, shoulders, thighs, and outer part of the legs and thighs are of a lead colour: the sides, as they approach the belly, become gradually more white: the belly, breast, and inner part of the legs and thighs are white, with a light shade of lead colour: the tail is round and bluntly pointed, covered with white, soft, fine fur, not quite so long as on the other parts of the body: the body is covered with a deep, fine, soft, close fur. The colours here described are those which the animal assumes from the middle of April to the middle of November; the rest of the year he is of a pure white,

383

except the black and reddish brown of the ears, which never change. A few reddish brown spots are sometimes intermixed with the white, at this season (February 26, 1806) on their heads and the upper part of their necks and shoulders: the body of the animal is smaller and longer in proportion to its height than the rabbit: when he runs he conveys his tail straight behind, in the direction of his body: he appears to run and bound with surprising agility and ease: he is extremely fleet, and never burrows or takes shelter in the ground when pursued. His teeth are like those of the rabbit, as is also his upper lip, which is divided as high as the nose. His food is grass, herbs, and in winter he feeds much on the bark of several aromatic herbs, growing on the plains. Captain Lewis measured the leaps of this animal, and found them commonly from eighteen to twenty-one feet: they are generally found separate, and are never seen to associate in greater numbers than two or three.

24. The rabbit is the same with those of our own country, and are found indifferently, either on the prairies or the woodlands, and are not very abundant.

25. The polecat is also found in every part of this country: they are very abundant on some parts of the Columbia, particularly in the neighbourhood of the Great falls and narrows of that river, where they live in the cliffs along the river, and feed on the offal of the Indian fishing shores. They are of the same species as those found in the other parts of North America.

The birds which we have seen between the Rocky mountains and the Pacific may be divided into two classes, the terrestrial and the aquatic. In the former class are to be arranged,

1. The grouse or prairie hen. This is peculiarly the inhabitant of the great plains of the Columbia, and does not differ from those of the upper portion of the Missouri. The tail is pointed, the feathers in the centre, and much longer than those on the sides. This species differs essentially in the formation of the plumage from those of the Illinois, which have their tails composed of feathers of an equal length. In the winter season this bird is booted to the first joint of the toes; the toes are curiously bordered on their lower edges with narrow hard scales, which are placed very close to each other, and extend horizontally about one eighth of an inch on each side of the toes, adding much to the broadness of the feet, a security which bounteous nature has furnished them for passing over the snows with more ease, and what is very remarkable, in the summer season these scales drop from the feet. This bird has four toes on each foot, the colour is a mixture of dark brown, reddish and yellowish brown, with white confusedly mixed. In this assemblage of colours, the reddish brown prevails most on the upper parts of the body, wings, and tail, and the white underneath the belly, and the lower parts of the breast and tail. These birds associate in large flocks in autumn and winter, and even in summer are seen in companies of five or six. They feed on grass, insects, leaves of various shrubs in the plains, and on the seeds of several species of speth and wild rye, which grow in richer soils. In winter their food consists of the buds of the willow and cottonwood, and native berries.

2. The cock of the plains is found on the plains of the Columbia in great abundance, from the entrance of the southeast fork of the Columbia to that of Clark's river. It is about two and three

quarter inches the size of our ordinary turkey: the beak is large, short, covered and convex, the upper exceeding the lower chop: the nostrils are large, and the back black; the color is an uniform mixture of a dark brown, resembling the dove, and a reddish and yellowish brown, with some small black specks. In this mixture the dark brown prevails, and has a slight cast of the dove-colour: the wider side of the large feathers of the wings are of a dark brown only. The tail is composed of nineteen feathers, and that inserted in the centre is the longest, the remaining nine on each side gradually diminish. The tail when folded comes to a very sharp point, and appears proportionably long, when compared with the other parts of the body. In the act of flying, the tail resembles that of the wild pigeon, although the motion of the wings is much like that of the pheasant and grouse. This bird has four toes on each foot, of which the hindmost is the shortest, and the leg is covered with feathers about half the distance between the knee and foot. When the wing is expanded there are wide openings between its feathers, the plumage being too narrow to fill up the vacancy: the wings are short in comparison with those of the grouse or pheasant. The habits of this bird resemble those of the grouse, excepting that his food is that of the leaf and buds of the pulpy-leafed thorn. Captain Lewis did not remember to have seen this bird but in the neighbourhood of that shrub, which they sometimes feed on, the prickly pear. The gizzard is large, and much less compressed and muscular than in most fowls, and perfectly resembles a maw. When this bird flies he utters a cackling sound, not unlike that of the dunghill fowl. The flesh of the cock of the plains is dark, and only tolerable in point of flavour, and is not so palatable either as that of the pheasant or grouse. The feathers about the head are pointed and stiff and short, fine and stiff about the ears; at the base of the beak several hairs are to be seen. This bird is invariably found in the plains.

3. The pheasant, of which we distinguish the large black and white pheasant, the small speckled pheasant, the small brown pheasant:

1. The large black and white pheasant differs but little from those of the United States; the brown is rather brighter, and has a more reddish tint. This bird has eighteen feathers in the tail, of about six inches in length. He is also booted to the toes: the two tufts of long black feathers on each side of the neck, so common in the male of this species inhabiting the United States, are no less observable in this pheasant: the feathers on the body are of a dark brown, tipped with white and black, in which mixture the black predominates.; the white are irregularly intermixed with those of the black and dark brown in every part, but in greater proportion about the neck, breast, and belly: this mixture makes this bird resemble much that kind of dunghill fowl, which the housewives of our country call Domminicker. On the breast of some of these species the white predominates: the tufts on the neck leave a space about two and a half inches long, and one inch in width, where no feathers grow, though concealed by the plumage connected with the higher and under parts of the neck; this space enables them to contract or dilate the feathers on the neck with more ease: the eye is dark, the beak is black, curved, somewhat pointed, and the upper exceeds the under chop: a narrow vermillion stripe runs above each eye, not protuberant but uneven, with

387

a number of minute rounded dots. The bird feeds on wild fruits, particularly the berry of the saca-commis, and exclusively resides in that portion of the Rocky mountains watered by the Columbia.

2. The small speckled pheasant resides in the same country with the foregoing, and differs only in size and colour. He is half the size of the black and white pheasant, associates in much larger flocks, and is very gentle: the black is more predominant, and the dark brown feathers less frequent in this than in the larger species: the mixture of white is more general on every part. This bird is smaller than our pheasant, and the body more round: the flesh of both this species is dark, and with our means of cooking, not well flavoured.

3. The small brown pheasant is an inhabitant of the same country, and is of the same size and shape of the speckled pheasant, which he likewise resembles in his habits. The stripe above the eye in this species is scarcely perceptible, and is, when closely examined, of a yellow or orange colour, instead of the vermillion of the other species: the colour is a uniform mixture of dark yellowish brown, with a slight aspersion of brownish white on the breast, belly, and feathers underneath the tail: the whole appearance has much the resemblance of the common quail: this bird is also booted to the toes: the flesh of this is preferable to the other two.

4. The buzzard is, we believe, the largest bird of North America. One which was taken by our hunters was not in good condition, and yet the weight was twenty-five pounds. Between the extremity of the wings the bird measured nine feet and two inches: from the extremity of the beak to the toe, three feet nine and a half inches;

from the hip to the toe, two feet; the circumference of the head was nine and three-quarter inches: that of the neck seven and a half inches; that of the body inclusive of two feet three inches: the diameter of the eye is four and a half tenths of an inch; the iris is of a pale scarlet red, and the pupil of a deep sea-green: the head and part of the neck are uncovered by feathers: the tail is composed of twelve feathers of equal length, each of the length of fourteen inches: the legs are uncovered and not entirely smooth: the toes are four in number, three forward, and that in the centre much the largest; the fourth is short, inserted near the inner of the three other toes, and rather projecting forward: the thigh is covered with feathers as low as the knee, the top or upper part of the toes are imbricated with broad scales, lying transversely: the nails are black, short, and bluntly pointed: the under side of the wing is covered with white down and feathers: a white stripe of about two inches in width marks the outer part of the wing, embracing the lower points of the plumage, covering the joints of the wing: the remainder is of a deep black: the skin of the beak and head to the joining of the neck, is of a pale orange colour; the other part, destitute of plumage, is of a light flesh colour. It is not known that this bird preys upon living animals: we have seen him feeding on the remains of the whale and other fish thrown upon the coast by the violence of the waves. This bird was not seen by any of the party until we had descended Columbia river, below the great falls, and he is believed to be of the vulture genus, although the bird lacks some of the characteristics, particularly the hair on the neck, and the plumage on the legs.

5. The robin is an inhabitant of the Rocky mountains: the beak is smooth, black, and convex; the upper chop exceeds the other in length, and a few small black hairs garnish the sides of its base: the eye is of a uniform deep sea-green colour: the legs, feet, and talons are white, of which the front one is of the same length of the leg, including the talon; these are slightly imbricated, curved, and sharply pointed: the crown, from the beak back to the neck, embracing more than half the circumference of the neck, the back, and tail, are all of a bluish dark brown: the two outer feathers of the tail are dashed with white near their tips, imperceptible when the tail is folded: a fine black forms the ground of their wings; two stripes of the same colour pass on either side of the head, from the base of the beak to the junction, and embrace the eye to its upper edge: a third stripe of the same colour passes from the sides of the neck to the tips of the wings, across the croop, in the form of a gorget: the throat, neck, breast, and belly, are of a fine brick red, tinged with yellow; a narrow stripe of this colour commences just above the centre of each eye, and extends backwards to the neck till it comes in contact with the black stripe before mentioned, to which it seems to answer as a border: the feathers forming the first and second ranges of the coverts of the two joints of the wing next to the body, are beautifully tipped with this brick red, as is also each large feather of the wing, on the short side of its plumage. This beautiful little bird feeds on berries. The robin is an inhabitant exclusively of the woody country; we have never heard its note, which the coldness of the season may perhaps account for.

The leather-winged bat, so common to the

United States, likewise inhabits this side of the Rocky mountains.

6. The crow and raven is exactly the same in appearance and note as that on the Atlantic, except that it is much smaller on the Columbia.

7. The hawks too of this coast do not differ from those of the United States. We here see the large brown hawk, the small or sparrow hawk, and one of an intermediate size, called in the United States, the hen hawk, which has a long tail and blue wings, and is extremely fierce, and rapid in its flight. The hawks, crows, and ravens are common to every part of this country, their nests being scattered in the high cliffs, along the whole course of the Columbia and its southeastern branches.

8. The large blackbird is the same with those of our country, and are found every where in this country.

9. The large hooting owl we saw only on the Kooskooskee under the Rocky mountains. It is the same in form and size with the owl of the United States, though its colours, particularly the reddish brown, seem deeper and brighter.

10. The turtle-dove and the robin (except the Columbian robin already described) are the same as those of the United States, and are found in the plains as well as in the common broken country.

11. The magpie is most commonly found in the open country, and resemble those of the Missouri, already described.

12. The large woodpecker or laycock, the lark woodpecker, and the common small white woodpecker, with a red head, are the inhabitants exclusively of the timbered lands, and differ in no respect from birds of the same species in the United States.

391

13. The lark, which is found in the plains only, and is not unlike what is called in Virginia, the old field lark, is the same with those already described as seen on the Missouri.

14. The flycatcher is of two species.

The first is of a small body, of a reddish brown colour: the tail and neck short, and the beak pointed: some fine black specks are intermingled with the reddish brown. This is of the same species with that which remains all winter in Virginia, where it is sometimes called the wren.

The second species has recently returned, and emigrates during the winter. The colours of this bird are, a yellowish brown, on the back, head, neck, wing and tail; the breast and belly are of a yellowish white; the tail is in the same proportion as that of the wren, but the bird itself is of a size smaller than the wren: the beak is straight, pointed, convex, rather large at the base, and the chops are of equal length. The first species is smaller, and in fact the smallest bird which captain Lewis had ever seen excepting the humming bird. Both of this species are found exclusively in the woody country.

15. Corvus. The blue-crested, and the small white-breasted corvus, are both natives of the piny country, and are invariably found as well on the Rocky mountains as on this coast. They have already been described.

16. The snipe, &c. The common snipe of the marshes, and the common sand snipe, are of the same species as those so well known in the United States. They are by no means found in such abundance here as they are on the coast of the Atlantic.

17. The leathern winged bat, so familiar to the

natives of the United States, is likewise found on this side of the Rocky mountains.

18. The white woodpecker, likewise frequents these regions, and reminds our party of their native country, by his approaches. The head of this bird is of a deep red colour, like that of the United States. We have conjectured that he has lately returned, as he does not abide in this country during the winter. The large woodpecker, and the lark woodpecker, are found in this country, and resemble those of the United States.

19. The black woodpecker is found in most parts of the Rocky mountains, as well as in the western and southwestern mountains. He is about the size of the lark woodpecker, or turtle-dove, although his wings are longer than the wings of either of those birds: the beak is one inch in length, black, curved at the base, and sharply pointed: the chops are the same in length; around the base of the beak, including the eye and a small part of the throat, there is a fine crimson red: the neck, as low down as the crook in front, is of an iron grey: the belly and breast present a curious mixture of white and blood-red, which has much the appearance of paint, where the red predominates: the top of the head, back, sides, and upper surface of the wings and tail, exhibit the appearance of a glossy green, in a certain exposure to the light: the under side of the wings and tail, is of a sooty black: the tail is equipped with ten feathers, sharply pointed, and those in the centre the longest, being about two and a half inches in length: the tongue is barbed and pointed, and of an elastic and cartilaginous substance: the eye is rather large, the pupil black, and the iris of a dark and yellowish brown: the bird in its actions when flying, resembles the small red-headed woodpecker

common to the United States, and likewise in its notes: the pointed tail renders essential service when the bird is sitting and retaining his resting position against the perpendicular sides of a tree: the legs and feet are black, and covered with wide imbricated scales: he has four toes on each foot, two in the rear and two in front, the nails of which are much curved and pointed remarkably sharp: he feeds on bugs and a variety of insects.

20. The calumet eagle, sometimes inhabits this side of the Rocky mountains. This information captain Lewis derived from the natives, in whose possession he had seen their plumage. These are of the same species with those of the Missouri, and are the most beautiful of all the family of eagles in America. The colours are black and white, and beautifully variegated. The tail feathers, so highly prized by the natives, are composed of twelve broad feathers of unequal length, which are white, except within two inches of their extremities, where they immediately change to a jetty black: the wings have each a large circular white spot in the middle, which is only visible when they are extended: the body is variously marked with black and white: in form they resemble the bald eagle, but they are rather smaller, and fly with much more rapidity. This bird is feared by all his carnivorous competitors, who, on his approach, leave the carcase instantly, on which they had been feeding. The female broods in the most inaccessible parts of the mountains, where she makes her summer residence, and descends to the plains only in the fall and winter seasons. The natives are at this season on the watch, and so highly is this plumage prized by the Mandans, the Minnetarees, and the Ricaras, that the tail feathers of two of these eagles will be purchased by the

exchange of a good horse or gun, and such ac-coutrements. Amongst the great and little Osages, and those nations inhabiting the countries where the bird is more rarely seen, the price is even double of that above mentioned. With these feathers the natives decorate the stems of their sacred pipes or calumets, from whence the name of the calumet eagle is derived. The Ricaras have domesticated this bird in many instances, for the purpose of obtaining its plumage. The natives, on every part of the continent, who can procure the feathers, attach them to their own hair, and the manes and tails of their favourite horses, by way of ornament. They also decorate their war caps or bonnets with these feathers.

As to the aquatic birds of this country, we have to repeat the remark, that, as we remained near the coast during the winter only, many birds, common both in the summer and autumn, might have retired from the cold, and been lost to our observation. We saw, however,

The large blue, and brown heron; the fishing hawk; the blue-crested fisher; several species of gulls; the cormorant; two species of loons; brant of two kinds; geese; swan; and several species of ducks.

1. The large blue and brown herons, or cranes, as they are usually termed in the United States, are found on the Columbia below tide-water. They differ in no respect from the same species of bird in the United States. The same may be observed of

2. The fishing hawk, with the crown of the head white, and the back of a mealy white, and

3. Of the blue-crested or king-fisher, both of which are found every where on the Columbia and

its tributary waters; though the fishing hawk is not abundant, particularly in the mountains.

4. Of gulls, we have remarked four species on the coast and the river, all common to the United States.

5. The cormorant is, properly speaking, a large black duck that feeds on fish. Captain Lewis could perceive no difference between this bird and those ducks which inhabit the Potomack and other rivers on the Atlantic coast. He never remembered to have seen those inhabiting the Atlantic states, so high up the river as they have been found in this quarter. We first discovered the corvus on the Kooskooskee, at the entrance of Chopunnish river: they increased in numbers as we descended, and formed much the greatest portion of the water-fowl which we saw until we reached the Columbia at the entrance of the tides. They abound even here, but bear no proportion to the number of other water-fowl seen at this place.

6. The loon: there are two species of loons: the speckled loon, found on every part of the rivers of this country. They are of the same size, colour and form, with those of the Atlantic coast.

The second species we found at the falls of Columbia, and from thence downwards to the ocean. This bird is not more than half the size of the speckled loon; the neck is, in front, long, slender and white: the plumage on the body and back of the head and neck are of a dun or ash colour: the breast and belly are white, the beak like that of the speckled loon: and like them, it cannot fly, but flutters along on the surface of the water, or dives for security when pursued.

7. The brant are of three kinds; the white, the brown, and the pied. The white brant are very common on the shores of the Pacific, particularly

below the water, where they remain in vast numbers during the winter: they feed like the swan-
geese, on the grass, roots, and seeds which grow
in the marshes: this bird is about the size of the
brown brant, or a third less than the common
Canadian wild goose: the head is rather larger,
the beak thicker than that of the wild goose,
shorter, and of much the same form, being of a
yellowish white colour, except the edges of the
chops, which are frequently of a dark brown: the
legs and feet are of the same form of the goose,
and are of a pale flesh colour: the tail is composed
of sixteen feathers of equal length as those of the
geese and brown brant are, and bears about the
same proportion in point of length: the eye is of
a dark colour, and nothing remarkable in size: the
wings are larger when compared with those of the
geese, but not so much so as in the brown brant:
the colour of the plumage is a pure uniform white,
except the large feathers at the extremity of the
wings, which are black: the large feathers at the
first joint of the wing next to the body are white:
the note of this bird differs essentially from that
of the goose; it more resembles that of the brown
brant, but is somewhat different; it is like the
note of a young domestic goose, that has not perfectly attained its full sound: the flesh of this bird
is exceedingly fine, preferable to either the goose
or brown brant.

2. The brown brant are much of the same
colour, form, and size as the white, only that their
wings are considerably longer and more pointed:
the plumage of the upper part of the body, neck,
head, and tail, are much the colour of the Canadian goose, but somewhat darker, in consequence
of some dark feathers irregularly scattered
throughout: they have not the same white on the

neck and sides of the head as the goose, nor is the neck darker than the body: like the goose, they have some white feathers on the rump at the joining of the tail: the beak is dark, and the legs and feet also dark with a greenish cast: the breast and belly are of a lighter colour than the back, and is also irregularly intermixed with dark brown and black feathers, which give it a pied appearance: the flesh is darker and better than that of the goose: the habits of these birds resemble those of the geese, with this difference, that they do not remain in this climate in such numbers during the winter as the others, and that they set out earlier in the fall season on their return to the south, and arrive later in the spring than the goose. There is no difference between this bird and that called simply the brant, so common on the lakes, on the Ohio and Mississippi. The small goose of this country is rather less than the brant; its head and neck like the brant.

3. The pied brant weigh about eight and a half pounds, differing from the ordinary pied brant in their wings, which are neither so long nor so pointed: the base of the beak is for a little distance white, suddenly succeeded by a narrow line of dark brown: the remainder of the neck, head, back, wings and tail, all except the tips of the feathers, are of a bluish brown of the common wild goose: the breast and belly are white, with an irregular mixture of black feathers, which give those parts a pied appearance. From the legs back underneath the tail and around its junction with the body above, the feathers are white: the tail is composed of eighteen feathers, the longest in the centre, and measures six inches with the barrel of the quill: those on the sides of the tail are something shorter, and bend with the ex-

tremities inwards towards the centre of the tail: the extremities of these feathers are white: the beak is of a light flesh colour: the legs and feet, which do not differ in structure from those of the goose or brant of other species, are of an orange colour: the eye is small, the iris of a dark yellowish brown, and pupil black: the note is much that of the common pied brant, from which in fact, they are not to be distinguished at a distance, although they certainly are of a distinct species: the flesh is equally palatable with that of common pied brant. They do not remain here during the winter in such numbers as the bird above mentioned: this bird is here denominated the pied brant, on account of the near resemblance, and for want of another appellation.

8. The geese are either the large or small kind: the large goose resembles our ordinary wild or Canadian goose; the small is rather less than the brant, which it resembles in the head and neck, where it is larger in proportion than that of the goose: the beak is thicker and shorter; the note like that of a tame goose. In all other points it resembles the large goose, with which it associates so frequently, that it was some time before it was discovered to be of a distinct species.

9. The swan are of two kinds, the large and the small: the large swan is the same common to the Atlantic states: the small differs only from the large in size and in note: it is about one fourth less, and its note is entirely different. It cannot be justly imitated by the sound of letters; it begins with a kind of whistling sound, and terminates in a round full note, louder at the end: this note is as loud as that of the large species; whence it might be denominated the whistling swan: its habits, colour, and contour, appears to be pre-

cisely those of the larger species: these birds were first found below the great narrows of the Columbia, near the Chilluckittequaw nation: they are very abundant in this neighbourhood, and remained with the party all winter, and in number they exceed those of the larger species in the proportion of five to one.

10. Of ducks, we enumerate many kinds: the duckinmallard; the canvass-back duck; the red-headed fishing duck, the black and white duck; the little brown duck; black duck; two species of divers, and blue-winged teal.

1. The duckinmallard, or common large duck, resembles the domestic duck, are very abundant, and found in every part of the river below the mountains: they remain here all winter, but during this season do not continue much above tidewater.

2. The canvass-back duck is a most beautiful fowl, and most delicious to the palate: it is found in considerable numbers in this neighbourhood. It is of the same species with those of the Delaware, Susquehannah and Potomack, where it is called the canvass-back duck, and in James' river it is known by the name of the shelled drake. From this last mentioned river, it is said, however, that they have almost totally disappeared. To the epicure of those parts of the United States, where this game is in plenty, nothing need be said in praise of its exquisite flavour, and those on the banks of the Columbia are equally delicious. We saw nothing of them until after we had reached the marshy islands.

3. The red-headed fishing duck is common to every part of the river, and was likewise found in the Rocky mountains, and was the only duck discovered in the waters of the Columbia within

those mountains. They feed chiefly on crawfish, and are the same in every respect as those on the rivers and the mountains bordering on the Atlantic ocean.

4. The black and white duck is small, and a size larger than the teal. The male is beautifully variegated with black and white: the white occupies the side of the head, breast and back, the tail, feathers of the wings, and two tufts of feathers which cover the upper part of the wings, when folded, and likewise the neck and head: the female is darker. This is believed to be the same species of duck common to the Atlantic coast, and called the butter-box: the beak is wide and short, and, as well as the legs, of a dark colour, and the flesh extremely well flavoured. In form it resembles the duckinmallard, although not more than half the size of that bird. It generally resorts to the grassy marshes, and feeds on grass seeds, as well as roots.

5. The black duck is about the size of the blue-winged teal; the colour of a dusky black; the breast and belly somewhat lighter, and of a dusky brown: the legs stand longitudinally with the body, and the bird when on shore, stands very erect: the legs and feet are of a dark brown: it has four toes on each foot, and a short one at the heel: the long toes are in front, unconnected with the web: the webs are attached to each side of the several joints of the toe, and divided by several sinews at each joint, the web assuming in the intermediate part an elliptical form: the beak is about two inches long, straight, fluted on the sides, and tapering to a sharp point: the upper chop is the longest, and bears on its base, at its junction with the head, a little conic protuberance of a cartilaginous substance, being of a red-

dish brown at the point: the beak is of an ivory colour; the eye dark. These ducks usually associate in large flocks, are very noisy, and have a sharp shrill whistle: they are fat and agreeably flavoured; feed principally on moss and vegetable productions of the water: they are not exclusively confined to the water at all seasons, captain Lewis has noticed them on many parts of the rivers Ohio and Mississippi.

6. The divers are the same with those of the United States. The smaller species have some white feathers about the rump, with no perceptible tail, and are very acute and quick in their motion: the body is of a reddish brown; the beak sharp, and somewhat curved, like that of the pheasant: the toes are not connected, but webbed, like those of the black duck. The larger species are about the size of the teal, and can fly a short distance, which the smaller but seldom attempt: they have a short tail; their colour is also a uniform brick reddish-brown: the beak is straight and pointed: the feet are of the same form with the other species: the legs remarkably thin and flat, one edge being in front. The food of both species is fish and flesh: their flesh is unfit for use.

7. The blue-winged teal is an excellent duck, and in all respects the same as those of the United States. One of our hunters killed a duck which appeared to be a male. It was of a size less than the duckinmallard; the head, the neck as low as the croup, the back, tail, and covert of the wings were all of a deep fine black, with a slight mixture of purple about the head and neck: the belly and breast are white: some long feathers which lie underneath the wings, and cover the thighs, were of a pale dove colour, with fine black specks: the large feathers of the wings are of a dove colour:

402

the legs are dark; the feet are composed of four
toes, of which three are in front connected by a
web: the fourth is short and flat, and placed high
on the heel behind the leg: the tail is composed of
fourteen short pointed feathers: the beak of this
duck is remarkably wide, and two inches in
length: the upper chop exceeds the under one,
both in length and width, insomuch, that when
the beak is closed, the under chop is entirely concealed by the upper: the tongue indenture on the
margin of the chops, are like those of the mallard:
the nostrils are large, longitudinal, and connected:
a narrow strip of white garnishes the base of the
upper chop: this is succeeded by a pale sky-blue
colour, occupying about an inch; which again is
succeeded by a transverse stripe of white, and the
extremity is a fine black: the eye is moderately
large, the pupil black, and of a fine orange colour:
the feathers on the crown of the head are longer
than those on the upper part of the neck and
other parts of the head, which give it the appearance of being crested.

The fish, which we have had an opportunity of
seeing, are, the whale, porpoise, skate, flounder,
salmon, red char, two species of salmon trout,
mountain, or speckled trout, bottlenose, anchovy,
and sturgeon.

1. The whale is sometimes pursued, harpooned
and taken by the Indians, although it is much
more frequently killed by running foul of the rocks
in violent storms, and thrown on shore by the
action of the wind and tide. In either case, the
Indians preserve and eat the blubber and oil;
the bone they carefully extract and expose to
sale.

2. The porpoise is common on this coast, and
as far up the river as the water is brackish. The

Indians sometimes gig them, and always eat their flesh when they can procure it.

3. The skate is also common in the salt water: we saw several of them which had perished, and were thrown on shore by the tide.

4. The flounder is also well known here, and we have often seen them left on the beach after the departure of the tide. The Indians eat this fish, and think it very fine. These several species of fish are the same with those on the Atlantic coast.

5. The common salmon and red char are the inhabitants of both the sea and rivers; the former are usually the largest, and weigh from five to fifteen pounds: they extend themselves into all the rivers and little creeks on this side of the continent, and to them the natives are much indebted for their subsistence: the body of the fish is from two and an half to three feet long, and proportionably broad: it is covered with imbricated scales, of a moderate size, and gills: the eye is large, and the iris of a silvery colour: the pupil is black, the rostrum or nose extends beyond the under jaw, and both jaws are armed with a single series of long teeth, which are subulate and inflected near the extremities of the jaws, where they are also more closely arranged: they have some sharp teeth of smaller size, and some sharp points placed on the tongue, which is thick and fleshy: the fins of the back are two; the first is placed nearer the head than the ventral fins, and has several rays: the second is placed far back, near the tail, and has no rays. The flesh of this fish is, when in order, of a deep flesh-coloured red, and every shade from that to an orange yellow: when very meagre it is almost white: the roes of this fish are in high estimation among the natives,

who dry them in the sun, and preserve them for a great length of time: they are of the size of a small pea, nearly transparent, and of a reddish yellow cast; they resemble very much, at a little distance, our common garden currants, but are more yellow. Both the fins and belly of this fish are sometimes red, particularly the male: the red char are rather broader, in proportion to their length, than the common salmon: the scales are also imbricated, but rather larger; the rostrum exceeds the under jaw more, and the teeth are neither so large or so numerous as those of the salmon: some of them are almost entirely red on the belly and sides; others are much more white than the salmon, and none of them are variegated with the dark spots which mark the body of the other: their flesh, roes, and every other particular, with regard to the form, is that of the salmon.

6. Of the salmon trout, we observe two species, differing only in colour; they are seldom more than two feet in length, and narrow in proportion to their length, much more so than the salmon or red char. The jaws are nearly of the same length, and are furnished with a single series of small subulate straight teeth, not so long nor as large as those of the salmon. The mouth is wide, and the tongue is also furnished with some teeth: the fins are placed much like those of the salmon. At the great falls we found this fish of a silvery white colour on the belly and sides, and a bluish light brown on the back and head; the second species is of a dark colour on its back, and its sides and belly are yellow, with transverse stripes of dark brown; sometimes a little red is intermixed with these colours on the belly and sides towards the head. The eye, flesh, and roe, are like those described of the salmon: the white spe-

405

cies found below the falls, were in excellent order, when the salmon were entirely out of season and not fit for use. They associate with the red char, in little rivulets and creeks: the Indians say that the salmon begin to run early in May. The white salmon trout is about two feet and eight inches long, and weighs ten pounds: the eye is moderately large, the pupil black, with a small admixture of yellow, and iris of a silvery white, and a little turbid near its border with a yellowish brown. The fins are small in proportion to the fish; are bony but not pointed, except the tail and back fins, which are pointed a little: the prime back fin and ventral ones contain each ten rays, those of the gills thirteen, that of the tail twelve, and the small fin placed near and above the tail has no bony rays, but is a tough flexible substance, covered with smooth skin. It is thicker in proportion to its width than the salmon: the tongue is thick and firm, beset on each border with small subulate teeth, in a single series: the teeth and the mouth are as before described. Neither this fish nor the salmon are caught with the hook, nor do we know on what they feed.

7. The mountain or speckled trout are found in the waters of the Columbia within the mountains: they are the same with those found in the upper part of the Missouri, but are not so abundant in the Columbia as on that river. We never saw this fish below the mountains, but from the transparency and coldness of the Kooskooskee, we should not doubt of its existence in that stream as low as its junction with the southeast branch of the Columbia.

8. The bottlenose is the same with that before mentioned on the Missouri, and is found exclusively within the mountains.

Of shell fish we observe the clam, periwinkle, common muscle, the cockle, and a species with a circular flat shell. The clam of this coast are very small; the shell consists of two valves, which open with hinges: the shell is smooth, thin, of an oval form like that of the common muscle, and of sky-blue colour. It is about one and a half inches in length and hangs in clusters to the moss of the rocks: the natives sometimes eat them. The periwinkle both of the river and the ocean, are similar to those found in the same situation on the Atlantic coast. The common muscle of the river are also the same with those on the rivers of the Atlantic coast: the cockle is small, and resembles much that of the Atlantic: there is also an animal that inhabits a shell perfectly circular, about three inches in diameter, thin and entire on the margin, convex and smooth on the upper side, plain on the under part, and covered with a number of minute capillary fibres, by means of which it attaches itself to the sides of the rocks: the shell is thin, and consists of one valve; a small circular aperture is formed in the centre of the under shell: the animal is soft and boneless.

The pellucid substance and fuci. The pellucid jelly-like substance, called the sea-nettle, is found in great abundance along the strand, where it has been thrown up by the waves and tide: there are two species of the fuci thrown up in that manner: the first species at one extremity consists of a large vesicle or hollow vessel, which will contain from one to two gallons: it is of a conic form, the base of which forms the extreme end, and is convex and globular, bearing at its centre some short, broad, and angular fibres: the substance is about the consistence of the rind of a citron melon, and three-fourths of an inch thick: the rind is smooth

407

from the small extremity of the cone; a long hollow cylindric and regular tapering tube extends to twenty or thirty feet, and is then terminated with a number of branches, which are flat, half an inch in width, rough, particularly on the edges, where they are furnished with a number of little ovate vesicles or bags of the size of a pigeon's egg: this plant seems to be calculated to float at each extremity, while the little end of the tube, from whence the branches proceed, lie deepest in the water: the other species seen on the coast towards the Killamucks, resembles a large pumpkin; it is solid, and its specific gravity is greater than the water, though sometimes thrown out by the waves: it is of a yellowish brown colour; the rind smooth, and its consistence is harder than that of the pumpkin; but easily cut with a knife: there are some dark brown fibres, rather harder than any other part, which pass longitudinally through the pulp or fleshy substance which forms the interior of this marine production.

The reptiles of this country are the rattlesnake, the gartersnake, lizard, and snail.

The gartersnake appears to belong to the same family with the common gartersnakes of the Atlantic coast, and like that snake they inherit no poisonous qualities: they have one hundred and sixty scuta on the abdomen, and seventy on the tail: those on the abdomen near the head and jaws as high as the eye, are of a bluish white, which, as it recedes from the head, becomes of a dark brown: the field of the back and sides black: a narrow stripe of a light yellow runs along the centre of the back; on each side of this stripe there is a range of small transverse, oblong spots, of a pale brick red, diminishing as they recede from the head, and disappear at the commencement of the tail: the pupil of the eye is black, with a narrow ring of white bordering on its edge; the remainder of the iris is of a dark yellowish brown.

The horned lizard, called, and for what reason we never could learn, the prairie buffalo, is a native of these plains, as well as those on the Missouri: they are of the same size, and much the same in appearance as the black lizard: the belly is however broader, the tail shorter, and the action much slower: the colour is generally brown intermixed with yellowish brown spots: the animal is covered with minute scales, interspersed with small horny points, like blunt prickles on the upper surface of the body: the belly and throat resemble those of the frog, and are of a light yellowish brown: the edge of the belly is likewise beset with small horny projections, imparting to those edges a serrate appearance: the eye is small and dark: above and behind the eyes there are several projections of that bone, and their extremities also being armed with a firm black substance, resemble the appearance of horns sprouting from the head: these animals are found in greatest numbers in the sandy open plains, and appear in the greatest abundance after a shower of rain: they are sometimes found basking in the sunshine, but conceal themselves in little holes of the earth in much the greatest proportion of the time: this may account for their appearance in such numbers after the rain, as their holes may thus be rendered untenantable.

9. The anchovy, which the natives call olthen, is so delicate a fish that it soon becomes tainted, unless pickled or smoked: the natives run a small stick through the gills and hang it up to dry in the smoke of their lodges, or kindle small fires

409

under it for the purpose of drying: it needs no previous preparation of gutting, and will be cured in twenty-four hours: the natives do not appear to be very scrupulous about eating them when a little foetid.

END OF VOLUME II.